The Fiscal Case against Statehood

The Fiscal Case against Statehood

Accounting for Statehood in New Mexico and Arizona

Stephanie D. Moussalli

LEXINGTON BOOKS
Lanham • Boulder • New York • Toronto • Plymouth, UK

Published by Lexington Books
A wholly owned subsidiary of The Rowman & Littlefield Publishing Group, Inc.
4501 Forbes Boulevard, Suite 200, Lanham, Maryland 20706
www.rowman.com

10 Thornbury Road, Plymouth PL6 7PP, United Kingdom

British Library Cataloguing in Publication Information Available

Library of Congress Cataloging-in-Publication Data

Moussalli, Stephanie D., 1953–
  The fiscal case against statehood : accounting for statehood in New Mexico and
Arizona / Stephanie D. Moussalli.
     p. cm.
  Includes bibliographical references and index.
  ISBN 978-0-7391-6699-4 (cloth : alk. paper) — ISBN 978-0-7391-6700-7 (electronic)
  1. Finance, Public—New Mexico—History. 2. Finance, Public—Arizona—History. 3.
New Mexico—Appropriations and expenditures—History. 4. Arizona—Appropriations
and expenditures—History. 5. New Mexico—Politics and government—1848–1950.
6. Arizona—Politics and government—To 1950. 7. Statehood (American politics—
History. 8. State governments—United States—History. 9. United States—Territories
and possessions—History. I. Title.
  HJ2423.M68 2012
  336'.01373—dc23
                                                                      2011052030

∞™ The paper used in this publication meets the minimum requirements of American
National Standard for Information Sciences—Permanence of Paper for Printed Library
Materials, ANSI/NISO Z39.48-1992.

Printed in the United States of America

Contents

Part I: The Money

Part II: The Books

List of Figures

List of Tables

Acknowledgments

There are not many doctoral programs that would allow research as interdisciplinary as this. It was my great fortune to find one that did, at the University of Mississippi.

The accounting faculty unanimously agreed that I could pursue the topic (even those who thought it not very promising, an open-mindedness not to be found at some schools). My committee—Dr. Dale Flesher, Dr. Tonya Flesher, and Dr. Karl Wang—not only provided essential guidance but were enthusiastic throughout the long process. The Department of Economics was hugely supportive, allowing me to minor in that field and providing me with the indispensable outside member of my committee, Dr. William Shughart, II. The Department of History not only accepted but welcomed the oddity of an accounting candidate who wanted to minor in history; members of that faculty made numerous important suggestions. I believe it is an unusual experience for a dissertation writer to have the expert advice and consistent good will of scholars from so many diverse perspectives.

Librarians at the University of Mississippi, the National Archives, and numerous state archives made this work possible by locating enormous amounts of primary source material. Dr. Royce Kurtz, at the University of Mississippi library, advised me at every stage and was unfailingly generous with his time and knowledge. Julie Doub, Rhodes College undergraduate *extraordinaire*, wrestled innumerable citations into shape so I could work with them. Finally, and far from least, my fellow doctoral students listened with good humor and patience for more than three years as the study developed through numerous versions.

I am also very grateful for the funding I received while working on the dissertation. The Graduate School of the University of Mississippi funded two terms of research; the Graduate Student Council paid for a trip to the National Archives; and the Graduate School, the Patterson School of Accountancy, the Government and Nonprofit Section of the American Accounting Association, and Dr. Barbara Merino of the University of North Texas provided travel monies that allowed me to present parts of this work at various conferences while still a student.

Weaknesses remaining in the book despite the generosity and attention of all of these people are due to my failures.

Chapters 1, 5, and 12 and figures 4.1, 5.1, 5.2, and 5.3 of this book contain material that appeared in a different version in *Public Choice*, vol. 137, 2008, pp. 119–126, "The Fiscal Effects of Statehood: New Mexico and Arizona, 1903–1919." Reprinted by kind permission of Springer Science and Business Media.

Chapter 6 of this book contains material that appeared in a different version in the *Accounting Historians Journal*, vol. 35, no. 1, 2008, pp. 167–195, "State and Local Government Accounting in 19th Century America: A Review of the Literature." Reprinted by kind permission of the Academy of Accounting Historians.

Introduction

"[T]he amount we require being small, [New Mexico] will be the lowest-taxed sovereign State in the nation,"[1] declared New Mexico statehood promoters to Congress in 1901. The promoters were actually continuing an argument with their fellow New Mexicans, who had voted statehood *down* by a two-to-one margin just a decade earlier. Miguel Otero, future governor, had opposed statehood too at the time because he "notice[d] all the politicians on both sides favor statehood, and all the business men and tax payers on both sides are not in favor," at least in 1890 when the election was held.[2]

It is not a widely known fact that many residents of American territories oppose statehood on the grounds that the new state government will be too expensive. I, for one, didn't know it until I was conducting research for my history master's thesis in the 1980s. In all six of the southern territories I studied, there was significant opposition to statehood within the territory, usually for fear of its expense.

Intrigued, I checked the secondary literature to see what scholars of statehood had to say about the phenomenon. Most of them didn't mention the pattern at all. An exception is Peter Onuf, whose study of statehood notes that in the past, fiscal policy often sparked territorial opposition to statehood. Residents feared the increased taxes and unrestrained spending they believed the change would bring.[3] Onuf thinks opponents exaggerated the costs, however.[4]

I was curious about this local opposition to statehood, but had neither the time nor the skills to determine whether the historians or the territorial residents were right. Decades later, though, I decided to tackle the question for my dissertation in accounting at the University of Mississippi. This book is a re-written version of that dissertation, with the addition of some subsequent research.

Roughly, I wanted to know two things for the dissertation:

1. Does statehood increase the fiscal burden of government?
2. Does statehood improve the government's accounting for its use of the
   public purse?

As best as I can tell, the answer to both questions is yes. There is a Leviathan dynamic of statehood, and it includes better accountability on the part
of the new state. One of the purposes of this book is to present the evidence
for these conclusions.

While no prior study has tried to answer these questions, several observers
have noted cases when a government simultaneously increased its power, fiscal size, and financial accountability on the occasion of war or the establish-
ment of a post-revolutionary government.[5] This work adds statehood to the
list of events that can lead to the same mix of changes.

I want to emphasize at the outset that this evidence does not address the
efficiencies with which territories and states supply public goods and other
government services. Instead, it is the first systematic test—albeit a limited
one using only two subject governments—of the claims of the opponents of
statehood that the loss of territorial status would bring substantial increases in
the tax burden. Whether the provision of additional public goods and services
that came with statehood justified the heavier state tax burden remains an
open question, one on which readers will differ.

A second purpose of the book is to tell the story of how fiscal politics
affected the history of some specific new states. I chose New Mexico and
Arizona, which became states in 1912, near the end of the period when most
American states joined the union. The financial records for their governments were easier to obtain than the records of the nineteenth century's new
states. To make sure that the changes I found were not just due to national or
regional trends, I used a control—Nevada, which had been a state for a long
time by 1912. The book thus tells fiscal policy stories about three Western
states from the 1880s to the 1920s.

I also hope the book will convince some people that accounting is *not* as
dull as they think it is. Much of human history, even in recent centuries, is
recorded only in the accounts. People often say one thing but do something
else. Government accounts record what politicians *do*, whereas our histories
sometimes rely on what they and others *say* about what they do. This book is
based on what the accounts show happened when two governments made the
transition from territory to state.

So part 1 of the book, "The Money," describes what I call the Leviathan
dynamic of statehood as it occurred in New Mexico and Arizona, including

the fiscal tensions between the territories and the national government. Then, analysis of the data series I created from those governments' financial statements shows what happened to the size of government, both before and after statehood. Part 1 is based on public choice economic theory.

Measuring fiscal behavior requires close examination of the government accounts of a set of territories and the succeeding states. Fortunately, the detailed data often still exist to be examined because state and territorial governments in this country have always been required to publish such information.

It is one thing, however, to put fiscal accountability into the law, and another thing actually to make the information accessible, consistent, and useful. Over the course of American history, the many state and local governments have differed widely in their accounting practices, in the degree to which they made the accounts public, and in their efforts to preserve the records. Comparing information across those governments lies in *terra incognita* for any period much before World War II. No nationally accepted formal accounting standards existed, and little prior research has been done on the informal development of state and local government accounting practices.

Thus, part 2, "The Books," deals with how the governments of New Mexico and Arizona (and Nevada) changed their accounting from the 1880s to the 1920s. This section includes many specific examples of what the governments were doing in those days. It is oriented around questions of accountability, and is largely written as accounting history.

This book will, I hope, interest accounting scholars as an examination of changes and the causes of changes in American government accounting techniques from the 1880s to the 1920s. Economists may be interested in its test of public choice theory; scholars of public administration in the differences in the "technologies of government"[6] between territorial and state governments; legal scholars and political scientists in the book's exploration of a key phenomenon of the U.S. federalist system—statehood; and historians in the controversial conclusions it draws about the range of local opinions and government actions when a territory becomes a state.

Like most Americans today, I see statehood as a Good Thing. I agree with the North Carolina representative who declared, in the congressional debate over Louisiana statehood in 1811: "I never would have consented to have taken [the Louisiana Purchase] to have kept [its people] in territorial government forever. I do not want provinces."[7]

But I learned something about a different and important point of view in doing this research, and I now think the question is more complex. As the people of New Mexico and Arizona celebrate the centennial of their statehood, they, and the rest of the nation, may be curious to know the story of why some of their forebears thought it was a *bad* idea.

In short, anyone who is interested in a contrarian historical example of how the American system of government works at the state level may enjoy this story.

NOTES

1. *Admission of Oklahoma*, HR 12543, 57th Cong., 1st sess., *Congressional Record* 35, part 5 (May 7, 1902) [Petition from convention held in Albuquerque on October 15, 1901]: H 5136.

2. Dargan, "New Mexico's Fight," 24. Otero refers to his early opposition on the grounds of poverty in *My Nine Years*, 200. See also Welsh, "Star," 36.

3. Onuf, "Territories and Statehood," 1284, 1298. See also Bakken, "Rocky Mountain," 6.

4. Onuf, "Territories and Statehood," 1283, 1284; Onuf, "New State Equality," 1988.

5. Brownlee, *Federal Taxation*; Daunton, *Trusting Leviathan*; Ezzamel, "Accounting Working for the State"; Peterson, "Why It Worked."

6. Miller, "Accounting and the State," 315–338.

7. *Annals of Congress*, 11th Cong., 3rd sess., 505.

I

THE MONEY

1

Statehood and Leviathan

The Treaty of Guadalupe-Hidalgo between the United States and Mexico (1848) declared that the Mexican-American inhabitants of the newly acquired lands "shall be incorporated into the Union of the United States, and be admitted at the proper time (to be judged of by the Congress of the United States) to the enjoyment of all the rights of citizens of the United States. . . . "[1] But the "proper time" for states to join the union from the new southwestern lands varied by more than half a century, from 1850 (California) to 1912 (Arizona and New Mexico). Why the difference in dates? What determined when a new state was created?

The usual answer to that question is that national politics controls the timing of statehood. For example, when Nevada was admitted in 1864, a key factor was Civil War politics; the Union wanted to admit new pro-Union states if at all possible.[2] So Congress granted statehood to Nevada when it had only about 21,000 to 40,000 inhabitants, many of them transient miners.[3]

This was fewer people than any other state except perhaps Illinois had when it entered the Union,[4] fewer than the next smallest state had at the time (67,460 in Oregon),[5] fewer than the 60,000 originally suggested in the Northwest Ordinance for statehood,[6] and far fewer than the 122,614 people then required for adding a congressional representative.[7] As historian Peter Onuf dubbed it, Nevada was the Union's "rotten borough."[8] National politics, and Nevada's role in those politics, trumped other concerns in timing statehood.

The congressional fight over admitting a new state, often dramatic, captures most historiographical attention.[9] But national politics is not the entire story. Territorial politics plays a major role, too, because the people of the territory must vote for statehood before the new state can be created. And at the territorial level, the argument turns primarily on fiscal questions—who

7

will control the public purse for what purposes, and how big the public purse should be.

Inside the territories, supporters of statehood think the new government will use its powers to make spending policy better suited to local needs, under stronger local control. Opponents think the new government will use its powers as a Leviathan, growing to burdensome size for no good purpose. The latter group, generally the argument's losers in the long run, have been almost forgotten.

But opponents of statehood have been numerous and vocal in U.S. territories. In the Missouri Territory in 1811, for instance, one writer estimated state government would cost 33.3 cents per capita as compared to 10 cents for the territorial government.[10] In the Territory of Florida, eastern residents lived in the middle of one of the most ferocious Indian wars in American history, which devastated the economy. Non-Seminoles bitterly resented being forced by the wealthier sections of Florida into a statehood they could not afford. They were "not disposed to invoke [the credit of the Territory] further for the elevation of political aspirants."[11] Among East Floridians, 73 percent voted against the proposed state constitution in 1839, and statehood nearly failed on the question; officially, the majority was only 113 votes.[12]

Even long after statehood, residents sometimes continue to attribute high fiscal burdens to the fact that the government involved is a state. Almost sixty years after Nevada became a state, the secretary of the state tax commission remarked a little bitterly that while public expenditures appeared

> grotesquely small, . . . [the] per capita tax . . . is the highest in the United States; and it is a source of wonder to people on the outside that less than one hundred thousand people should be burdened with a state government. That came about from the fact that a state government was wished on Nevada by a war congress . . . with less than one inhabitant to the square mile, it is easy to see that the per capita cost of state government cannot fail to remain much above the average.[13]

Opposition to statehood also springs from fear of losing the subsidies given to the territories by the U.S. government. The United States paid, for territories but not for states, the costs of the governors' and secretaries' salaries, their contingent expenses, and many of the legislatures' expenses.

This fear for subsidies has retarded many statehood movements during the centuries of American growth.[14] In 1835, for example, Arkansas's territorial governor argued for extracting as much money from Congress as possible before statehood shut down federal aid.[15] In 1903, Teddy Roosevelt told New Mexico's governor, "If I were in your place I would remain a territory as long as the United States government will pay your running expenses."[16] In the late twentieth century, Puerto Ricans continued to be ambivalent on the statehood question, partly due to their fear of losing the preferential tax treatment given to corporations operating in their territory.[17]

Individual state histories often mention this sort of detail, but only a few observers discuss the fear of the cost of statehood as a general phenomenon. Those who do describe it, downplay it. Peter Onuf and Jack Eblen are among the scholars who discuss the issue, but they regard the fiscal objections to statehood as weak. They both argue that the federal subsidies amounted to no more than 10 percent of the total cost of territorial government, so replacing them with local revenues (as states had to do) would not have been burdensome.[18] Eblen adds that although the territorial governments did raise local salaries and exercise patronage irresponsibly, an important reason for their notorious financial difficulties was that they did not set tax rates high enough or collect them efficiently enough.[19] Onuf considers the opposition to raising enough taxes to pay for statehood "surprising." He remarks that "[t]ax-conscious electorates were easily swayed by exaggerated estimates of the cost of statehood."[20]

Gordon Bakken, too, in his study of Rocky Mountain state constitution-making, notes that all convention delegates "recognized the increased financial burden of statehood," but they disagreed on how to handle it. Bakken asserts that "economy-in-government proponents . . . and . . . anti-statehood forces . . . tried to achieve their ends through scare tactics."[21] Thus, Bakken implicitly agrees with Onuf and Eblen that statehood opponents exaggerated the potential for fiscal expansion under state government.

Who is right? Does statehood substantially increase the price of a government, as opponents contend, or does it not, as supporters and historians believe? To investigate this question, I analyzed the financial statements of two of the most recent additions to the union, New Mexico and Arizona, and compared them to the records of Nevada as a control. Discussion of the general context of the argument, the model I tested in the research, and the methodology, follows.

THE STATEHOOD PROCESS

In 1787, the U.S. Confederation Congress passed the Northwest Ordinance, which established the process by which new states would be admitted to the Union.[22] Under this act, territories acquired progressively greater powers of self-government as their populations grew, until they achieved, in statehood, full political equality with the original thirteen states. The Northwest Ordinance process recapitulated the movement towards stable self-government that had occurred in the English colonies. It was a brilliant exploitation of the nation's federalist structure,[23] and with some modifications the same basic scheme controls the admission of new states to this day.[24]

The legal process leading to statehood in the last century and a half has included, roughly speaking, seven steps.[25] The territorial legislature requests statehood and Congress passes an enabling act that allows the next steps to take place. In the territory, a constitutional convention is called and delegates are elected who write the constitution. The territorial electorate ratifies the constitution, the president approves it, state officers are elected, and the president proclaims the existence of the new state.

Problems and delays can occur at each step, prolonging the process over many decades. This is what happened in the cases of New Mexico and Arizona. They became together a single organized territory named "New Mexico" in 1850.[26] From that point, it took over six decades for the two to accomplish the steps required to join the union in 1912.

THE MODEL

Statehood, as it is intended to do, dramatically shifts power from the national government to the local level. U.S. territories are fiscally subordinate to Congress. Although territorial residents vote for their own representatives to territorial legislatures that have taxing and spending powers, Congress can annul any territorial laws it does not like[27]—and sometimes did so in the cases of New Mexico and Arizona. States cannot be controlled in this way, nor is the federal government responsible for state debts.

Thus, statehood causes two important changes: an expansion in sovereignty for a territorial government and the decentralization of the national government's fiscal authority. Both these events may be fitted into the economic paradigm known as public choice.

The public choice paradigm applies the theories and methods of economics to politics, broadly defined. In this view, public policy is created in a political marketplace in which all the actors, including politicians and bureaucrats, act in their rational self-interest—that is, in economically predictable ways.[28] For politicians, control over the largest possible amount of resources is the equivalent of a vendor's charging the highest price the market will bear. Voters prefer to pay as little as possible for their government, and those with a lower demand for government will object the most to the increases they believe statehood will bring.

Particularly applicable to this study is Geoffrey Brennan and James Buchanan's work, in which they argue that the "natural proclivities of government," lead it to behave as a "revenue-maximizing Leviathan."[29] If, as Brennan and Buchanan maintain, a government tends to charge the highest possible price for its services consistent with the electoral and non-electoral constraints it faces,[30] then a government that increases its powers—obtains more sovereignty—can be expected to charge the citizens more (other things being equal). Statehood confers substantially greater power on a former territorial government, so Brennan and Buchanan's Leviathan model would predict that a new state will use its broader taxing and spending powers to raise the relative "price" it charges the economy for its services.[31]

Figure 1.1 depicts this Leviathan dynamic of statehood as a positive relationship between sovereignty and the fiscal size of government.

Most American states began as territories.[32] In those cases, the horizontal axis in the figure can be re-labeled to indicate the change from territory to state across time, as shown in Figure 1.2. The model in figure 1.2 predicts that, around the time of statehood, the price the government charges the private economy for its services rises at a significantly faster rate than it does before or after that time.

Note that what happens to the relative price of government before and after the statehood period is irrelevant (which is why those sections of the graph are drawn with dotted lines). The model simply predicts that, some time around the period when a territorial government assumes the powers of a state, it uses those powers to increase the share of the private economy that it controls. It grows not just absolutely, but relative to the total available

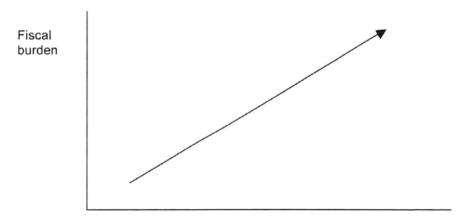

Fiscal burden

Degree of sovereignty of the government

Figure 1.1. Leviathan dynamic of statehood: Hypothesized relationship between degree of sovereignty and relative fiscal burden of government.

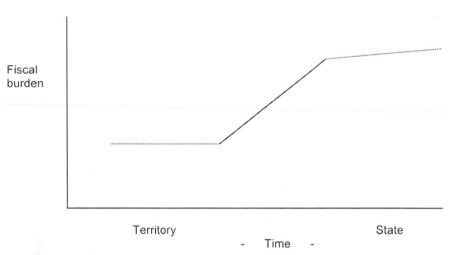

Figure 1.2. Hypothesized change in relative fiscal burden as government changes from territory to state.

resources in the state. In short, figure 1.2 depicts a relationship from which the fiscal predictions of pre-statehood citizens can be derived.

Interestingly, the model also predicts that if statehood involves a *decline* in sovereignty, the fiscal bite of government will decline, too. This is just what the people of the independent Republic of Texas predicted would happen when they voted almost unanimously to join the United States as a state.[33] That is, it is the change in the government's degree of sovereignty that triggers the change in its cost according to this model, not statehood *per se*.

There is an alternative theory from the public choice paradigm that would *not* predict the fiscal jump when a territory becomes a state. As mentioned above, statehood devolves fiscal power from the federal government to a lower level of government, and in that sense involves the decentralization of power. The public choice literature generally predicts that fiscal decentralization will *restrain* government spending and taxing, by introducing competition among governments. But empirical testing has produced mixed results.[34]

Historically, even statehood's proponents did not argue that the transition would *reduce* spending, though they sometimes did claim that the increases would be quite modest,[35] and they wrote strict fiscal restraints into new state constitutions in an attempt to ensure this.[36] At least one historian, Gordon Bakken, believes that these restraints probably worked to control the cost of new states.[37]

So there are two theoretical predictions about the price of statehood, each backing a different territorial faction. This study predicts that the Leviathan hypothesis is the better model. If so, then statehood opponents in New Mexico and Arizona were right in expecting statehood to cause substantially higher government costs.

Any answers this test provides are important because if statehood critics are right, then widespread voter opposition, even sometimes majority opposition (as in Puerto Rico), can be expected within territories. After all, popular support for a government is affected by changes in the relative size of government, as various studies have found.[38] On the other hand, if the tests fail to find evidence of a jump in the fiscal bite around the time of statehood, this would suggest that statehood's opponents exaggerate the cost of statehood, as contemporary supporters and many of today's scholars believe.[39]

THE STATES

The aim of this study was to test the model's predictions on a sample of states that began as territorial governments—the case shown in figure 1.2. There have been dozens of such transitions in American history, from Tennessee in 1796 to Hawaii in 1959. I chose Arizona and New Mexico. Both became states in 1912, near the end of the period of state formation, when data are more easily available. In fact, substantial fiscal data are available for the New Mexico and Arizona governments from the 1880s on.

It is possible that fiscal trends in New Mexico or Arizona simply resulted from general economic conditions rather than from statehood. To control for this possibility, I also studied a government that did not change its sovereignty status in the study period.

Nevada is a good control for this purpose. Geographically and economically similar in many ways to Arizona and New Mexico, Nevada was admitted to statehood long before them, in 1864. Any effects statehood had on its finances had presumably vanished by 1912. Nevada records for the 1880s to the 1920s are also good—easily available, reasonably informative, fairly consistent over time, and concise.

VARIABLES AND HYPOTHESES

The "price" of a government is, generally speaking, measured by its revenues or expenditures. However, an absolute dollar measure of these variables is unsatisfactory. The real value of a currency fluctuates over time, and changes in government's receipts and expenditures normally coincide with changes in population and wealth. For example, a statement that the states collectively spent $4 million on highways in 1902 but $6,635 million in 1962, as they did,[40] conveys little useful information. The reader needs to know more—the constant-dollar increase, perhaps, or the accompanying changes in population, technology, or the economy. Given that this study deals with a forty-five-year period of enormous economic and demographic changes, it was necessary to use a measure of government's price that controls for these factors.

Therefore, the study uses a ratio—the ratio of the government's revenues to the total size of the state's economy. That is, the fiscal burden is measured as the percentage of the economy that the state or territorial government directly controls. Versions of this fiscal measure are widely used in the economics literature.[41] I call it the "F-ratio" after the terminology in Cuzán's work.[42]

The numerator is the government's revenues from its own sources—that is, excluding transfers from the federal government. In the denominator, the size of the economy is measured by assessed property values, the only annual measure of states' and territories' economies available in the nineteenth and early twentieth centuries.

Specifically, the main variable is:

F-Rev = total own-source (i.e., excluding transfers from the federal government) territorial or state revenues / assessed property values

To control for the possibility that assessed property values are a systematically flawed measure, and to control for fluctuations in the national economy, I also used an F-ratio in which the denominator is the size of the *U.S.* economy. This variable is:

F-GNP = total territorial or state own-source revenues / gross national product

The behaviors of F-Rev and F-GNP were employed to test two hypotheses:

Hypothesis 1: A territory that becomes a state experiences a greater increase in F-Rev around the period of statehood than in the periods before or after statehood.

Hypothesis 2: A territory that becomes a state experiences a greater increase in F-Rev around the period of statehood than do political entities that do not change their status over the same historical period.

In other words, I hypothesize that statehood's opponents are correct in expecting that when a territorial government becomes a state, it takes a bigger fiscal "bite" from the local economy as the price of its services.

Primary sources for this study are the published reports of territorial and state financial officers, such as auditors, treasurers, and tax officials from the 1880s to the 1920s. That is, the story is told from the point of view of insiders, people who worked for or in close association with the governments involved. For the most part, they are accountants or other fiscally knowledgeable individuals.

In addition, the annual *Account of the Receipts and Expenditures of the United States* presented by the U.S. executive branch to the House of Representatives provided information on transfers made to the territories.[43] Annual gross national product from 1889 on is available in the Census's *Historical Statistics*. Supplementary data (generally derived from state and territorial reports) were used when available.[44] Occasionally I also consulted other sources, such as legislative records, memoirs, and newspapers.

Numerous methodological issues arose during the project, including how the data series were developed, the details of the choice of variables, the development of a number of alternative fiscal ratios, and advantages and disadvantages of the data sources. These issues are discussed in the appendix. The various data series I created also appear there.

The next two chapters recount New Mexico's and Arizona's internal fiscal and political travails on the road to statehood.

NOTES

1. "Treaty of Guadalupe Hidalgo," *Statutes at Large of USA* 9 (February 2, 1848): 922–932, art. 9.

2. Onuf, "Territories and Statehood," 1300.

3. *Enabling Act and Admission of Nevada, Stats at Large of USA* 13 (March 21, 1864): 30; Onuf, "Territories and Statehood," 1300. Population range from: Eblen, *First and Second,* 230–231, who estimates 21,140; Onuf, "Territories and Statehood," 1300, who estimates 30,000; U.S. General Accounting Office, "Experiences of Past Territories," 19, which estimates 40,000.

4. U.S. General Accounting Office, "Experiences of Past Territories," 19. Illinois may have had 34,620 people or fewer (ibid.).

5. Eblen, *First and Second,* 230–231.

6. *An Ordinance for the Government of the Territory of the United States Northwest of the River Ohio,* U.S. Confederation Congress (July 13, 1787), *Journals of the Continental Congress,* ed. Ford et al., 32: 334–343, art. 5.

7. U.S. Bureau of the Census, *Historical Statistics of the United States,* 1975, part 2, series Y 215–219.

8. Onuf, "Territories and Statehood," 1300.

9. Lamar's *Far Southwest* has lengthy bibliographic essays listing much of the statehood literature. For New Mexico, see pp. 451–453 and 462–464; for Arizona, pp. 502–503, 505, and 508. An interesting primary source for these events is the congressional debate of 1911 (U.S. Congress, House Committee on the Territories, Constitutions of New Mexico and Arizona, 1911). Melzer, "New Mexico in Caricature," is a good study of anti-Hispanic bias.

10. Letter to *Louisiana Gazette,* November 23, 1811, cited in Eblen, *First and Second,* 156.

11. Florida Territorial Legislative Council, "Report of a Minority," *Legislative Council Journal*, 358–359.

12. Reid, "Statement of the Votes," 376–378.

13. Fletcher, F. N. "Budget and State Taxes in Nevada," 113–114.

14. Onuf, "Territories and Statehood," 1296–1299; Eblen, *First and Second*, 139.

15. "Governor's Message to the Legislative Council and House," *Arkansas Advocate*, October 9, 1835.

16. Otero, *My Nine Years*, 216.

17. Santana, *Puerto Rican Newspaper Coverage*.

18. Onuf, "Territories and Statehood," 1298; Eblen, *First and Second*, 222.

19. Eblen, *First and Second*, 207.

20. Onuf, "Territories and Statehood," 1284, 1283.

21. Bakken, "Rocky Mountain," 38.

22. *An Ordinance for the Government of the Territory of the United States Northwest of the River Ohio*, U.S. Confederation Congress (July 13, 1787), *Journals of the Continental Congress*, ed. Ford et al., 32: 334–343.

23. For excellent discussion of the interaction of sovereignty and form of government in the American system, see Briffault, "Federalism"; Elazar, "Federalism: Theory"; and Scheiber, "Federalism: History."

24. Although Peter Onuf ("Territories and Statehood," 1283) argues that the reasoning behind the original scheme, "the territory-to-state developmental model—and the idea of a state as a true political community—had collapsed and was finally discarded" by the early twentieth century.

25. "How States Are Admitted."

26. *Territorial Government for New Mexico, Stats at Large of USA 1789–1873* 9 (September 9, 1850): 446.

27. Eblen, *First and Second*, 195–200.

28. Shughart and Razzolini, *Elgar Companion*, xxi–xxiv.

29. Brennan and Buchanan, *Power to Tax*, 17, 29.

30. Brennan and Buchanan, *Power to Tax*, chap. 2.

31. "Price" and "cost" of government are used interchangeably, in either sense meaning the share taken from the private economy by the government. Multiple measures of receipts and expenditures were recorded (see appendix).

32. For dates of territorial acts and enabling acts, see U.S. General Accounting Office, *Experiences of Past Territories*, 8. This report has a good summary of the statehood process.

33. Fehrenbach, *Lone Star*, 267, chap. 15.

34. Oates, "Essay on Fiscal Federalism," 1140–1141.

35. E.g., U.S. Congress, House, *Admission of Oklahoma, Arizona, and New Mexico*, HR 12543, 57th Cong., 1st sess., *Congressional Record* 35, part 5 (May 7, 1902) [Petition from convention held in Albuquerque on October 15, 1901]: H 5136.

36. E.g., New Mexico Constitution of 1912, art. 4, 5, 8, 9.

37. Bakken, "Rocky Mountain."

38. E.g., Cuzán and Bundrick, "Fiscal Policy and Presidential Elections"; Cuzán and Heggen, "Expenditures and Votes"; Peltzman, "Voters as Fiscal Conservatives."

39. Onuf, "Territories and Statehood"; Onuf, "New State Equality."

40. U.S. Bureau of the Census, *Historical Statistics of the United States*, 1989, tab. 5, "Finances of State Governments: 1902 to 1962."

41. E.g., Cuzán and Bundrick, "Fiscal Policy and Presidential Elections," 142; Nelson, "Empirical Analysis"; Ott and Shadbegian, "Centralized versus Decentralized Provision," tab. 12.1, 36–37; Sylla, "Long-Term Trends," tab. 16.2, 828. For a criticism of the validity and usefulness of all such measures, see Cullis and Jones, *Microeconomics*, chap. 7.

42. E.g., Cuzán and Heggen, "Expenditures and Votes."

43. U.S. Dept. of the Treasury, *Receipts and Expenditures.*

44. Sylla, Legler, and Wallis, *Sources and Uses of Funds*; Sylla, Legler, and Wallis, *State and Local Government*; U.S. Bureau of the Census, *Wealth, Debt, and Taxation*, 1907 and 1913; U.S. Bureau of the Census, *Financial Statistics of the States.*

2

New Mexico's Rocky Fiscal Road to Statehood

Congress created the Territory of New Mexico in 1850 and then carved the Territory of Arizona out of it in 1863. Achieving statehood took another half century.[1]

New Mexicans attempted to join the Union more than once during their six decades of political infancy, although the early attempts may not have been supported by the majority of the residents. The first occasion was in 1850, when, amidst alarming signs of an attempt by Texas to add New Mexico to its own territory, the military governor and other leaders called an election for a constitutional convention, wrote a free-state constitution,[2] held an election in which they claimed with "suspicious solidarity" 6,371 votes for ratification against only 39 votes opposed,[3] and petitioned Congress for immediate statehood.

Meanwhile, President Zachary Taylor, who might have supported the move, died. His successor, Millard Fillmore, inclined more to compromise in the incessant battle between North and South for control of the Senate. As a result, New Mexico (which then included Arizona) acquired a "temporary" second-degree territorial government instead of statehood in 1850.[4] The fact that New Mexico already had in that census year 62,000 inhabitants,[5] far more than Nevada and more than the old Northwest Ordinance had required for statehood, was irrelevant. The politics of the approaching civil war controlled the question.

THE PEOPLE AND THE ECONOMY

Territorial New Mexico was always predominantly Mexican-American. Although the Anglo newcomers held a great deal of power from the beginning, wealthy Hispanics were a major political and economic force. The most powerful Anglo in territorial New Mexico was Thomas B. Catron. Catron arrived just after the Civil War, learned to speak Spanish immediately, set up the most important law partnership in the territory, and founded the notorious Santa Fe Ring. The Santa Fe Ring, an extraordinarily powerful group of attorneys, wealthy Hispanics, and innumerable politicians (including nearly every governor), had the support of the leading territorial newspaper, the *New Mexican*, and of key people in Washington and New York. Adapting smoothly to economic changes, open to adding any useful newcomers to its circle, and untroubled by much ethnic or partisan bias, the Ring more or less ran New Mexican politics and business until well into the 1900s.[6]

New Mexico's economy was dominated by land. Land titles were hopelessly confused and almost universally fraudulent to some degree, attracting national attention and inspiring constant conflict both in and out of court throughout the territorial period.[7] Ring members personally acquired huge tracts. Thomas Catron himself owned hundreds of thousands of acres.[8]

After the Civil War, and particularly after the first railroad crossed the territory in 1879–1880, the New Mexico economy changed dramatically, from frontier primitiveness to a far more modern economic mix. Where there had been few towns, suddenly there were many.[9]

The railroad went from Las Vegas to Albuquerque, making of Albuquerque the commercial capital of the territory. Santa Fe, the political capital, languished economically as a result. When the railroad first reached Albuquerque in 1880, Santa Fe had a population of 6,600 compared to Albuquerque's 2,300. By 1910, the eve of statehood, Santa Fe had actually dropped to 5,100 residents, while Albuquerque had soared to 11,000.[10]

Both territorial leaders and the railroad relentlessly promoted New Mexico as a tourist and health mecca. The territorial legislature created the Bureau of Immigration in 1880[11] and the legend of New Mexico as the "birthplace of Montezuma" swept the United States. The Fred Harvey Company created a chain of hotels and restaurants along the railroad, William Henry Jackson (the father of the picture postcard) promoted the region on behalf of the railroad, and the School of American Archeology (today the School for Advanced Research) helped jumpstart American archeology.[12]

Mining and commercial development boomed, at least 46 new banks opened before the turn of the century,[13] and newcomers flocked to the territory.[14] By 1890, 160,000 people lived there.[15] At century end, however, and even as late as 1910, land and ranches still dominated the economy and provided the occupations of the majority of the people.[16]

PARTISAN POLITICS AND STATEHOOD EFFORTS

The 1871–1872 legislature made a second attempt at statehood, writing a constitution and sending it to the voters for approval, but the referendum was so conflicted and confused, as was the legislature that drafted it, that the governor aborted the process.[17] The next year, territorial delegate and Ring member Stephen Elkins introduced a statehood bill into what seemed to be a receptive Congress, but made the mistake of appearing to approve of an anti-South speech by one of the radical Republican remnant. Southern senators killed the bill.[18]

New Mexicans generally adhered to the Republican Party. It was an allegiance steady enough to win the support of a predominantly Republican Washington in the post-bellum period, but not so passionate as to alienate newcomers with Democratic or Southern sympathies.

However, in 1885 Washington sent the territory its first Democratic governor since the war, and an uproar ensued. Edmund Ross was a crusader, a champion of small farmers against large landowners, and a former Radical Republican who had cast one of the deciding votes against the removal by impeachment of President Andrew Johnson.[19] A new broom bent on sweeping clean, Ross attempted to abolish Catholic and Hispanic control of education in the territory, tried to destroy the Santa Fe Ring as the root of all New Mexican corruption, and joined the surveyor-general in declaring essentially every land title in the territory fraudulent.[20] Many of his remaining supporters likely were alienated when he vetoed nearly every bill the legislature passed, more than any other territorial governor.[21]

Most factions in New Mexico united against Ross. The legislature overrode every one of his vetoes and refused to confirm many of his patronage appointments, including that of the treasurer.[22] New Mexicans deafened Washington with cries that Ross had shut down the state's economy by rendering all land titles suspect and worthless.[23] Finally, in 1889, Ross was removed.

The lesson most New Mexican politicians drew was that they needed statehood to protect them from national political interference. Ring members believed statehood would multiply the value of their land holdings.[24] They believed, as they told the U.S. Senate Committee on Territories, that they represented "Democrats and Republicans . . . all parts of the Territory and every interest in it. . . ."[25] A constitutional convention met under the Santa Fe Ring's tight control and presented a constitution to the voters for ratification in 1890. By a margin of two to one, they rejected it.[26]

Historians speculate about the reason for this anti-state vote. Perhaps the largely Republican Hispanics objected to the constitution's disfranchisement of non-English speakers and promotion of non-Catholic public schools. Perhaps the largely Democratic Anglos objected to the constitution's fixing the tax burden almost entirely on the mining and railroad industries and gerrymandering the electoral districts in favor of Republicans.[27] Some have speculated that Hispanics feared statehood would bring higher taxes and the loss of even more land.[28] Robert Larson notes that "lumber barons in New Mexico opposed statehood because their large land holdings . . . were assessed at less than one-tenth their true value" and statehood might bring an increase in assessments and therefore higher taxes.[29]

Perhaps the problem was simply that, as future governor Miguel Otero put it, "the territory was too poor to pay the expenses of a state government."[30] Certainly, the 1880s were a period of economic decline in New Mexico, and the 1890s brought more than one serious economic panic, as, indeed, occurred in the nation as a whole.[31]

Otero became New Mexico's first Hispanic governor in 1897.[32] By the middle of his nine-year tenure, times had improved.[33] Historian Robert Larson notes that the improving economy of the early twentieth century "was generally regarded as a good omen for statehood."[34] By that time, a majority of New Mexicans may have supported statehood. In fact, the territorial delegate to Congress who was elected in 1900, Bernard Rodey, won on a statehood platform.[35]

In 1901, the Arizona and Oklahoma congressional delegates joined Rodey in a promising push for triple statehood. Arizona and New Mexico, however, fell at the stone wall erected by the Senate chairman of the Committee on Territories, Albert Beveridge.[36] Beveridge, like many of his fellow Progressives, was an ethnic chauvinist; he did not like Hispanic Americans. Furthermore, Republicans had only held a plurality of the Senate seats in the Congress of 1897–1899; they did not care to add states that might not be rock-solidly Republican.[37] Among Washington Republicans there had long been a suspicion, reasonably well-founded, that New Mexico harbored numerous Southern sympathizers.[38]

In 1904, Beveridge almost succeeded in cutting the future Senate representation of Arizona and New Mexico in half by having the two territories admitted as one state.[39] That plan was torpedoed by Arizona voters. Mostly Democratic and Anglo, Arizonans overwhelmingly opposed joining themselves to their Republican, Hispanic, and far more numerous neighbors.[40]

A majority of New Mexicans may have voted for the measure. For one thing, joint statehood would require paying for only half the number of officials and a smaller share of taxes than separate statehood.[41] Officially, the New Mexico vote was 64 percent for jointure, but serious questions about the validity of the results were raised after the election.[42] In any event, New Mexico's vote was irrelevant given Arizona's opposition.

By 1908, President Roosevelt had come to support statehood, and the Republican Party put the admission of New Mexico and Arizona into its national platform.[43] Beveridge, who bitterly believed that both states would ultimately swing Democratic, blocked their entry as long as he could, and he outlasted Roosevelt's tenure. But President Taft took office determined to add the new states.[44]

In 1910, Congress passed an act enabling New Mexico and Arizona to hold constitutional conventions.[45] A hasty election was held in New Mexico and a constitution was written, ratified by 70 percent of the voters,[46] and submitted to Washington for approval. The president and Congress required a change to the constitution making future amendments easier to pass, but otherwise accepted the document and statehood.[47] Taft signed the proclamation in January of 1912 that added the State of New Mexico to the union and ended over sixty years of political subordination.[48]

SPENDING IN THE TERRITORY OF NEW MEXICO

Based on the behavior of their territorial and local governments, New Mexicans had good reason to suspect that statehood would bring explosive fiscal growth. Local officials and lawmakers frequently handled the public purse irresponsibly, and sometimes criminally. The New Mexico Territory had to issue scrip to its vendors in the 1870s as a result of such actions, and citizens returned the favor, paying their taxes in scrip. The courts nearly shut down.[49]

Santa Fe County, Thomas Catron's county, issued half a million dollars of bonds to fund a railroad at a time when the total bonded debt at the territorial level was only $1.1 million. The bond issue was of doubtful legality, heavily litigated, and the subject of a great deal of attention from Congress.[50] In the end, Congress paid for these bonds by granting New Mexico lands to sell for that purpose upon statehood.[51]

In another instance, the speaker of the territorial House of Representatives was also the secretary of the board of trustees for a "deaf and dumb" asylum (as such institutions were then widely known). As speaker he sponsored a bill to pay himself as secretary of the asylum board an annual salary of $1,800 (the governor's salary was then $3,500). Governor Otero, a presidential appointee, vetoed the act.[52]

TERRITORIAL-FEDERAL FISCAL RELATIONS

Fiscal scandals, whether official policy or outright theft, probably did lead some residents to conclude that their territorial officials were not up to the responsibilities of statehood.[53] In defense of these officials, however, their general irresponsibility was actually mandated by Congress. The federal government, after all, controlled much of what happened in the territories.

The act creating the Territory of New Mexico stated the situation quite bluntly: "All the laws passed by the legislative assembly and governor [of New Mexico] shall be submitted to the Congress of the United States, and, if disapproved, shall be null and of no effect."[54] Floridians bitterly remarked during their own statehood debates in the 1830s that Congress's nullification power meant territorial citizens possessed no political rights and territorial councils possessed no real authority; the territories were only "a plantation of the states and the council the *overseer*."[55]

The Floridians were right. Congress's nullification power was not a mere formality. On the contrary, U.S. legislators disapproved territorial acts on many occasions.[56] In the late 1890s, for example, Congress took two years to allow the issue of New Mexican bonds beyond the limit it had previously imposed, so that New Mexicans could build a new capitol to replace the one arsonists had burned.[57]

In 1903, New Mexican legislators passed a law limiting corporate liability for personal injuries occurring in the territory. Five years later, the U.S. House Committee on the Territories delivered an outraged report to the full chamber on the iniquities of the law. The Committee added insult to its report: "This legislation of New Mexico, to say the least, is unique and demonstrates the wisdom of the law giving Congress absolute control over the legislation of the Territories."[58] In May, Congress threw the act out by joint resolution.[59] In 1910, another joint resolution threw out the New Mexican assembly's re-drawing of the boundaries of one of its counties.[60]

As Congressman William Knox of Massachusetts put it in the 1902 debate over admitting New Mexico, Arizona, and Oklahoma:

> The unreasonable provision [of Congress's power] is that no time is fixed in which Congress may disapprove of a Territorial enactment. . . . It is never settled that the law of the Territorial legislature shall remain . . . The evidence was conclusive that that is the opinion in the financial centers of the world—in New York, in London, in Berlin, and everywhere securities are examined. Capitalists will not invest in a Territory. They want a State law, and the reason is because of the power which Congress has to unmake the Territorial law.[61]

This is one of the main reasons the Santa Fe Ring supported statehood—they believed it would raise their property values and bring about a boom in business.[62]

Congress sometimes used its power directly to micromanage the territories, often on the subject of money. For instance, before recommending that the full House validate a New Mexico bond issue in 1908, the Committee on Territories asked the U.S. Secretary of the Interior for suggestions. The Secretary requested the New Mexico governor to explain why the territorial auditor had collected excess taxes to repay railroad bonds and what had happened to the extra revenues.[63]

At other times, Congress left the micromanagement to the Department of the Interior.[64] For example, a 1907 Interior memorandum divided the New Mexico governor's report into five different subjects and assigned each to the appropriate office for study.[65] Commissioner Elmer Ellsworth Brown, at the Bureau of Education, replied at length with tables and commentary comparing detailed educational statistics from New Mexico to statistics from each region of the country. Brown thought the territory's average length of school term "altogether too short," its expenditure "far too low," and its "compulsory school law . . . inadequate."[66]

The federal government not only supervised a territory's fiscal policy but also subsidized it. When Congress passed the act creating the Territory of New Mexico, it listed the regular subsidies the territory would receive. These included specified salaries for the governor, the federal judges, and the territorial secretary, a specified stipend for legislators when in session or in transit to and from sessions, and some monies for the contingent expenses of the governor and the assembly.[67]

In his indispensable study of the federal administration of the territories, Earl Pomeroy notes that the U.S. Treasury, which was responsible for delivering the subsidies mandated by Congress, sometimes scrutinized the financial requests of territorial officers in minute detail and inevitably became involved to some degree in management and policy.[68] The Interior and Agricultural Departments also micromanaged the territories by exercising the power of the purse.

Such financial supervision by federal departments often caused conflict. In 1908, the New Mexico territorial secretary and the Department of the Interior exchanged sharp letters after the postmaster denied New Mexico the frank for sending its session laws to Washington. The postmaster said the frank was for national business only; the territory said Congress had made territorial laws national business.[69]

The federal government sometimes stood on firmer ground in denying funds, though the amounts were occasionally trivial. In 1912, the Acting Assistant Secretary of the Interior refused to pay Western Union 34 cents for a telegram because its subject was the participation of a New Mexico rifle team in a national competition; the governor's annual report had claimed the team represented the territory, so this was not, said the assistant secretary, national business.[70]

Despite the oversight, the territories did not disdain their financial dependence on Washington. Sometimes, they simply requested funds for a local need in the hope that a federal agency would fit it into an existing appropriation. This is probably what happened when New Mexico Governor George Curry asked the U.S. Department of Agriculture for seed wheat to distribute to the poor in dry farming areas suffering a drought.[71] The Agriculture Department denied the request on the grounds that the seed wheat appropriation was "for experimental and testing purposes only."[72]

As the early twentieth century wore on, Washington began funding more and more projects in both states and territories. For all states, federal aid as a percent of total revenue grew from 1.6 percent in 1902 to 7.9 percent in 1922.[73] Major irrigation projects and the Good Roads movement of the first decades of the 1900s both pumped enormous amounts of money into New Mexico.[74] Thus, some of New Mexico's dependence on the federal government was simply part of the twentieth century's shift of power to Washington, not a function of territorial status per se.

On the other hand, the fiscal transition from territory to state was sharply demarcated in some instances. The Treasury Department refused to pay the salaries of the New Mexican governor and secretary and their staffs for even one day after statehood. "There is no law," stated the U.S. Comptroller, "of which I have any knowledge that will justify the payment of the salaries of the Territorial officers after said State is admitted to the Union."[75]

Similarly, Congress appropriated $100,000 each to New Mexico and Arizona for the expenses of electing the constitutional convention delegates, holding the constitutional conventions, and ratifying the constitutions.[76] When New Mexicans were required to add a later constitutional amendment before statehood, in 1911, they asked that the costs of ratifying that amendment be paid from the same appropriation. Treasury refused; the later ratification process had not been mentioned in the 1910 appropriating act.[77] As for the office furniture, typewriters, and so forth bought under that statehood appropriation, Interior required that they be sold when the constitution had been ratified, and the money returned to the U.S. Treasury.[78]

THE CONSTITUTION AND STATEHOOD

As illustrated above, Congress and the federal executive departments acted as fiscal brakes on territorial spending. With statehood, that brake vanished. Anticipating a problem with their nascent state governments as a result, distrustful delegates to the constitutional conventions usually wrote numerous fiscal restraints into the new state constitutions.[79]

The first New Mexico constitution certainly had such restraints. The state could not incur debt without simultaneously levying an adequate tax for repayment,[80] could not require any county to help pay the debts of another county (this was protection against counties like Grant and Santa Fe, which had tried to shift their own extraordinary debt burdens to the rest of the territory),[81] and could not borrow more than $200,000 for any reason (except defense), unless a popular majority approved of the debt; even then, the total post-territorial indebtedness could not exceed 1 percent of all property assessments.[82]

Taxes in the new state could not exceed 12 mills on assessed valuation for the first two years, nor exceed 10 mills thereafter (except for levies for the state debt).[83] The entities eligible for tax exemptions were enumerated.[84] The legislature could not assess large landholdings for tax purposes at a lower value per acre than small tracts, nor could plowed land be assessed at a higher value than unplowed land.[85] Nor could the legislature authorize bonds without simultaneously levying a tax sufficient for the interest and repayment of principal.[86]

Suspicious convention delegates wrote into their constitution many provisions aimed at impeding individual officials' dishonesty. For instance, the state treasury could not pay out any monies except for the public debt or by legislative appropriation, and all appropriations had to specify their sums and purposes.[87] If anyone used public funds illegally, the legislature could not retroactively legalize the crime.[88]

The constitution set the salaries of the major executive officials, which were unchangeable for the first ten years of statehood.[89] Legislators could not hold other civil offices while sitting in the legislature or for one year after their terms were over hold any office that had been created, or the compensation for which had been increased, while they were in the legislature.[90] The legislature could not give officers, contractors, or agents any additional compensation after services were rendered.[91]

In 1912, one of the questions facing New Mexicans, whether supporters or opponents of statehood, was: Would these constitutional rules restrain government spending as well as congressional oversight had done? Would the people come to regret or celebrate their decision to raise their government to the status of a state?

NOTES

1. Lamar, *Far Southwest*, chaps. 18, 19.
2. I.e., slavery would be prohibited in the new state.

3. Lamar, *Far Southwest*, 68.

4. Lamar, *Far Southwest*, 65–70; "Boundary of Texas. Territory of New Mexico," *U.S. Statutes at Large* 9 (September 9, 1850): 446, "temporary" in §2. For a brief description of the specifics of the administrative system Congress set up for the territories of New Mexico and Arizona, see Willoughby, *Territories and Dependencies*, 53–60. Pomeroy, *Territories and the United States*, has more detail, but includes many states and stops at 1890. Van Cleve, *Office of Territorial Affairs*, almost exclusively covers the administration of the possessions acquired after 1898.

5. U.S. Bureau of the Census, *Historical Statistics*, part 1, series A 195.

6. Dargon, "New Mexico's Fight," 19–22; Lamar, *Far Southwest*, 122–134; Larson, "Statehood for New Mexico," 162–166; Larson, "Territorial Politics," 249–255; Otero, *My Nine Years*, 142–147; Owens, "Pattern and Structure," 170.

7. Jenkins, *Guide to the Microfilm Edition*, 12; Lamar, *Far Southwest*, 159; Larson, *Forgotten Frontier*, 180; Larson, "Territorial Politics," 263–267.

8. Lamar, *Far Southwest*, 131.

9. Riskin, *Train Stops Here*, chap. 2.

10. Dye, *All Abroad for Santa Fe*, chap. 2.

11. Weigle, *Alluring New Mexico*, 14.

12. Lewis and Hagan, *Peculiar Alchemy*; Weigle, *Alluring New Mexico*.

13. Schweikart, "Early Banking in New Mexico," 16.

14. Jenkins, *Guide to the Microfilm Edition*, 11–13; Larson, *Forgotten Frontier*, 67; Montoya, "Dual World," 16; Seligmann, "El Paso and Northeastern Railroad."

15. U.S. Bureau of the Census, *Historical Statistics*, part 1, series A 195.

16. Lamar, *Far Southwest*, 172; Fowler, "Constitutions and Conditions," 55.

17. Jenkins, *Guide to the Microfilm Edition*, 15; Lamar, *Far Southwest*, 127–143.

18. Lamar, *Far Southwest*, 144.

19. Larson, "Territorial Politics," 255.

20. Jenkins, *Guide to the Microfilm Edition*, 19–20; Lamar, *Far Southwest*, 155–160. Before 1883, there were only three indictments for land fraud in New Mexico; in 1886, the year after Ross took office, 351 cases were filed (Sálaz Márquez, *Santa Fe Ring*, 59).

21. Lamar, *Far Southwest*, 159.

22. Eblen, *First and Second*, 189.

23. Lamar, *Far Southwest*, 159–160.

24. Dargon, "New Mexico's Fight," 28; Lamar, *Far Southwest*, 144; Larson, "Statehood for New Mexico," 166; Melzer, "New Mexico in Caricature," 343.

25. Quoted in Prince, *New Mexico's Struggle*, 76.

26. Lamar, *Far Southwest*, 135; Jenkins, *Guide to the Microfilm Edition*, 21. The anti-statehood vote included large majorities in the counties of Santa Fe, Bernalillo (Albuquerque), Dona Ana (Las Cruces), and San Miguel (Las Vegas) (Prince, *New Mexico's Struggle*, 55).

27. Lamar, *Far Southwest*, 165.

28. Lamar, *Far Southwest*, 164.

29. Larson, "Statehood for New Mexico," 185.

30. Otero, *My Nine Years*, 200. See Dargan, "New Mexico's Fight," 1–6, for similar arguments.

31. Schweikart, "Early Banking in New Mexico," 16; Larson, "Statehood for New Mexico," 178; Larson, *Forgotten Frontier*, 84–84; Jenkins, *Guide to the Microfilm Edition*, 23.

32. Jenkins, *Guide to the Microfilm Edition*, 24.

33. Schweikart, "Early Banking in New Mexico," 17; Larson, "Statehood for New Mexico," 178; Larson, *Forgotten Frontier*, 84–85.

34. Larson, "Statehood for New Mexico," 178.

35. Lamar, *Far Southwest*, 171, 425. U.S. territories are allowed one popularly elected representative to Congress. The representative has no congressional vote, though traditionally he holds a good deal of power on questions concerning the territory.

36. Braeman, "Albert J. Beveridge"; Lamar, *Far Southwest*, 425–426; Larson, "Taft, Roosevelt."

37. Martis, *Historical Atlas*, 151.

38. Larson, *Forgotten Frontier*, 71–72; Larson, "Territorial Politics," 248–253; Onuf, "Territories and Statehood," 1300.

39. Braeman, "Albert J. Beveridge," 321–335; Harrison, "Congressional Insurgents," 5; Leopard, "Joint Statehood: 1906."

40. Lamar, *Far Southwest*, 428–429. The anti-jointure vote in Arizona was 84 percent to 16 percent (calculated from Leopard, "Joint Statehood," 246.)

41. Larson, "Statehood for New Mexico," 185.

42. Leopard, "Joint Statehood," 246–247.

43. Dargon, "New Mexico's Fight," 26.

44. Braeman, "Albert J. Beveridge," 334–338.

45. *Statehood of New Mexico and Arizona*, Public Law 61–219, *U.S. Statutes at Large* 36 (June 20, 1910), 557; Jenkins, *Guide to the Microfilm Edition*, 8.

46. Calculated from New Mexico (Territory), Governor, Secretary, and Chief Justice, "Certificate of the Governor," 6.

47. The original amending article had made it "almost impossible" to change the constitution, in the words of one participant (Tiltman, "New Mexico Constitutional Convention," 182).

48. U.S. General Accounting Office, *Experiences of Past Territories*, 8; Larson, "Taft, Roosevelt," 114.

49. Ball, *Desert Lawmen*, 259–261.

50. NM Traveling Auditor, *Report 1918–1919*, 9; "Governor's Message to . . . the 38th Legislative Assembly of the Territory of New Mexico," *Terr. Pap: NM*, reel 15, p. 8; Otero, *My Nine Years*, 385; Lamar, *Far Southwest*, 154.

51. *Statehood of New Mexico and Arizona*, Public Law 61–219, *U.S. Statutes at Large* 36 (June 20, 1910), § 7.

52. Otero, *My Nine Years*, 75–76; Eblen, *First and Second*, 311.

53. See remarks of some New Mexicans in 1890, cited in Dargan, "New Mexico's Fight," 6.

54. *Territorial Government for New Mexico, Stats at Large of USA 1789–1873* 9 (September 9, 1850), 446 and § 7.

55. Alfred Woodward at Florida constitutional convention in 1838, in Knauss, "Reports of Convention," 205, emphasis in the original. New Mexico Governor Miguel Otero made the same point, albeit as a presidential appointee in less inflamed language (*My Nine Years*, 28). See also Onuf, *Statehood and Union*, 72.

56. Eblen, *First and Second*, 195–200, discusses Congress's use of this power in the territories generally.

57. Otero, *My Nine Years*, 68.

58. U.S. House Committee on the Territories, *Disapproval of Certain Laws*, 1908, *Terr. Pap.: NM*, reel 13.

59. *New Mexico, Legislative Act Disapproved*, Pub. Res. 22, 60th Cong., 1st sess. *U.S. Statutes at Large* 35 (May 13, 1908), 573.

60. *New Mexico, Law Disapproved*, Pub. Res. 29, 61st Cong., 2nd sess., *U.S. Statutes at Large* 36 (May 10, 1910), 879.

61. U.S. Congress, House, *Admission of Oklahoma*, 5140.

62. See also Prince, *New Mexico's Struggle*, 90.

63. Sec. James Garfield to Gov. New Mexico, April 1, 1908, *Terr. Pap.: NM*, reel 13.

64. Pomeroy, *Territories and the United States*, 6; Van Cleve, *Office of Territorial Affairs*, 6. According to Van Cleve, micromanaging the territories is a popular activity at Interior, right up to the Secretarial level (ibid., 201–202). The Department of the Interior took over supervision of the territories from the Department of State in 1873.

65. "Memorandum for Mr. Parker," Nov. 14, 1907, *Terr. Pap.: NM*, reel 10.

66. "Memorandum from Elmer Ellsworth Brown, Commissioner, Bureau of Edu., U.S. Dept. Interior," Nov. 29, 1907, *Terr. Pap.: NM*, reel 10.

67. *Territorial Government for New Mexico, Stats at Large of USA* 9 (September 9, 1850): 446, and § 12.

68. Pomeroy, *Territories and the United States*, 30–33. Pomeroy's fourth chapter, on territorial finances, contains a wealth of detail on the fiscal relations of Washington with the territories from 1861 to 1890.

69. Sec. of NM to Sec. of the Interior, July 21, 1908, *Terr. Pap.: NM*, reel 13.

70. Clement S. Ucker, Acting Assistant Sec., Dept. Interior, to James H. King, Cashier, Western Union Telegraph Company, Aug. 12, 1912, *Terr. Pap.: NM*, reel 13.

71. George Curry, Gov., New Mexico, to James R. Garfield, Sec. of the Interior, Aug. 22, 1908, *Terr. Pap.: NM*, reel 10.

72. Acting Sec., U.S. Dept. of Agriculture, to U.S. Sec. of the Interior, Aug. 18, 1908, *Terr. Pap.: NM*, reel 13.

73. Inman, "Federal Assistance," 37.

74. Nash, "New Mexico in the Otero Era," 7–8; Jenkins, *Guide to the Microfilm Edition*, 25.

75. Comptroller, U.S. Treasury Dept., to Sec., U.S. Dept. of the Interior, Dec. 13, 1911, *Terr. Pap.: NM*, reel 14.

76. *Statehood of New Mexico and Arizona*, Public Law 61–219, *U.S. Statutes at Large* 36 (June 20, 1910): 557, § 17 (New Mexico), § 35 (Arizona).

77. Comptroller, U.S. Treasury Dept., to Sec., U.S. Dept. Interior, September 11, 1911, *Terr. Pap.: NM*, reel 14.

78. Chief Clerk and Chief Executive Officer, U.S. Dept. Interior, to Nathan Jaffa, Sec., Terr. of NM, Nov. 17, 1911, *Terr. Pap.: NM*, reel 14.

79. See for example, Louisiana Constitution of 1812, art. 2, § 23; art. 6, § 5; Texas Constitution of 1845, art. 3, § 26; art. 7, § 8. In 1886, the Senate Committee on Territories made exactly this argument in support of the Harrison Act, which restricted the territories' fiscal behavior. U.S. Congress, Senate, Committee on Territories, *Prohibiting Passage*, 1.

80. NM Constitution of 1912, art. 4, § 29.

81. NM Constitution of 1912, art. 9, § 2.

82. NM Constitution of 1912, art. 9, §§ 7, 8.

83. NM Constitution of 1912, art. 8, § 4. A 1914 amendment raised the millage limits and made the new limits open to change by popular majority vote.

84. NM Constitution of 1912, art. 8, §§ 7, 8, 11.

85. NM Constitution of 1912, art. 8, § 12.

86. NM Constitution of 1912, art. 1, § 29.

87. NM Constitution of 1912, art. 4, § 30.

88. NM Constitution of 1912, art. 4, § 25.

89. NM Constitution of 1912, art. 5, § 21.

90. NM Constitution of 1912, art. 4, § 28.

91. NM Constitution of 1912, art. 4, § 27.

3

Arizona's Rocky Fiscal Road to Statehood

Congress cut the Territory of Arizona out of New Mexico in 1863.[1] In the territory, a little desultory discussion of statehood occurred in the late 1870s, but it was not very serious. Neither the territory's newspapers nor its political parties called for statehood before the late 1880s. Things changed quickly after that, and by 1891, perhaps a decade before most New Mexicans wanted a state, a majority of Arizona residents approved statehood.[2] But Congress stalled for another two decades before admitting Arizona to the union.

As with New Mexico, the historiography of Arizona statehood focuses on the long struggle between the territory and Congress.[3] The controversy within the territory has occupied a lot less of historians' attention.[4] This chapter details some of that controversy, beginning with a little political background.

POLITICS, PEOPLE, AND THE ECONOMY

Politically, Arizona was divided. Its governors were usually Republican, as their appointment was in presidential hands. The Mexican-Americans were also solidly Republican.[5] However, most Arizona voters were Democratic and Anglo. They generally elected a Democratic territorial delegate to Congress, usually Marcus Aurelius Smith in the later decades.[6]

In the year of statehood, Arizonans were far more likely to be Progressive and Socialist than were voters in New Mexico and the rest of the country. Over 13 percent of Arizona voters cast their ballots for Socialist Party presidential candidate Eugene Debs in 1912, versus only 5.8 percent in New Mexico and 6 percent in the nation as a whole.[7]

The mining companies and railroads were the territory's economic powerhouses, with concomitant political influence. More than a third of the labor force worked in mines and manufacturing by the eve of statehood.[8] Labor unions constituted an important interest group in Arizona, unlike New Mexico.[9] Ranchers and farmers were important, too, though not the dominant force they were in New Mexico.

After the railroads arrived to serve the mines in the 1870s and 1880s,[10] people from everywhere poured into Arizona. From 10,000 people in 1870, to four times that number in 1880, the population of Arizonans doubled again by 1890 to 88,000. By 1930, the end of the period of this study, there were more than 10 times as many people in Arizona as there had been at the beginning of the period in 1880.[11]

These numbers were far smaller than New Mexico's in the territorial years. Arizona had only about 10 percent of its neighbor's population in 1870. As late as 1910, there were 60 percent more New Mexicans than Arizonans. New Mexico soon lost its lead after statehood, though; Arizona had more people by 1930 (436,000 vs. 423,000).

Anglos already outnumbered Mexican-Americans in Arizona in 1883.[12] Therefore, Mexican-Americans had far less political power in Arizona than they did in New Mexico, where they were always a majority. To ensure their political control, the Democrats of Arizona, mostly Anglos, succeeded in passing a voter qualification law in 1909 (over the Republican governor's veto) that was intended to disfranchise Spanish speakers and thereby reduce Republican opposition.[13]

Arizona was a very different place on the eve of statehood than it had been in 1870. Phoenix consisted of 200 people in 1870 (Tucson had 3,200). The railroad reached Maricopa County in 1879; and by the 1880s, Phoenix had streetcars, a water system, an insane asylum, and an opera house. The Roosevelt Dam boosted agriculture in the early 1900s and the territory became a haven for tuberculosis patients. At statehood, Phoenix had over 11,000 people and gas lights, and the state had 1,800 automobiles with a string of dealerships and repair shops.[14] Arizona was no longer a frontier.

STATEHOOD EFFORTS

Statehood opponents within the Territory of Arizona objected on the grounds that the territory could not afford it, according to Mark Pry.[15] The powerful railroads and mining companies feared that statehood would bring them a higher tax burden, as well.

On the other hand, some Arizonans wanted a state. A bill was introduced in Congress in 1889 to take both Arizona and Idaho into the union. Governor Meyer Zulick, a Democrat, supported the idea in his annual message that year on the grounds that "our progress would be more rapid" as a state.[16] As in New Mexico, this argument was based on the belief that Congress's power to annul territorial laws starved the territories of investment capital.

The legislature complied with Zulick's suggestion and called for a constitutional convention despite a general lack of interest among the people. But the next governor was a Republican, Lewis Wolfley. He opposed statehood because Arizona "can ill afford this expense," and he refused to implement the legislation. Other statehood opponents, including some Democrats, spoke up to agree. The convention alone, argued many, would be an excessive expense.[17]

Just a few years later, however, in 1891, the opposition had died down enough that an informal convention was held without a prior enabling act from Congress.[18] A large majority of Arizonans voted to ratify the constitution the convention wrote, thus approving of entering the union.[19] The document was never implemented because Congress delayed two more decades before granting Arizona statehood. But the territorial debate over statehood had ended by the early 1890s.

That majority sentiment did not embrace just any type of statehood, however. When Congress attempted to admit Arizona and New Mexico as a single state in 1906, more than 16,000 Arizonans voted against the plan (a majority of 84 percent).[20] New Mexicans would have overwhelmed the Arizona minority in a joint state at the time. Since New Mexicans were predominantly Republican and Arizona was controlled by Democrats, Arizona naturally opposed the idea. Of course, the congressional majority supported the plan for the same reason.

FISCAL PROBLEMS

Arizonans had even more reason to fear extravagance from their local lawmakers than did New Mexicans. From 1879 to 1883, territorial debt soared. The legislature of this period issued bonds to build five roads ($60,000) and a prison ($30,000), and to fund the floating debt[21] ($30,000) and 1884's operating expenses ($230,000). Meanwhile, the counties issued over a million dollars worth of debt, including, notoriously, Pima County bonds for a railroad that was never built.[22]

By the last half of 1884, the territory was so short of cash that it stopped honoring warrants when they were presented for payment. As E. P. Clark, the Arizona auditor, put it, "We are endeavoring to live at an expense of $208,784.04 with an income of less than $150,000.00." Clark recommended that tax rates and assessments be increased.[23]

Instead of cutting back on expenditures in this fiscal crisis, in the very next year (1885) the Thirteenth Legislature overspent the legal limits on its own expenses by $45,000 and sent the territory's debt into the stratosphere.[24] The "Thieving Thirteenth," as it was known for years in the territory,[25] issued a cool $100,000 in bonds to build an insane asylum and threw in another $25,000 for the university. Legislators also issued two more road bonds of $27,000 and territorial funding bonds of $150,000.[26] This was at a time when the total *two-year* revenues of the territory were expected to be about $151,000.[27]

In his remarks to Benjamin Harrison, the chairman of the Senate Committee on Territories who wanted a report on the territory's debt, Democratic governor Meyer Zulick characterized the expenses as:

> useless and extravagant legislation, a wanton misappropriation of public funds to purposes from which the people receive no corresponding benefit. The insane of the Territory are cared for in asylum at Stockton, Cal., for $6 per week each patient, which is much less than we could keep them for ourselves had we the asylum built. We require neither a university, normal school, nor any of the things provided for in these schedules, the wagon-road and bridge bonds being properly county, not Territorial charge.
> . . . In conclusion permit me to say we have a debt, when all the appropriations of the last assembly are provided for, of nearly $700,000, upon which the Territory must pay an annual interest of over $50,000, as a result of recklessness and extravagance in our Territorial and legislative government.[28]

What scandalized some people even more than this borrowing spree was the extraordinary ballooning of patronage.[29] The Thieving Thirteenth overspent the congressional appropriation for its own expenses by almost $24,000, spent on dozens of clerks. Another $20,000 was spent on printing. Only Dakota, of all the western territories required to report to Congress on their fiscal situations in 1886, had numbers as shocking as Arizona's.[30] In 1885, Arizona was not able even to pay the interest on territorial debt, and a cumulative total of over $120,000 of warrants on the general fund had not been paid.[31] As for the legislators of the Thieving Thirteenth, all but one lost his job at the next election.[32]

THE HARRISON ACT OF 1886

Exasperated by Arizona's egregious fiscal irresponsibility,[33] as well as by trouble from other territories, Congress passed the Harrison Act of 1886, to tie up all the territories' purse strings. The Harrison Act forbade the legislatures to issue debt exceeding 1 percent of the assessed value of taxable property for most purposes. Total debt at all levels of territorial government could not exceed 4 percent of assessed values. The territories could not pass special or local acts, including bills for managing common schools, for laying out the roads, or for remitting fines. In particular they could not pass special acts incorporating businesses or towns or "granting to any corporation, association, or individual any special or exclusive privilege, immunity, or franchise whatever."[34]

The Harrison Act also reminded the territories who the boss was: "Nothing in this act contained shall be construed to abridge the power of Congress to annul any law passed by a Territorial legislature, or to modify any existing law of Congress requiring in any case that the laws of any Territory shall be submitted to Congress."[35]

The Harrison Act exemplifies the reason territorial officials of this period so often, bitterly, called the federal government's attitude "colonial." As the Montana delegate put it, "the present Territorial system . . . is the most infamous system of colonial government that was ever seen on the fact of the globe," far worse, he said, than the English colonial system had ever been.[36]

TERRITORIAL-FEDERAL FISCAL RELATIONS

The federal government's appointments of officials, control of the courts, land survey laws, and Indian relations all evoked constant complaints in the territories.[37] But federal control of the purse strings was what probably sparked the most outrage among territorial officials and politicians.[38]

No other federal department was as strict as Treasury in its monitoring of territorial activities, according to historian Earl Pomeroy.[39] Treasury's justification was that the national government subsidized the territories and occasionally bailed them out of their fiscal crises, so close oversight was necessary. Such oversight inevitably entailed interference in local policy, so that local policy-makers were enraged by restraints on both the uses and amounts of territorial moneys.

In Arizona, fiscal relations with federal officials may have been more fraught than in most territories, because its late nineteenth-century elected legislators were so often Democratic while their Washington overseers were typically Republican.[40] Still, even the federally appointed Democratic governor Meyer Zulick sought and obtained an opinion from a U.S. assistant attorney general that the Thirteenth Legislature's expenditures in excess of congressional limits were illegal.[41]

The Thieving Thirteenth and its predecessors knew that their expenditures and debt issues were unsustainable when they decided on them. Territorial debt had already exceeded the Harrison Act limits in both Arizona and New Mexico before the law was signed. So dubiously did the market view the New Mexico fiscal situation that the territorial floating debt (warrants for expenditures that holders had not yet presented for payment) traded at two-thirds of its face value.[42]

The Fourteenth Arizona Legislature issued new bonds to re-fund its debt, but everyone knew these were not worth their printing since they exceeded Harrison Act limits. Arizona's floating warrants, too, quickly plummeted in value. The legislature attempted to restrain spending by, for instance, not publishing the journal of its proceedings among other economies, but still could not cover its current expenses.

The next governor, Republican Wolfley, lobbied Congress successfully to authorize the 1890 issue of $1,250,000 in new bonds to cover the deficit. Despite this implicit federal guarantee, Arizona's credit was so poor that the bonds were hard to move.[43]

The territorial auditor of 1891–1892 estimated that the excess of expenses over receipts was still $78,000.[44] By 1894, Arizona territorial warrants were worthless, and Congress agreed to back all outstanding warrants through 1895.[45] In January of 1897, Congress bailed Arizona out yet again by retroactively validating most of its bonds because of court decisions arising from the interminable litigation over the semi-fraudulent 1883 Pima County railroad bonds.[46]

The federal government directly subsidized a small part of territorial activities in addition to being ultimately responsible for the territories' fiscal excesses. For example, Washington directly paid the salaries of appointed territorial executive and judicial officials. But it seldom paid as much salary as the law allowed. An Arizona governor of the early 1900s asked the Secretary of the Interior to persuade Congress to pay him the full amount statutorily allowed, $3,500, as opposed to the $2,600 he actually received, an amount "so manifestly inadequate that . . . [it] hardly pays the necessary incidental expenses of the office, and no Territorial Governor can conduct the office properly without more or less pecuniary loss to himself."[47]

Insufficient salaries were a constant bone of contention on the nation's frontier.[48] Both the federal and the territorial governments were extraordinarily stingy, as a rule, seeming almost to expect service on a charitable basis. But the territories often took advantage of Washington's parsimony by illegally augmenting officials' salaries.[49] These payments were at best legally dubious; Congress outlawed territorial supplements for its major officials' salaries for fear the territories would emulate their revolutionary forefathers, who had wrested control of colonial officials away from England by paying (or withholding) their salaries.[50]

Salary supplements sometimes took the form of additional legislative appropriations. For instance, in the year ending June 30, 1899, Arizona paid $124 towards the governor's contingencies, $2,173 to his other office expenses and rewards, and $300 for his private secretary. The territory also paid $1,600 for district judges' expenses.[51]

The salary subsidies were paid automatically. But some direct federal subsidies were paid only upon request, which had to be properly documented. The U.S. Treasury argued with Arizona officials about such expenses throughout the territorial period, just as it argued with New Mexicans.

For example, a Treasury auditor in 1908 denied $197.50 of reimbursement for Navajo and Yuma County printing expenses related to the 1906 joint statehood election. Yuma had published the statehood proclamation for twelve weeks instead of only four weeks, as the law stipulated. Furthermore, Yuma and Navajo had both added election questions to the ballot that did not concern statehood, which increased printing costs.[52]

This attention to printing costs may strike today's reader as excessive, but "no other charge . . . was such a temptation" to territorial legislatures, as Earl Pomeroy points out. The legislators patronized politically supportive newspapers and also received kickbacks from the chosen printers.[53]

Economic times had improved a great deal by 1909. Arizona's Twenty-fifth Legislature undertook new capital projects for the normal schools, the university, the industrial school, the prison, and a new Pioneer's Home, among other projects entailing "the most extraordinary appropriations ever made in the history of the Territory," according to the enthusiastic report of Governor Richard Sloan.[54] So good were tax revenues that no additional bonds were issued and he thought the legislature should also accelerate the retirement of the territorial debt.[55]

Arizona's new optimism concerning its debt was crucial as Congress began, finally, serious consideration of taking Arizona into the union. Perhaps because of the impending statehood, a series of tense fiscal incidents between the territory and the national government occurred as statehood approached.

On April 12 of 1909, Arizona governor Joseph Kibbey received a telegram from the Secretary of the Interior asking that he "[f]orward soon as possible statements showing in detail all outstanding indebtedness bonded or otherwise territorial and county when incurred for what purpose and whether or not they have been validated by congressional or territorial legislation also what county debts are assumed by the territory."[56] The governor telegraphed back the next day that his 1908 report had supplied the requested information, that more of the debt had since been redeemed, and "[n]et Territorial debt [was] now $997,972.43."[57]

Interior scorned the reply in an April 14 telegram: "Statement in Annual Report not satisfactory. Please furnish detailed statement by mail requested by former telegram."[58]

Arizona could not possibly ignore this request. Congress was determining the amount of public lands Arizona would receive from the federal government to cover its outstanding bonds, a crucial issue for the soon-to-be state. Governor Kibbey spent a month collecting the information and replied by mail. He summarized the history of the controversial and onerous railroad bonds and argued that Congress's 1896 validation of these bonds also obliged Congress to cover the debts. After all, without that validation, the counties had no legal liability, since Congress had made its approval a requirement for territorial debt issues.[59]

Thus did the federal government's attempts to restrain irresponsible territorial assumptions of debt furnish the territories with a rationale for offloading all the debt onto the nation. The argument worked for Arizona; it was to receive more lands upon statehood than any state except Florida, according to Interior Department documents.[60]

Despite the final support of Arizona's territorial debts on a grand scale, the Treasury Department continued its close scrutiny of expense claims up to the end. On the eve of statehood, when expense claims for the upcoming constitutional convention arrived in Washington, Treasury often denied them. For instance, the Treasury auditor refused payment for 16 ballot boxes, because they could be used at future elections. He denied reimbursement for the publication of the statehood proclamation for eight of the twelve weeks it was published, because the law had allowed for only four. He refused to pay for three of the four precinct marshals at Yuma because Arizona's own statutes required only one.[61]

In 1910 Territorial Secretary George Young requested $1.50 for post office box rent and $100 for his messenger, and Treasury refused. This seems to have been the last straw. Young complained to the Secretary of the Interior that the Treasury auditor "seems to be suffering with a spasm of economy."[62] He told the auditor that since he was not allowed to pay the box rent until the last day of the month and the post office would close the box if the rent were not paid on time, he had paid the rent himself. "Someone has to pay the bills," he pointed out.[63]

As for the messenger, Young informed Treasury that he was really the Assistant Secretary of Arizona. The territory had sent vouchers to Treasury under that designation, and "had the mortifying experience of having the same returned to them from the Department with instructions that he must be rated as a Messenger. There is no more connection between the term 'messenger' and the duty that a messenger does in this office than there is between the Pesident [*sic*] and a constable of some Ohio village."[64]

And finally, to a request to know who did the typewriting of Arizona's vouchers, Secretary Young answered that:

> the vouchers are typewritten because . . . in the West we consider the day of long hand writing and the quill pen as past and forgotten. This service is performed by one of the neatest and most thorough business women found . . . [and] does not cost the Government one cent . . . all this must come from the menial stipend paid the Secretary. . . . As we are on this subject, permit me to state that both the Governor and myself accepted these representative places with the distinct understanding that our salaries would be what the law calls for and allowed us; that has not been done. The appropriation allowed this office per quarter to meet the state expenses required by the Department falls short just $22.50 every three months which I must make up. The Secretary's salary is $150.00 per month; from that must be paid the stenographer which ranges from $60.00 to $75.00 per month. Not one cent is allowed for incidentals. At the present time, I am carrying personally $116.00 account material and supplies for the office which I have no way of collecting or receiving my money for until the Legislative appropriation is made in 1911. . . . Permit me to be a little personal and say: You need have no fear of $1.50 being filched. This office pays me at the rate of about $150.00 per month. My daily expense account averages about $250.00 per day [*sic*]. You are sufficient mathematician yourself to make the proper deduction.[65]

Thus ended, fractious to the last, the fiscal relations between the United States and the Territory of Arizona.

THE CONSTITUTION AND STATEHOOD

The 1891 constitutional convention in Arizona—which Congress derailed by refusing to consider statehood at the time—created a constitution packed with fiscal constraints.[66] Legislators could not introduce appropriations bills within the last five days of a session. The delegates more or less adopted all the Harrison Act's prohibitions on local and special laws. In a slap at the Thieving Thirteenth, contracts to print government documents had to be let by bid and were restricted to a statutory maximum. The legislature could not authorize any debt in aid of businesses, except for internal improvements approved by two-thirds of the voters. Maximum tax millage rates were set at a level even stricter than the Harrison Act.

The pro-statehood Democrats who dominated Arizona in 1911, at the time of the constitutional convention, were not as worried by the prospect of an increased cost of government as the anti-statehood factions were. Nevertheless, the delegates to the convention made sure to pack the Constitution of 1912 with numerous fiscal constraints, including strict maximum millage rates for the local governments.[67] The state government was forbidden to incur state debts of more than $350,000 for operating expenses, and loans had to be repaid within twenty-five years. Legislators were constitutionally restricted to a maximum of 20 cents per mile for travel reimbursements.

The people of the new State of Arizona would soon discover how well these restraints worked.

NOTES

1. *Territory of Arizona*, 37th Cong., 3rd sess., *US Statutes at Large 12* (February 24, 1863), 664.

2. Lamar, *Far Southwest*, 414.

3. For the battle with Congress over statehood, see Lamar, *Far Southwest*, chaps. 18 and 19; Braeman, "Albert J. Beveridge"; Fazio, "Marcus Aurelius Smith," 1970; Palsson, "Arizona Constitutional Convention"; Sheridan, *Arizona: A History*, 173–181.

4. For exceptions, see Pry, "Statehood Politics"; and Lamar, *Far Southwest*, 413–416.

5. Sheridan, *Arizona: A History*, 173–181; Trimble, *Arizona: A Panoramic History*, 316; Palsson, "Arizona Constitutional Convention."

6. Lamar, *Far Southwest*, 412.

7. Leip, *United States Presidential Elections*.

8. Fowler, "Constitutions and Conditions Contrasted," 53.

9. Lamar, *Far Southwest*, 394–395, 402–406; Trimble, *Arizona: A Panoramic History*, 316.

10. Fowler, "Constitutions and Conditions Contrasted," 53.

11. U.S. Bureau of the Census, Historical Statistics, part 1, series A 195.

12. Lamar, *Far Southwest*, 411.

13. Palsson, "Arizona Constitutional Convention," 116–117. The law required a voter to be able to read the Constitution in English "in such manner as to show he is neither prompted nor reciting from memory. . . ."

14. Watts, *Legal History*; Peterson, *Danger Sound Klaxon*; VanderMeer, *Desert Visions.*

15. Pry, "Statehood Politics," 399–400.

16. Pry, "Statehood Politics," 399.

17. Pry, "Statehood Politics," 399–400.

18. Lamar, *Far Southwest*, 413.

19. Lamar, *Far Southwest*, 414.

20. Gov. of Arizona to Sec. of Interior, Nov. 6, 1906, *Terr. Pap.: AZ*, reel 5.

21. The floating debt consisted primarily of warrants issued but not yet presented for payment.

22. Lyon, "Arizona Territory," 212; U.S. Senate, Committee on Territories, *Prohibiting Passage, Appendix* (*Report of Governor of Arizona*, 3).

23. AZ Terr. Auditor, *Report*, 1884, 6, 7, 47–50.

24. Pry, "Statehood Politics," 402.

25. Pry, "Statehood Politics," 402; Trimble, *Arizona: A Panoramic History*, 319–320.

26. AZ Terr. Auditor, *Report*, 1888, 32–35.

27. AZ Terr. Auditor, *Report*, 1884, 7.

28. U.S. Senate, Committee on Territories, *Prohibiting Passage, Appendix* (*Report of Governor of Arizona*, 4).

29. See also Trimble, *Arizona*, 319–320.

30. U.S. Senate, Committee on Territories, *Prohibiting Passage, Appendix* (*Report of Governor of Arizona*, 10–12).

31. U.S. Senate, Committee on Territories, *Prohibiting Passage, Appendix* (*Report of Governor of Arizona*, 3).

32. Trimble, *Arizona: A Panoramic History*, 320.

33. Lyon, "Arizona Territory"; Pry, "Statehood Politics."

34. *Harrison Act, U.S. Statutes at Large* 24 (July 30, 1886): 170.

35. *Harrison Act, U.S. Statutes at Large* 24 (July 30, 1886): 171.

36. Quoted in Pomery, *Territories*, 104.

37. See, e.g., Guice, "Role of the Territorial Supreme Courts," 108; Alexander, "Federal Land Survey," 145–160.

38. Oddly, the fiscal tensions are the least studied historiographically. An outstanding exception is Pomeroy's richly detailed chapter 4 in *Territories*.

39. Pomeroy, *Territories*, 34.

40. Owens, "Pattern and Structure," 171.

41. Lyon, "Arizona Territory," 213.

42. Lyon, "Arizona Territory," 213–218.

43. Lyon, "Arizona Territory," 221, 218.

44. AZ Terr. Auditor, *Report*, 1891–1892, 4.

45. Lyon, "Arizona Territory," 221.

46. Lyon, "Arizona Territory," 222–223; Gov. of Arizona to Sec. of Interior, May 12, 1909, *Terr. Pap.: AZ*, reel 8.

47. Gov. to Sec. of Interior, January 17, 1906? [year illegible], *Terr. Pap.: AZ*, reel 5.

48. Pomeroy, *Territories*, 35–39; Moussalli, "Florida's Frontier Constitution," 85.

49. Guice, "Cement of Society," 95; Pomeroy, *Territories*, 36–39.

50. Pomeroy, *Territories*, 47–49; see also Gov. to Sec. of Interior, January 17, 1906? [year illegible], *Terr. Pap.: AZ*, reel 5.

51. AZ Terr. Auditor, *Report*, 1900, 98.

52. "Statement of Differences," Department of Treasury, May 29, 1908, *Terr. Pap.: AZ*, reel 8.

53. Pomeroy, *Territories,* 31–32.

54. U.S. Department of Interior, *Report of Governor of Arizona*, 1909, 550, 547.

55. U.S. Department of Interior, *Report of Governor of Arizona*, 1909, 549, 550.

56. Private Sec., Dept. of Interior, to Gov. of Arizona, April 12, 1909, *Terr. Pap.*: *AZ,* reel 8.

57. Gov. of Arizona to Sec. of Interior, April 14, 1909, *Terr. Pap.*: *AZ*, reel 8.

58. Private Sec., Department of Interior, to Gov. of Arizona, April 14, 1909, *Terr. Pap.*: *AZ*, reel 8.

59. Gov. of Arizona to Sec. of Interior, May 12, 1909, *Terr. Pap.*: *AZ*, reel 8.

60. Letter to Mr. Clements, January 24, 1910, *Terr. Pap.*: *AZ*, reel 8.

61. "Statement of Difference," Acting Sec. of Interior to Sec. of Arizona, June 2, 1908, *Terr. Pap.: AZ*, reel 8. See also Sims Ely, Sec. to Gov. of Arizona, to Sec. of Interior, March 19, 1908, *Terr. Pap.: AZ*, reel 7, remarking that "in practice it has been found that congressional sanction gives county and city bonds a better standing in the bond market."

62. Sec. of Arizona to Sec. of Interior, June 6, 1910, *Terr. Pap.: AZ*, reel 7.

63. Sec. of Arizona to Acting Auditor, Dept. of Treasury, June 6, 1910, *Terr. Pap.: AZ*, reel 7.

64. Sec. of Arizona to Acting Auditor, Dept. of Treasury, June 6, 1910, *Terr. Pap.: AZ*, reel 7.

65. Sec. of Arizona to Acting Auditor, Dept. of Treasury, June 6, 1910, *Terr. Pap.: AZ*, reel 7.

66. Pry, "Statehood Politics," 399–400; U.S. Congress, House, *Admission of Arizona, Exhibit A Constitution for the State of Arizona, as Adopted by the Constitutional Convention Friday October 2, 1891*, art. 4, §§ 27, 31, 39, and arts. 6, 7.

67. Constitution of Arizona, 1912, art. 9.

4

The Statehood Gamble

Statehood arguments formed a similar pattern in both New Mexico and Arizona, two states with somewhat different demographics, politics, and economies.

Opponents of statehood objected to the higher price of government that they believed they would have to pay. The territorial governments had handled the public purse unwisely and profligately, in the opinion of many citizens. A state government, thought the critics, would use its greater powers to take and spend even more money, also unwisely. Government operates as a Leviathan, in this view. A government that receives more power, as does a new state, will take a much larger share of the economic pie because it can.

Supporters of statehood argued in both New Mexico and Arizona that local economies had prospered to the point where the people could afford state governments, statehood itself would improve the local economy, and in any case the costs could be kept under control. On their side was the fact that the region's economy was improving in the decade before statehood (see fig. 4.1).

Both sides agreed that if statehood came, the people should severely restrict the fiscal power of the new government and require of it strict public accountability. Almost no one claimed the fiscal conservatives were totally mistaken about the coming increases in the size of the government. Everyone understood that the partially free ride they had enjoyed at the federal expense would end with statehood. In essence, the argument pitted those who believed that statehood would entail little more than raising local revenues to replace federal subsidies against those who believed that statehood would grant new and uncontrollable fiscal powers to a young Leviathan.

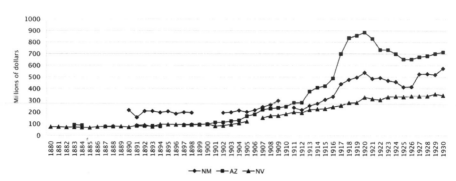

Figure 4.1. Total adjusted-to-true property values, New Mexico, Arizona, Nevada, 1880–1930. For data see tables A.2, A.3, A.4.

A territorial government's fiscal power is constrained by Congress, which can and does interfere with local tax, debt, and spending laws. Congress forbids some territorial laws and imposes others on the grounds that the nation ultimately pays for a territory's fiscal irresponsibility.

When the pro-statehood factions won, they changed the rules of the game for everyone. Statehood unleashed the taxing and spending power of the local government by abolishing congressional oversight. In place of Congress, the new states had two defenses against a fiscal Leviathan: elections in which state voters knew that only they would now restrain profligate politicians, and state constitutions with numerous restrictions on the size and use of the state purse. Opponents of statehood predicted that the increased electoral oversight and constitutional limits of statehood, however stringent they might be, would fail to stop dramatic increases in the price of government.

Statehood proponents probably wanted more government—i.e., more spending—and were willing to pay for it, within reason. Cuzán and Heggen argue that, like any normal good, the public's demand for government services shifts over time. Increased wealth or a national emergency such as war will shift the demand curve to the right, and wealthier residents would then be willing to risk the greater costs of a more powerful state government.[1] On the other hand, if demand among the public in general or among some part of the public is stable (or declining), then these people will oppose a government's getting bigger.

Back in 1787, when the Confederation Congress set up the process by which new states would be admitted to the Union, congressmen were attempting to re-create the gradual political maturation experienced by the British colonies. It worked amazingly well in New Mexico and Arizona. Their experience with political subordination recapitulated many of the same fiscal strains and economic changes as were experienced by their colonial forebears. In the eighteenth century, these strains led to independence for the American colonies. In the twentieth century, they led to statehood for Arizona and New Mexico.

So after more than sixty years, New Mexico and Arizona achieved their political adulthood in 1912. They cast off the restraining hand of the federal government, especially its control of money. Soon their people would learn who was right about the price.

NOTE

1. Cuzán and Heggen, "Expenditures and Votes."

5

The Birth of Leviathan

Recall what New Mexico statehood promoters told Congress in 1901: "[T]he amount we require being small, [New Mexico] will be the lowest-taxed sovereign State in the nation."[1] The question asked in this part of the book is—were they right or wrong?

Statehood came in 1912 and so did the answer. The promoters were wrong. The naysayers who thought statehood would be expensive were right. In both New Mexico and Arizona, the cost of government soared immediately after statehood in 1912. In absolute dollars across the three years spanning statehood, New Mexico's own-source revenues increased from $831,000 (1911) to $1,695,000 (1913).[2] Arizona's collections rose from $1,014,000 to $1,719,000.

These increases were far greater than the federal subsidies lost at statehood. In the last full year of territorial status, 1911, this subsidy amounted to about $30,000 for New Mexico.[3] By 1913, New Mexico was collecting $864,000 more from its people than it had in 1911, more than 28 times the federal subsidy lost at statehood. Arizona's federal subsidy as a territory, lost upon statehood, had amounted to about $25,000 a year.[4] Its increase in collections was $705,000, or thirty-five times the erstwhile federal subsidy. That is, as the opponents had predicted, citizens of the new states had to pick up far more than the subsidies they lost.

It is true that following statehood the New Mexico and Arizona economies grew (see fig. 4.1), just as statehood advocates had predicted. But government collections grew a lot more, as a glance at figure 5.1 will confirm. The fiscal "bite" the governments took from the local economies, F-RevA, is the ratio of the government's own-source revenues to the size of the economy.

Chapter 5

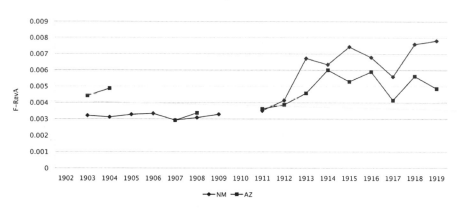

Figure 5.1. Relative fiscal size of government (F-RevA), New Mexico and Arizona, 1903–1919. For data, see tables A.2 and A.3.

From 1911 to 1913, F-RevA jumped from 0.35 percent to 0.67 percent of the economy in New Mexico and from 0.36 percent to 0.46 percent in Arizona.

Nor were the increases transitory. For the first seven years of statehood, the mean fiscal bite was substantially higher than it had been during territorial days in both states. In New Mexico, the state government's fiscal share was more than twice as high as the territorial government's had been, rising from 0.33 percent to 0.69 percent. In Arizona, the territorial government took an annual mean of 0.38 percent of property values from 1903 to 1912, while the state took 0.52 percent on the average annually from 1913 to 1919.

Meanwhile, in neighboring Nevada, no such increase in collections occurred. Nevada, a state since 1864, collected a mean F-RevA of 0.55 percent from its citizens both before and after 1912 (see fig. 5.2).

The new receipts were spent on many things, from new projects to increases in old budget items. The New Mexico penitentiary's bath house fund spent $67.65 in 1914. The University of New Mexico budget went from $32,000 in 1910 to $45,000 in 1914. The road fund more than doubled, from $60,000 to $142,000.[5]

In Arizona, license and inspection fees soared after statehood, from $18,000 in 1911 to $41,000 in 1914. The state school fund benefited spectacularly from the new government, increasing from about $62,000 in 1911 to $566,000 in 1914. Even the general fund almost tripled, from $243,000 to $663,000. The state auditor in 1914 protested the "appropriation of large sums of money, (in some cases, unlimited sums) to entirely new purposes of government," such as the Corporation Commission, the Inspector of Weights and Measures, and the Mine Inspector.[6]

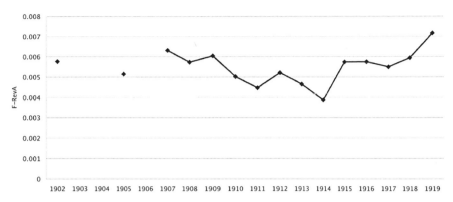

Figure 5.2. Relative fiscal size of government (F-RevA), Nevada, 1902–1919. For data, see table A.4.

SUMMARY OF REGRESSION ANALYSES

Regression analysis confirms what the graphs show.[7] SOVEREIGNTY, a dummy variable distinguishing the territorial years (1903–1912) from the statehood years (1913–1919), explains about 92 percent of the variation in F-RevA in New Mexico and about 58 percent of the variation in Arizona.

SOVEREIGNTY has no significant effect on the control government. That is, Nevada, which did not change its governmental status in or around 1912, had a pattern of fiscal behavior that cannot be explained by comparing the years before 1912 to those after.

Another possible explanation for at least some of the change in the governments' size is that regional economic phenomena were affecting the F-RevA ratio, either the property values in the denominator or the revenue collections in the numerator. Nevada was included in this study in part to control for such regional effects. To test for this possibility statistically, the residual variation in the Nevada regression equation that simply corrects for autocorrelation (see appendix) was entered as an explanatory variable into the New Mexico and Arizona equations.

The results show that the regional economic processes captured in the Nevada residual term do *not* account for the behavior of F-RevA in New Mexico or Arizona. Furthermore, SOVEREIGNTY—that is, the 1912 statehood change—remains a highly significant explanatory variable in both states.

It is also conceivable that F-RevA simply rises over time as governments grew in the early twentieth century, and that the dummy variable SOVEREIGNTY captures some part of that rise. Although the graphs of F-RevA in New Mexico and Arizona do not seem to the naked eye to support that explanation, I regressed F-RevA on YEAR as well as SOVEREIGNTY to test this possibility.

F-RevA did rise modestly with the simple passage of time in New Mexico from 1903 to 1919, if one accepts a statistical significance level of 0.10. However, the fiscal bite of the government jumped much more sharply with statehood; SOVEREIGNTY has a larger coefficient and much higher probability level. Adding YEAR to the regressions does not add much explanatory power; an equation using SOVEREIGNTY alone explains about 92 percent of the variance; adding YEAR brings the R^2 up to 93 percent.

In Arizona, time was also a minimally significant variable, but in this case the relative cost of government *declined* slightly over time. This decline was overwhelmed by the fiscal jump at statehood. When YEAR was added to the equation, SOVEREIGNTY remained highly significant, showing a large increase in the fiscal bite upon statehood. The model as a whole, including the term for time, accounts for 67 percent of the variance in F-RevA, as opposed to the 58 percent explained by the change in sovereignty alone.

In Nevada, the control state, adding YEAR to the model was not helpful. Neither the passage of time nor sovereignty explains the fiscal size of Nevada's government from 1903 to 1919.

Another way to measure fiscal size is F-GNP, the ratio of a government's own-source revenues to the gross national product. Using GNP as the denominator controls for trends in the national economy. It also controls for any biases in the property value data series that forms the denominator in F-RevA.

All three governments collected similar fractions of GNP in taxes through 1912. But 1913 brought much bigger fiscal bites to the two territories that had just become states.[8] The difference between them and the long-time state, Nevada, is vividly illustrated in figure 5.3.

Again, regression analysis tells the same story as the graphs. SOVEREIGNTY is a statistically significant explanatory variable in every equation for New Mexico and Arizona, but not for Nevada.

Recall that 58 percent of F-RevA changes are explained by SOVEREIGNTY alone in Arizona. In contrast, 92 percent of F-GNP changes are explained by SOVEREIGNTY. In New Mexico, SOVEREIGNTY explains almost all the variation in the government's fiscal behavior no matter which measure is used (92 percent of F-RevA; 87 percent of F-GNP).

F-GNP is an alternative measure of the relative cost of the subject and control states' governments. Its denominator, GNP, is quite different from the property value denominator of the study's main dependent variable, F-RevA. The data for national GNP and for local property values are collected and measured by different entities, for different purposes. Thus, the results of the

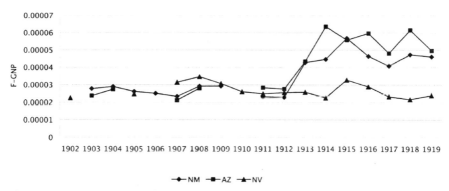

Figure 5.3. **F-GNP (ratio of own-source collections to GNP), New Mexico, Arizona, and Nevada, 1902–1919.**

F-RevA analysis were not spuriously caused by inaccurate measurements of property values (a threat to validity that is discussed in detail in the appendix).

I calculated a number of other measures of the governments' size, including several different measures of revenues and several of expenditures (see appendix for descriptions and analyses). Instead of using Revenue A as the numerator for the fiscal measure, any of the other revenue or expenditure measures may be used. All of these versions of "F" support the main analysis—that 1912 made a big difference to New Mexico's and Arizona's fiscal sizes, but not to Nevada's. The fact that all the ratios are affected the same way by the sovereignty status of their governments strongly suggests that the basic model is robust.

THE PEOPLE REACT

It is unlikely that many New Mexico and Arizona voters consulted the published financial reports to reach their conclusions, either before or after statehood. After all, there is only a little evidence that most voters of today or the past read governmental financial statements at all.[9]

In that case, how does one explain the fact that the statehood opponents acted as though they *had* read the financials? On what did they base their strongly held expectations of how a state government would behave financially, if not on the reports?

Sanders points out that people dissatisfied with their local government do not have to read financial reports to know they are dissatisfied. "Even the most politically unaware citizen-resident," he notes, "can observe whether his property has increased or decreased in value, whether the condition of streets and other public properties has changed, whether there are jobs, and whether snow is removed quickly."[10]

Certainly, the people of New Mexico and Arizona had opinions about the spending behavior of their new state governments, whether they read the financial reports or not. In 1916, the New Mexico Taxpayers' Association began publishing the *New Mexico Tax Review*, dedicated to monitoring and analyzing the fiscal policy of the state. The association declared as its premise that "the people are moreover beginning to be appalled at the extent of the demands made on them, and in general at the comparative inadequacy of the results attained."[11]

The 1920 Special Revenue Commission in New Mexico, too, discussed the fiscal situation of the young state at length:

> As to the increased costs to the taxpayers because of the change to statehood it may be said that while the amounts formerly paid the territory for administrative charges by the Federal Government were not large and are now met at home, the increase in administrative costs due to unnecessary elaboration entailed by the change are entirely out of proportion to the benefits received.[12]

In Arizona in the very year of statehood, the first state auditor fulfilled the naysayers' fears by calling for an increase in spending and taxes in many areas. In particular, he supported re-allocating the tax burden:

> It is to be hoped that [the Legislature] will succeed in formulating an enactment which will . . . without being drastic, secure from [the mining industry], as a whole, the payment of its fair share of taxes into the treasury, thus lightening the excessive tax burden, too long borne by the farmer, home-owner, and the small business interests.[13]

But when state taxes did in fact explode, the auditor felt things had gone too far. In 1914 he commented disapprovingly:

> The transition from territorial to state government carried with it the assumption of certain expenses formerly borne by the National Government, but the total of these would not approximate ten per centum of the above increase, so that it must be stated that the increase is entirely out of proportion to ordinary expectation, or to the growth of population in the state.[14]

Even in Nevada, a state since 1864, awareness of the fiscal effects of statehood lingered for more than fifty years. In 1922, the secretary of the Nevada Tax Commission, F. N. Fletcher, wrote that while Nevada expenditures were in his opinion small, nevertheless:

the per capita tax . . . is the highest in the United States; and it is a source of wonder to people on the outside that less than one hundred thousand people should be burdened with a state government. That came about from the fact that a state government was wished on Nevada by a war congress, at the earnest desire of President Lincoln. . . .[15]

It appears that some New Mexicans and Arizonans and even Nevadans did not welcome the Leviathan that statehood awakened.

SUMMARY AND DISCUSSION

This study tests two fiscal hypotheses: that a new state takes a larger fiscal share from its local economy as the price of its services than that government did as a territory; and that the statehood fiscal jump is greater than any simultaneous increases made by governments that did not increase their level of sovereignty at that time.

Examination of the fiscal behavior of New Mexico and Arizona supports these hypotheses. The ratio of the governments' revenues to property values in both places was much higher after statehood in 1912 than before. Furthermore, a neighboring control state, Nevada, which was a state throughout the study period, experienced no increase in its relative fiscal price.

Specifically, the government of Arizona increased the fiscal bite it charged for its services from a mean of 0.38 percent of the economy when it was a territory (1903–1912) to 0.52 percent as a state (1913–1919). The government of New Mexico charged even more, increasing its annual share of the economy from a mean of 0.33 percent to 0.69 percent. Meanwhile, the Nevada government took about 0.55 percent of the annual property value both before and after 1912.

Thus, the answer to the question—does the fiscal size of a government vary directly with the degree of sovereignty it possesses?—in the cases of New Mexico and Arizona is yes. As statehood's opponents had warned in both places, when the territorial government became a state, it took more money from the local population. The increase was greater than the increase in the size of the local economy, much greater than the amount required to replace lost federal subsidies, and large in absolute dollars.

The question of whether statehood *caused* the increase is harder to answer. Some alternate explanations have been ruled out by this study. The increase did not occur in Nevada, nor did the residual variation in the Nevada regression equation significantly affect New Mexico or Arizona, suggesting that the fiscal jump in New Mexico and Arizona was not a function of regional economic trends.

Furthermore, when I controlled for the U.S. GNP by creating a new dependent variable, F-GNP (the ratio of own-source revenues to GNP), the graphical and regression analyses gave similar results to those found for F-RevA: SOVEREIGNTY was a significant variable in every equation for New Mexico and Arizona, explaining almost all the variation in F-GNP. SOVEREIGNTY had no significant effect on the control government's F-GNP (Nevada). Therefore, the post-statehood jump in the price of government was not just an effect of national economic trends.

Two alternative explanations were ruled out by the use of the F ratio itself. The increase in the governments' size cannot be a simple function of having a larger economy. F-RevA controls for the size of the local economy by putting total property values in the denominator. F-GNP provides a related control for the size of the national economy. The governments' price grew not just in absolute terms but as a fraction of the local and national economies.

Similarly, the increase in the government's price is not purely nominal, a function of inflation or deflation. Any inflation from 1903 to 1919 would have affected the dollars in the denominator as well as the numerator.

Throughout the Western world in the twentieth century, there was general growth in the size of the public sector.[16] However, the post-1912 jump in F in New Mexico and Arizona was different from that general growth. Regressing New Mexico's F-RevA on YEAR as well as the dummy variable for the change in the level of sovereignty found that the passage of time probably (at a .10 significance level) had a modest positive effect on F-RevA. In Arizona, the effect of time was modestly negative. In both equations, the effect of the increase in sovereignty was much larger, highly significant, and positive.

The post-1912 increase in the cost of government was not an idiosyncratic event particular to one state. It occurred in both New Mexico and Arizona. The phenomenon common to both governments in 1912 was statehood.

A final possibility, that the model's constructs were poorly operationalized, is unlikely. For each state, two different denominators and at least six different numerators were used in a variety of combinations to create a number of F ratios. All of the ratios showed similar graphical patterns and those on which regressions were run produced similar analytical results. In short, the simplest, and quite robust, explanation of the finding that the price of government increased in New Mexico and Arizona after 1912 is that statehood caused it.

Indeed, the phenomenon appears to be so large and distinctive that it cannot be missed. The F ratio data series are very noisy. There were frequent gaps in the data, many inaccuracies, and innumerable occasions when I had to make judgment calls about which numbers to use from the reports. Yet all of the ratios created from these numbers tell the same story: the New Mexico and Arizona governments (but not the Nevada government) substantially increased their fiscal prices after statehood in 1912, both absolutely and relative to the size of the economy.

This finding supports Brennan and Buchanan's Leviathan model of government. The model treats government as an entity whose goal is to increase taxes, a goal that is "independent of the demand for publicly provided goods and services."[17] Elevating a government from territory to state confers a great deal more sovereign power on that government in the American system. Brennan and Buchanan would predict just such a fiscal jump as this study finds. Statehood unleashed the New Mexico and Arizona governments. They increased the size of their fiscal "bites" from the economy because they could.

Recall that public choice theory predicts two different tax effects of the change from territory to state: that the tax burden will (1) increase as a result of increases in the government's power (the Leviathan effect), and (2) decrease as a result of the decentralization of power experienced when the nation hands over some of its power to a new state. Statehood combines both effects: greater sovereignty for a former territory and devolution of power from the federal to the state level. The limited evidence from two governments suggests that statehood *unleashes* government rather than restraining it. That is, the Leviathan dynamic trumps the effects of decentralization in this context.

This study supports the existence of what may be called a Leviathan dynamic of statehood. But the specific mechanisms and motives that enable the dynamic are not clear. What restrained the growth of F when New Mexico and Arizona were territories? Why did territorial residents so confidently predict fiscal expansionism in the new states?

Perhaps it was simply the loss of Congress's power of review upon statehood. Territories have little or no power at the national level. Their representatives, lacking votes in Congress, cannot engage in vote-trading or logrolling. A territory has nothing to offer politicians representing the states in return for budget requests that will add to the federal government's liabilities should the territory default on its debts. Members of Congress uninterested in a territory's pet projects pay no political costs for imposing fiscal discipline, but they do protect the taxpayers in their own states from territorial free-riders. For these reasons, the federal government may act as a fiscal brake rather than a spur for territorial governments.

The fiscal restraint of territorial governments could spring from more than just Congress's hand on the reins. Perhaps the relative poverty of many territories, especially in their early years, contributed to the restraint. Whatever the spur for fiscal caution may be, it is something that vanished with statehood.

Given the Leviathan dynamic, then, why statehood? Pro-state voters at least vaguely knew about the financial scandals created by their governments, including the frequent bond issues to cover appropriations in excess of tax levies. Yet in 1891, just a few years after Arizona's infamous "Thieving Thirteenth" legislature had adjourned, a majority of the residents voted to elevate their government to the status of a state.

It seems likely that rising wealth brings a rightward shift in the demand for government. That is, when the majority is well-to-do, they are willing to spend a greater proportion of their wealth on government services. Pro-statehood citizens presumably seek benefits they believe a more powerful local government will supply.

In both New Mexico and Arizona, total property values rose in the half-decade before statehood, at least nominally (see fig. 4.1). Growing territorial wealth is often cited by contemporaries as a reason to support statehood. If rising wealth shifts the demand for government to the right, then the pro-statehood factions may have been willing to pay the price of joining the Union. Indeed, wealth in New Mexico and Arizona continued to grow after 1912, justifying the hopes of the pro-state majority. Of course, the nay sayers' fears that the price of government would grow even faster also were justified.

The new state governments provided more goods and services to the citizenry. Perhaps expenditures such as New Mexico's larger cattle indemnity fund ($17,000 in 1910; $32,000 in 1914) and Arizona's larger school fund ($62,000 in 1911; $566,000 in 1914) satisfied popular demands for a greater supply of public goods and local control of budgetary resource allocation decisions that were not completely capitalized in property values. No evidence is offered here on whether the citizens—either proponents or opponents of statehood—found that the greater benefits provided by the new states were proportionate to their cost.

Possibly some New Mexicans and Arizonans just did not believe that a Leviathan dynamic would occur, or they may have trusted constitutional restraints to impede it. If so, they would not be the only ones to disbelieve in fiscal expansionism in new states—the few historians who have commented on the costs of statehood agree. Onuf and Eblen argue that opponents exaggerated the costs of statehood; they suggest the only new costs were to replace lost federal subsidies.[18] Gordon Bakken asserts that the western states did in fact control costs upon statehood because they put strict fiscal provisions in their first constitutions.[19] As it turns out, he mistakes legalities for reality, at least in the cases of New Mexico and Arizona.

Another explanation for the pro-state majorities is that the thesis of Daunton's *Trusting Leviathan* applies to the American statehood process. Daunton notes the British government's low fiscal price in conjunction with excellent and careful public accounting during the half-century between 1840 and 1890. When the twentieth century and World War I came, Britain increased the fiscal burden to levels its people had never seen before, far higher than the fiscal burden in Germany or France at the same time. And the people continued to support the government, at least for awhile.

Like the British government of the late nineteenth century, most territorial New Mexico and Arizona legislatures practiced great fiscal restraint, although it may have been against their will. Perhaps this created enough trust among the citizens that they were willing to risk statehood. It would be interesting to know if the level of public support for the new state dropped as its fiscal price soared after 1912.

The findings presented here for the effect of statehood on New Mexico and Arizona cannot be generalized to other governments with any measurable degree of probability. One limit on generalizability is that the study covered only one historical era. In other times, different circumstances may have changed the dynamic. Perhaps in the early days of the republic, when Tennessee, Ohio, and Louisiana became states, or in the later twentieth century, when Hawaii and Alaska entered the union, there were differences in the territorial and state experiences significant enough to prevent the Leviathan effect.

On the other hand, in the cases of New Mexico and Arizona the statehood explanation for the post-1912 bump in the relative cost of government is robustly supported. In those places, the Leviathan dynamic of statehood seems to have been a powerful phenomenon, one that was predicted by contemporaries and was supported by the post-statehood facts. Residents of other territories have predicted the same effect. Perhaps they were right, too.

This is the first empirical support for the prediction commonly made by residents of U.S. territories that statehood will bring much more expensive government. That the amounts involved are small by today's standards is irrelevant; in contemporary and relative terms they were huge. The government of New Mexico more than doubled its fiscal bite with statehood (comparing the 1903–1912 mean to the 1913–1919 mean); the government of Arizona increased its bite by 37 percent. Popular political opinion often reacts more strongly to the relative than to the absolute size of a fiscal increase.[20] Certainly it has mattered to the American opponents of statehood, from Tennessee to Puerto Rico.

NOTES

1. U.S. Congress, House, *Admission of Oklahoma* [Petition from convention held in Albuquerque on October 15, 1901]: H 5136.

2. See appendix for data series containing the numbers mentioned throughout this chapter.

3. U.S. Congress, House, *Receipts and Disbursements*, 36. The New Mexico Special Revenue Commission of 1920 agreed that the federal subsidy lost at

statehood was about $30,000. NM Special Revenue Commission, *Report*, 18. As far as I have determined, the governors', secretaries', legislatures', and possibly some of the courts' expenses were the only subsidies the New Mexico and Arizona territories lost at statehood. Each received $100,000 for the expenses of the statehood vote and first constitutional convention, but that was a one-time event. *Statehood of New Mexico and Arizona*, Public Law 61-219, *U.S. Statutes at Large* 36 (June 20, 1910): 557, §§ 17 and 35. Many other subsidies to the territories continued after statehood, including support for the Agricultural Colleges and internal improvements. Subsidies of this sort to the states (though not to the territories) had been extremely controversial in the first half of the nineteenth century, but were fairly common by the early twentieth century. It is possible that other territorial subsidies ended at statehood that have not been identified by this study, because no government annually reported such totals in one place until the U.S. Census began doing so in 1915. There is some definitional question of what to include as federal subsidies when considering items such as national forest proceeds, land transfers, postal roads, fort provisions, and so forth.

4. U.S. Congress, House, *Receipts and Disbursements*, 36.

5. NM Terr. Auditor, *Report*, 1910; NM Auditor, *Report*, 1914.

6. AZ Auditor, *Report*, 1914, 10.

7. For details of regression models, see appendix.

8. The correlation between New Mexico's and Arizona's *F-GNP* values was 93 percent during the post-1912 study period.

9. Similarly, some studies have found little evidence that the bond market reacts to government reports. Inman, Raman, and Wilson, "Information in Governmental Annual Reports." In contrast, Kwiatkowski's survey results suggest that various groups do use public sector financial reports. Kwiatkowski, "Infrastructure Assets," 100. Brackenborough recounts an early nineteenth-century citizen campaign to improve the maintenance of the River Tyne in England in which the protesters' main ammunition was the published financial statements. Brackenborough, "'Pound Foolish Penny Wise.'"

10. Sanders, "Tiebout Migrants," 144. Ingram and Robbins make the same point. They explained part of the election results for city mayors with a city's accounting ratios, but they explicitly reject the idea that voters read the financials, arguing that the published data simply express what voters have experienced personally. Ingram and Robbins, "Partial Validation of the GASB," 840–881.

11. Hagerman, "Foreword," 1.

12. New Mexico, Special Revenue Commission, *Report*, 18.

13. Arizona, Auditor, *Report*, 1912, 41, 64–68.

14. Arizona, Auditor, *Report*, 1914, 9.

15. Fletcher, "Budget and State Taxes," 113.

16. Ott and Shadbegian, "Centralized versus Decentralized Provision."

17. Nelson, "State and Local Tax Structure," 289.

18. Eblen, *First and Second*, 139, 207, 222; Onuf, "Territories and Statehood," 1283–1284, 1297–1298.

19. Bakken, "Rocky Mountain," 48, 38–39.

20. Cúzan and Bundrick, "Fiscal Policy."

II

THE BOOKS

6

Accountability and Statehood

When it comes to money and government, Americans have expected accountability since colonial days. And governments have usually complied. Arizona's founding fathers, for instance, wrote this into their first constitution: "An accurate statement of the receipts and expenditures of the public money shall be published annually . . ."[1] The citizens of two centuries ago expected financial accountability, too, even on the frontier; new states' constitutions from the early nineteenth century had requirements nearly identical to Arizona's.[2]

The Governmental Accounting Standards Board (GASB) of today firmly supports such accountability. Declaring that "financial reporting plays a major role in fulfilling government's duty to be publicly accountable in a democratic society,"[3] the GASB added:

> Accountability is the cornerstone of all financial reporting in government and the term *accountability* is used throughout this Statement. . . . Accountability requires governments to answer to the citizenry—to justify the raising of public resources and the purposes for which they are used. Governmental accountability is based on the belief that the citizenry has a "right to know," a right to receive openly declared facts that may lead to public debate by the citizens and their elected representatives. . . . the Board considers [accountability] to be the paramount objective from which all other objectives must flow.[4]

This notion—that governments must formally account to the people for the public purse—is old in American history. Certainly it was widely believed at the time of this study.

John Tanner, writing in the *Journal of Accountancy* in 1914, asserted that "*right thinking on the part of the public is the hope of democracy. Indeed*

it seems evident that right thinking cannot prevail until the people receive
in proper form true reports of costs and results."[5] In their influential 1918
Principles of Accounting, Paton and Stevenson made the argument for fiscal
accountability: "In order to cast an intelligent vote at the municipal elections,
a citizen should have information in regard to the financial standing of the
city and a history of the results of financial transactions during the preceding
period."[6]

And on the occasion of the American Institute of Accountants' 50th an-
niversary in 1937, President Franklin Roosevelt said:

> The business of government is surely the most important business in the world.
> For its proper dispatch it is absolutely essential that there shall be a microscopic
> scrutiny of all government accounts not only to prevent irregularities and dis-
> honesty but as a guarantee that the will and intent of the Congress—the sole
> appropriating power—shall be carried out in all disbursements of public funds.[7]

In short, people believe that governments must publish their financial statements to show how they have handled the public purse. But to what end do
governments provide all this accountability? Do governments simply supply
financial transparency by popular demand? In the next section, I argue that
statehood supplies governments with a motive for better financial reporting.

ACCOUNTABILITY AND STATEHOOD

Many players in the public sector value good financial data. After all, it is not
only the people, from investors to lobbyists, who use a government's financial
reports. The governments themselves—the legislators and executive branch officials who make the budgets—also benefit from clear records. The information
in the reports makes the work of officialdom possible, just as accounting information makes the work of business managers in the private sector possible.[8]

Governments further benefit from the public's approval of the fact that
they publish transparent descriptions of their handling of the public purse. Indeed, there is a small body of research suggesting that dramatically improved
accounting and honest fiscal procedures sometimes accompany the growth of
Leviathan. The researchers conclude that the former enable the latter.

An example is the administration of the property tax in ancient Egypt.
Scholar Mahmoud Ezzamel believes that the New Kingdom adopted meticulous records supporting property assessments and tax collections in aid of its
expansionist wars. The scribes (bookkeepers) also prospered. Designated as
experts by the government, and expected to produce "fair" valuations, they
became quite powerful.[9]

Similarly, John Brewer tells a compelling tale of England's rise from insignificance to world-striding hegemon in the seventeenth and eighteenth centuries on the shoulders of its accountants and other government clerks.[10] Not the quick-wittedness of its military officers, the agile enterprise of its merchants, or even the dogged courage of its troops, but the orderly and voluminous accounting for every dull detail of a booming public sector, Brewer says, explains the creation of a fiscal-military state capable of making an empire out of a small island. And "at the seat of dullness," observes Brewer, "were the clerks."[11]

The clerks tracked every aspect of their target businesses, to an extent that would be unacceptable to most twenty-first-century businesses. They were very competent practical mathematicians and obsessive record-keepers. Their internal controls were admirable even by today's standards. The number of clerks employed by the government soared.

Because eighteenth-century Englishmen ceaselessly voiced their fears that the government would use its new powers of fiscal control to crush its own people, Parliament saw to it that its accounts were regularly published. These accounts, widely regarded as accurate, were the basis for an enormous growth in the tax burden relative to the size of the economy, huge deficits, and explosive government spending (both absolutely and relative to the economy). England thus prevailed over its previously more powerful neighbors. Paradoxically, suspicion of an excessively strong state produced in the end an amazingly strong state.[12]

Martin Daunton, too, argues that the high-quality public financial transparency of the nineteenth-century British government earned enough trust from the people to increase its revenues to unheard-of heights in the early twentieth century, far higher than the governments of Germany and France could do. England prevailed in World War I in part because of this.[13]

Expansionist wars are the nexus of these examples of huge tax and accounting improvements coinciding with fast government growth. Elliott Brownlee generalizes the phenomenon: new tax regimes occur on the occasion of national emergencies. The reforms enhance the public's trust in the government changes that accompany emergencies and thus facilitate the growth of government.[14]

My argument is that statehood ranks with war and emergencies as a creator of dramatically improved tax and government accounting procedures and reports. This extends my argument from the first part of the book that statehood, like war, enables Leviathan. Improvements in accountability were an important part of the means by which Leviathan was created in New Mexico and Arizona.

As might be expected of any complex human cultural system, government accounting evolves over time.[15] How it does so has not been much studied, in part because scholars seldom study the technological intangibles—the recording of property, the voting mechanisms, the accounting for government, and so forth—that are prerequisites for the development of modern liberal democracy (though they do occasionally acknowledge their necessity). Many seem to assume that somehow such technologies will appear as needed.[16]

Peter Miller points out in his study of the interrelations between accounting and the state that "it is through technologies of government that the programmatic realm of political rationalities is made operable."[17] These technologies of government, he argues, develop in particular ways due to complex interactions with the programmatic realm of government. Far from being purely technical, "the calculative practices of accounting are intrinsically and irredeemably social."[18]

Waymire and Basu take this reasoning a step farther. They argue that:

Economic crises likely play a role similar to major shocks in biological environments by selecting accounting practices . . . for survival based on how well they adapt to post-crisis environments . . . [W]e hypothesise accounting evolution around crises as bursts of rapid change amidst periods of relative stasis consistent with punctuated equilibrium theory . . .[19]

Statehood, my evidence suggests, acts as an economic crisis does. It dramatically changes and improves the financial reporting of a government. It punctuates the former accounting equilibrium, if one accepts a period of gradual small improvements as a state of equilibrium.

I also rely on earlier scholarship linking the structure of a government to the quality of its accounting.[20] Jerold Zimmerman applied agency theory for his groundbreaking 1977 analysis of why many cities did not supplement their reports with full accrual-based numbers. He found that city managers report better to city councils than mayors do to voters, and argued that it is because the city councils monitor managers more intensely than voters monitor mayors.

Appointed fiscal officers in a state faced only one set of authorities—officials elected by local residents. Fiscal officers in a territory, on the other hand, served under authorities who were variously elected by local residents (the legislature) and appointed by the federal government (the governor, territorial secretary, and judges). Monitoring of appointed territorial fiscal authorities was thus diluted compared to the monitoring experienced by their successors in the new states.

Furthermore, territorial fiscal officials who were elected, as auditors usually were, faced not only local voters but also monitors in the federal government, who could and did overrule territorial actions on occasion. This dilution of authority in a territory is an important part of why the rise in a government's sovereignty that accompanies statehood should lead to better accounting.

In fact, a government of a lower degree of sovereignty might be expected to create "fiscal illusions," to use Picur and Miranda's term,[21] more often than a government of higher sovereignty. Obscuring the revenues and costs of the public sector may partly deceive territorial residents, who are not able to exercise sole authority over their government.

The people of a state require more fiscal transparency because the greater sovereignty of a state endows the government with more independent responsibility for its fiscal situation.[22] Washington would no longer routinely bail New Mexico and Arizona out after statehood. Their partly free ride on the federal taxpayers ended in 1912. The greater financial transparency demanded of a state government should eliminate some of those illusion-creating practices.

As for the government of an infant state, it requires better reports to maintain public support as it grows. And it is going to be raising and spending much more money, if the results in part 1 of this book are correct. Leviathan requires to be fed a lot of information.

Thus, one question I address in part 2 is: Did New Mexico's and Arizona's financial reporting improve significantly around 1912 as power shifted from Washington to the state capitols?

ACCOUNTABILITY IN THE ERA OF PROGRESSIVISM

Another question concerns the Progressive movement. New Mexico and Arizona became states in 1912, the heyday of Progressivism. That was the year that a Socialist Party candidate, Eugene Debs, won the highest percentage of votes his party ever received for the presidency of the United States (5.8 percent) and Socialists won numerous local elections across the country. Progressives, for their part, agreed that governments should be far larger and more active than in the American past, an antidote to what they saw as the corrupt power of corporations. Arizonans in particular tended to support Progressivism.[23]

A. K. Mehrotra pinpoints 1900 to 1910 as the decade in which the American administrative capacity to support the modern (meaning much larger than previously known) state developed.[24] Accountants of the Progressive decades in the United States enthusiastically supported these developments in the name of good-government reforms.

With the dawn of the Progressive era, articles poured out of accountants' offices across the country, mostly concerned with the reform of municipal accounting. They sought cleaner and more transparent fiscal processes, help-ing to reform much of municipal accounting practice.[25]

Intended to effect changes in how governments accounted for the public purse, this profusion of articles was generally more polemical than descrip-tive. Yet the writers also provided their interested descendents with first-hand information on the accounting practices of the late 1800s and early 1900s, to which we can compare the quality of New Mexico's and Arizona's financial reporting.

Contrary to common opinion, frontier governments like New Mexico and Arizona were generally not slow to adopt the political techniques of the day. Arizona extended the right to vote to women just after statehood, in 1912.[26] Both New Mexico and Arizona were among the twenty-eight states (and terri-tories) that had installed a uniform system of accounts for state institutions and/ or counties before 1913.[27] Arizonans elected their first female auditor in 1927, Ana Frohmiller, and returned her to office at every election until 1950.[28] There is no reason to expect the public accounting practices of these two governments to be unusual for their times, even though they were on the frontier.

So the second question is: Did the New Mexico and Arizona governments participate in the Progressive "good government" improvements of public accounting that swept the nation in the early twentieth century?

To provide a background against which to judge the accounting practices of New Mexico and Arizona, the next section describes some of the practices and reforms in government accounting that took place around the country during the study period, the Progressive years.

GOVERNMENT ACCOUNTING PRACTICES DURING THE PROGRESSIVE ERA

Accountants of a Progressive persuasion were particularly active reformers. But I should note from the start that not all the accountant-reformers of this era shared the Progressive passion for curbing the private sector. A different view was espoused by Elijah Watts Sells, a founder of Haskins & Sells (now Deloitte, Touche, Tohmatsu):

[I]t is the unassailable truth that almost any one of the men who stand at the head of our great business institutions is far more competent to run the Government, and would run it more economically, more wisely, and more honestly than any of those who are in the business of running governments.

I know as a matter of fact that the management of our great properties is gen-erally intelligent and economical, and that the management of our Government bureaus is generally loose, irregular, and frequently dishonest . . .[29]

Sells knew whereof he spoke. He had personally evaluated the books of many companies and governments. But his speech was intended to be provocative. It was not what Sells said about government officials that was so controversial—muckraking was a favorite pastime of the period. What was controversial was his claim that private corporations were more honest and competent than government.

Whatever their views of the private sector, accountants certainly found a lot of muck to rake in the governments of this period. Chicago was a scandalous example, as Charles Waldo Haskins chronicled after his firm's 1900 audit of Chicago's books.[30] In Cook County, there were perhaps 317 tax-levying entities. Collectors' reports of unremitted taxes were not audited; receipts were often reported late and not audited or itemized; and special assessment accounts went unposted for five years in the 1890s. A previous auditor had found half a million dollars missing from the special assessments fund. He also found a vault containing a jumbled mass of bonds and interest coupons for the city.

According to the *Engineering Record*,[31] Chicago trust funds had been raided for operating expenses; the balance of collections for school taxes was unknown; departmental books did not balance with the controller's books; the controller was forbidden to investigate before authorizing disbursements; funds were commingled; and the special assessment books of original entry were regularly destroyed.

Chicago was not alone in shoddy bookkeeping. Massachusetts city books contained "ill-digested" material;[32] Wisconsin towns failed to list all their debts or account for servicing them.[33] Cleveland's government in the 1880s was "a growth, not an organization . . . no system of accounts of city affairs was possible."[34] In Portland, Oregon, accounting was so lax and the public so inattentive that few knew what the tax rates were, invoices were paid for goods not received, over $300,000 of public funds were lost in bank failures, and contracts were overpaid to employers who could deliver votes.[35] According to Frederick Clow, a scholar at the State Normal School in Oshkosh, Wisconsin, most cities published "worthless" financial reports, often consisting of a simple list of expenditures that extended for hundreds of pages if necessary.[36]

Reforms

But reform was in the air. A movement for uniform public sector accounting started in Minnesota in the 1860s.[37] An 1865 law required Minnesota counties to publish annual financial statements containing specific information, and an 1878 supplement required the state examiner to be an accountant with the power to force the counties to comply with correct bookkeeping. Within ten years, observed the U.S. Census Bureau's statistician LeGrand Powers, financial administration had improved so much that the counties' new interest income more than equaled the examiner's salary.

Massachusetts followed with similar reforms in 1879 and 1887, eliminating customary "gross abuse of the fee system" by county officials (presumably, bribes).[38] In 1887, Ohio began a massive municipal reform, including departmental annual financial reports, city council approval of all contracts over $250, and some separation of financial powers.[39] In New York in the 1890s, the state began supervising county trust fund accounts, vetting the details of all bond issues, and requiring uniform accounting for all cities with populations under 250,000.[40]

The District of Columbia accounting system created by Congress in the 1870s and 1880s was better than most. The chart of accounts was modern, transactions were booked promptly, appropriations and revenue accounts were integrated with expenditures and collections, a daily cash flow statement was maintained, and a daily statement of funds from the U.S. Treasurer was kept. Furthermore, the District had made an important technological improvement—loose-leaf ledgers, which allowed the subsidiary account expenditures to be summarized easily and balanced to the monthly control account.[41]

Reform headed west about the same time.[42] San Francisco limited monthly expenditures from any fund to one-twelfth of the amount appropriated for the year. This reform did not operate perfectly; some vendors stopped deliveries in the last two months of the fiscal year because of invoices outstanding for two years.[43] In 1892, Wyoming placed an examiner over the state and county accounts. H. B. Henderson, the state examiner, averred that whereas once only two Wyoming counties had kept within their budgets, by 1899 all did so.[44] Indeed, so much more efficient did government become that expenses dropped significantly despite a population increase. Both the Dakotas followed the Minnesota and Wyoming leads.[45]

One of the most popular reforms of this period, strongly backed by the National Municipal League, was the push to standardize accounting and financial reporting by local governments. In 1896, Frederick Clow, a scholar at the State Normal School in Oshkosh, Wisconsin, recommended that good municipal reports would require, among other improvements, classification of expenditures by function, statements of assets and liabilities, and comparability across reports.[46] In 1899, the NML published a model city charter with a proposed uniform accounting system and specific controls for municipal debt, franchises, and contracts.[47] Two years later, the NML set up the Committee on Uniform Municipal Accounting and Statistics.[48] Frederick Cleveland, one of the main creators of these proposals, favored accrual-basis accounting for cities rather than the cash-basis accounting that he found prevalent.[49]

Numerous organizations joined in the campaign to standardize municipal accounting.[50] The American Association of Public Accountants, a predecessor of the AICPA, began publishing the *Journal of Accountancy* in 1905, which included, nearly from the beginning, occasional articles on municipal accounting and the need to standardize it.[51] The Association of American Government Accountants (AAGA) began publishing *The Government Accountant* in 1907.

At first, *The Government Accountant* covered only the federal government. However, LeGrand Powers, the chief statistician of the Bureau of the Census,[52] was an early AAGA president. The Bureau had begun collecting details of state and local government finances in 1880, a Herculean task. Under Powers' leadership, the journal soon advocated uniformity in public sector accounting practices.

The Bureau of the Census itself also published essays on the quality of state and local government accounting in the early twentieth century, based on its experience trying to collect and report comparable statistics for all the states. These essays provided extensive, systematic information about turn-of-the-century differences in the states' handling, recording, and reporting of public monies, as well as their taxation and property valuation systems.[53]

The Bureau found many differences among states. Some states allowed offices other than the treasurer's to collect and spend public funds. Some states recorded trust fund expenditures in the trust funds themselves; others simply passed the money through to the general fund, where it was finally spent. In some states, private trust fund obligations were classified as state debt, while in others such obligations were not. Some states used modified accrual-basis accounting, while others used "antiquated" cash receipts and payments only. Some states collected local governments' revenues and passed them on to the counties or towns; elsewhere, the counties collected all money and forwarded the state's share to the capital.[54]

These and other differences between the states are what make research using early state and local records difficult. Certainly the differences rendered the job of the Census Bureau gargantuan. In its own defense, the Bureau developed and published detailed definitions of government accounting terminology.[55] State and local governments had to use these definitions at least minimally in their reports to the Bureau, which contributed to the growing uniformity in public sector reporting in the early twentieth century. The Census Bureau essays and the articles by Powers are probably the most systematic and detailed information available about turn-of-the-century government accounting in the United States.

General acceptance of the nascent government accounting standards advanced state by state and often city by city. Powers reported by 1909 that about one-third of U.S. cities with populations over 30,000 had made substantial progress toward uniformity by using the Census account classifications.[56] The other large cities had made some progress, while smaller towns continued in their old ways. By contrast, Marwick, Mitchell & Co. took a rather gloomier view that "no properly defined system of accounting [was] in use" in cities as of 1908, a terrible situation given that "the management of a city can be judged in a very large measure by the books it keeps."[57]

According to Chase, a pre-eminent municipal accounting expert,[58] in the beginning of the standards movement:

> the prospect for uniform municipal accounting was . . . sufficiently discouraging . . . and it was only by leaving uniformity of *accounting* severely alone for the time being, and devoting all available energies to the simpler side of the question, namely, uniform municipal *reports* based upon a re-distribution of the city treasurer's accounts at the end of the year—this re-distribution being made upon uniform and comparative schedules—that any progress could be achieved.[59]

Accounting reformers had produced the core of a model uniform municipal chart of accounts by the turn of the twentieth century[60] and a scattering of municipal accounting handbooks by the 1910s.[61] Agreement on public sector reporting reached the point that Paton and Stevenson included a chapter on local government accounting techniques in their important 1918 textbook, *Principles of Accounting.*

In 1923, James McKinsey, whose interest in accounting always lay primarily in its management value, wrote that municipal accounting should serve administrative needs, such as understanding cash flow, planning and controlling revenues and expenditures, judging employees, displaying profit and loss for enterprise activities, and providing reports "for the guidance of executives and the enlightenment of the public." These objectives, said McKinsey, require a budget, performance measurements, cost accounting, and reports that will answer a lengthy checklist of questions.[62]

Frederick Cleveland and Lloyd Morey also wrote and spoke often during this period on the goals and techniques of municipal accounting.[63] In short, by the 1920s, public discussion of state and local government accounting had become specific and prolific.

Reform-minded accounting writers, however, remained very dissatisfied with the actual progress made by the early twentieth century. According to LeGrand Powers (1904), chief statistician of the Census Bureau at the turn of the century, published municipal reports varied so widely in quality and underlying methodology that "any comparisons . . . are bound to be more or less misleading."[64]

Even at the end of my study period in 1930, the quality of local government accounting left a lot to be desired. R. P. Hackett remarked on "the marked absence of any general improvement" in municipal accounting in a 1933 article for the *Accounting Review*. He noted that two recent studies of the accounting practices of Illinois cities found most of them had seriously deficient accounting systems. Only thirteen of fifty-six cities, for instance, "properly segregated items by funds"; only twelve prepared budgets.[65]

GOVERNMENT ACCOUNTABILITY AND EXPERIENCE

In addition to the two broad questions described above—how statehood and Progressivism affected New Mexico's and Arizona's accounting—this study also explores a more basic question: How did New Mexico, Arizona, and Nevada governmental financial reports develop over time?

What nascent generally accepted government accounting practices appeared from the 1880s to the 1920s in these state and territorial governments? Were there periods or examples of backsliding, when reporting became noticeably less informative? What elements or techniques stayed the same, or were used by more than one government?

It may be that a government's reporting improves with experience, so that older governments publish better financial statements than do new ones. A number of authors claim that the centuries preceding the twentieth were times of great experimentation and adaptation in accounting.[66] Was this so for American frontier governments like New Mexico and Arizona? The fact is, we have no clear picture of how state and local government financial reporting changed from the 1880s to the 1920s.

FILLING A RESEARCH GAP

Prior research does not explore these questions. They address two of the three least-covered areas of government accounting historiography, according to Philip Colquhoun: longitudinal and comparative studies.[67] There are no studies at all of statehood's effect on accounting, or of frontier and territorial accounting in general. Even the broader topic of the history of American state and local government accounting across the whole nineteenth century through the first decade of the twentieth century is largely untouched by researchers.[68]

Few government accounting standards or regulations existed in the United States until the mid-1900s. While American governments from the early national period on routinely published their financial records, there was no nationwide uniformity in the reports until sixty or seventy years ago.

Because of the early lack of formal standards, it is widely believed that the history of government accounting in the United States began a century or so ago. According to the Governmental Accounting Standards Board, "[s]ystematic governmental financial reporting in the United States traces its beginnings to the last decade of the nineteenth century and early part of the twentieth century" when "the growth in the number and size of cities, coupled with corruption in municipalities, led to a demand for financial accountability."[69] Figlewicz, Anderson, and Strupeck agree: "[s]ince little in the way of nonbusiness accounting systems developed earlier than the turn of the century, the history of governmental . . . accounting can be considered to have begun around 1900 . . . "[70]

This belief is mistaken. A great deal of development occurred in government accounting before 1900. A variety of reporting styles existed and changed and became customary across the territories and states. State laws of the nineteenth century also occasionally imposed specific reporting requirements on those in charge of the public purse. The federal government sometimes did the same via less formal means, trying to impose some degree of uniformity on the territories and, in the late 1800s, even on the states through such tools as census forms.

One reason that public sector accounting techniques largely developed in obscurity until the mid-twentieth century is that government accounting as a whole, and its history in particular, are stepchildren in accounting scholarship. Other disciplines such as public administration and economics have done almost as much work on the nineteenth century history of government accounting as accounting scholars have done, which is to say, only a little.[71]

Previts and Brown find that in the *Journal of Accountancy*'s first eighty-five years, fewer than 5 percent of the articles concerned any aspect of public sector accounting.[72] In his *History of Accounting* (2000), Edwards concluded that there was not enough information available on the history of government accounting to include it as a subject heading, as he had originally intended to do.[73] Sargiacomo and Gomes found only thirty-three scholarly articles on public sector accounting that had ever been published on local government accounting through 2009.[74]

In defense of accounting scholars, it must be admitted that the primary source material for early state and local government accounting research is difficult to use. Frederick Clow explained the methodological problem more than a century ago:

Material, indeed, exists in great abundance. There are tons of auditors' and comptrollers' reports, treasurers' statements, debt statements, . . . But its crudity is appalling. City documents seem compiled to meet the requirement of the law or to make a job for the city printer,—anything except to give intelligible and desirable information . . . each state has its municipal system. . . . Thus . . . we have a myriad of financial systems to take into account.[75]

Of the studies that have been done, almost all concern municipal accounting rather than any other level of government. The 1920 first edition of the *Accountants' Index*, produced by the American Institute of Accountants,[76] attempted to list all the publications related to accounting for the previous few decades. The indexers found about 700 items to put under the heading "Municipal Accounting," but only 19 for the subject "State Accounting"—that is, state literature was less than 3 percent of the whole.

In short, the basic work of describing frontier government accounting techniques remains to be done. Gary Previts and Barbara Merino remark that "[t]he financing and fiscal administration of the growing cities and towns during [the antebellum] period is less than well documented."[77] The same could be said of state and territorial government accounting at any time through the early 1900s.

In the United States today, governmental accounting standards are sometimes called by the (slightly odd) acronym "GAGAS." This stands for "generally-accepted government accounting standards." Nowadays, these are formal standards promulgated by authoritative bodies.

It is much easier to study standards than it is to study evolving norms, as Shyam Sunder pointed out in a plenary address to a regional meeting of the American Accounting Association in 2006. But GAGAS became "generally accepted" in the first place by customary usage. It is how these nascent, informal, public sector accounting techniques became customary that interests me in this study.

METHOD

In light of the tradition of fiscal accountability by American governments, it is not surprising that there should have been long and serious consideration in this country of exactly what such accountability means in practice. For more than a century, extensive discussion has taken place and, in recent decades, systematic studies have been conducted, of the needs that American governments' financial reports should serve and of the accounting methods that should underlie those reports.[78]

The Governmental Accounting Standards Board sponsored a series of studies in the 1980s and 1990s. In particular, Jones and others published *The Needs of Users of Governmental Financial Reports*, a carefully developed survey of three groups of users: citizens, legislators and other oversight officials, and investors and creditors.[79]

The study found that users strongly preferred to see fund information as opposed to just consolidated information; they strongly desired information comparing the budget to actual expenditures (for citizens, this item approached 100 percent agreement); they preferred modified accrual data to full accrual; they supported extensive classification of the statements nearly unanimously; and very large majorities of every group wanted information about tax rates, limits, and tax base trends.[80]

Following this survey, Ingram and Robbins studied the extent to which local government reports satisfy the needs of users. They found that GAAP was legally required for most local governments, and the number experiencing this requirement had been increasing substantially. "Over 80 percent compliance was observed for most items [on the list of GAAP requirements]," they note. The requirement most often neglected was GAAP-compliant fixed assets reporting. Items desired by users but not required by GAAP were not as often disclosed.[81] It is this research from which I drew a list of reporting practices observed in my subject governments (see discussion below).

Data Sources

The financial reports of New Mexico, Arizona, and Nevada from the 1880s to 1930 supply the data for this study. For Nevada, the reports of the state controller were used throughout. For New Mexico and Arizona, the main financial officers were the auditors and treasurers.

Auditors had many duties, the most important of which during most of the study period was to issue warrants for the expenses approved by government legislation. Recipients of the warrants presented them to the treasurer for payment. The two officials—auditor and treasurer—prepared separate financial reports and normally operated independently of each other. In addition, New Mexico created the position of traveling auditor, an official who performed duties that today would be understood as auditing, examining the financial records of state entities such as local governments and state institutions (hospitals, universities, prisons, and so forth).

Additional information came from state and territorial tax commissions and comptrollers, some federal government records such as the census, and a few other sources.[82] Most of these ultimately derived their data from the territorial and state auditors and treasurers.

I attempted to obtain at least one officer's report—usually the auditor's, the treasurer's, or the controller's—for every year from the early 1880s to 1930 for each state. However, if data were not easily obtainable for some years, I made no extraordinary attempt to locate them. I did not examine ledgers, books of original entry, or legislative reports.

Nevada is included because it was a state throughout the study period. It serves as a control for factors other than the change in sovereignty. I examined Nevada reports cursorily, for the sake of comparison only.

Thus, the conclusions in this section are tentative due to several limitations: information may have appeared in reports I did not obtain; the information about Nevada's reporting practices is sparse; and techniques relevant to my conclusions may appear in books of original entry that I did not see.

Instruments

For each financial report, I systematically observed a set of characteristics in a checklist loosely drawn from Ingram and Robbins' 1987 survey of the reporting practices of local governments.[83] I truncated the list to suit the simpler reporting of a century ago and also modified it to eliminate anachronistic elements such as vacation pay accruals.

The reporting practices observed in the records of Arizona and New Mexico, and, to a much lesser extent, Nevada, were:

- Assets—fixed, infrastructure, cash, etc.
- Debt—floating, bonded, schedule of outstanding bonds
- Funds used—revenues and expenses classified by funds, fund balances
- Revenues by source, expenditures by function, annual difference between revenues and expenditures
- Budget information
- Subventions and grants from federal government
- Interfund subsidies
- Assessed value of taxable property and tax rates
- Explanatory material

To this list, I added report timing and fiscal year-end dates. For each item on the list, its presence or absence, and quality if present, were noted for New Mexico and Arizona. I make brief comparisons to the practices of the control state, Nevada, where possible.

CONTENTS OF PART 2

The primary purpose of this part of the book is simply to describe the technologies used by some governments to account for their collection and use of public monies as they transitioned from territory to state. I am also interested in patterns and peculiarities that appear as the reporting governments changed status, and in the extent to which they participated in the general improvements in public sector reporting of the times. As often as possible, I let the records speak with examples and anecdotes.

I begin with the last item from the list above, explanatory material. These are the narratives written by the financial officials; they are so illuminating that I spend all of chapter 7 on them. Chapter 8 expands the topic of tax assessments to discuss the early twentieth-century reforms of property tax administration in all three states.

Chapters 9 and 10 split up the remaining elements from the list. Chapter 9 covers funds, assets and liabilities, and fiscal years as well as report timing. Chapter 10 covers the items most closely related to revenues and expenditures, from interfund subsidies to tax rates and budgets.

We begin, in the next chapter, with the voices of the auditors and other fiscal officials of New Mexico and Arizona from a century ago.

NOTES

1. Arizona Constitution of 1912, art. 9, § 4.
2. E.g., Louisiana Constitution of 1812, art. 6, § 5; Mississippi Constitution of 1817, art. 6, §8; Alabama Constitution of 1819, art. 6, §7; Arkansas Constitution of 1836, art. 7, §3; Florida Constitution of 1845, art. 8, §3; Texas Constitution of 1845, art. 7, §8.
3. Governmental Accounting Standards Board, "Concepts No. 1," ii.
4. Governmental Accounting Standards Board, "Concepts Statement No. 1," 20–21, 27, par. 56, 57, 76. Appendix A in this Concepts Statement discusses the nineteenth- and twentieth-century historical roots of public sector accountability.
5. Tanner, "Governmental Profit and Loss," 269, emphasis in the original. For more recent expressions of the same opinion, see Chan, "Decisions and Information Needs." See also Dworak, *Taxpayers, Taxes,* 181 and chap 11. Such insistence on "the democratic financial accountability of public sector organizations" continues to be commonly expressed in the United Kingdom as well, as in Wynne's "Public Sector Accounting."
6. Paton and Stevenson, *Principles of Accounting*, 620.
7. Roosevelt, "Message from the President," 1937, 331.
8. See Waymire and Basu, "Economic Crisis," 210 and footnote 4, p. 226.
9. Ezzamel, "Accounting Working," especially p. 38.

10. Brewer, *Sinews of Power*.

11. Brewer, *Sinews of Power*, xvi.

12. This paradox of the coexistence of opposition to the Leviathan state with support for its meticulous public accountability is neatly personified in Adam Smith. Famous for centuries as the author of the free market treatise *An Inquiry into the Nature and Causes of the Wealth of Nations* (1776), Smith also spent the last 12 years of his life as a commissioner of Scottish customs. In this position, he scrupulously enforced the detailed mercantilist trade regulations of his time. Anderson, Shughart, and Tollison, "Adam Smith in the Customhouse."

13. Daunton, *Trusting Leviathan*.

14. Brownlee, *Federal Taxation*, Introduction.

15. Waymire and Basu, 2011.

16. E.g., Heller et al., "Political Structure," 152–153.

17. Miller, "On the Interrelations," 318.

18. Miller, "Governing by Numbers," 395.

19. Waymire and Basu, "Economic Crisis," 207, 208.

20. Zimmerman, "Municipal Accounting Maze"; Giroux and McLelland, "Governance Structures and Accounting."

21. Picur and Miranda, "Fiscal Information Illusion," 163–165.

22. The "people" in this case refers to citizen groups, government creditors, and investors contemplating increased business in the state.

23. Key, "Progressivism and Imperialism."

24. Mehrotra, "Producing Tax."

25. Fleischman and Marquette, "Municipal Accounting Reform"; Fleischman and Marquette, "Chapters in Ohio Progressivism."

26. Hayostek, "Douglas Delegates," 362.

27. "State Supervision."

28. Jones, "Ana Frohmiller."

29. Sells, "Corporate Management," 59.

30. Haskins, "Municipal Accounts of Chicago." See also Previts and Merino, *History of Accountancy*, 169–170.

31. "Municipal Accounting."

32. Hartwell, "Financial Reports of Municipalities," 129.

33. Sparling, "Importance of Uniformity." See also Winkler, "Municipal Government of Milwaukee," 120.

34. Blandin, "Municipal Government," 112–113.

35. Strong, "Municipal Condition."

36. Clow, "Suggestions for the Study," 460, 465.

37. Powers, "Standardizing Governmental Accounts," 256. See also Chase, "A Brief History of the Movement"; Woodruff, "Uniform Municipal Accounting."

38. Powers, "Standardizing Governmental Accounts," 256.

39. Blandin, "Municipal Government of Cleveland," 113–115; Kibler, "The Work of the Ohio Municipal Code Commission," 192. See also Fleischman and Marquette, "Municipal Accounting Reform."

40. Holls, "State Boards"; Powers, "Nature and Aims," 257.

41. Tweedale, "Accounting System."

42. Hartwell, "Report of Committee," 210.

43. Milliken, "Municipal Condition of San Francisco."

44. Henderson, "Uniform Accounting."

45. Powers, "Standardizing Governmental Accounts."

46. Clow, "Suggestions for the Study."

47. National Municipal League, "Municipal Corporations Act," 220, 230–233. See Rowe, "Public Accounting," for a detailed explanation of the proposed accounting system, including a chart of accounts. For an NML committee description of the municipal evils standardized accounting should help cure, see Wilcox, "Examination of the Proposed," 51–54.

48. Hay, "State and Local Governments," 553. A predecessor committee had started operations in 1897 and had produced a working plan of municipal accounting by 1898. Hartwell, "Report of Committee."

49. Matika, "The Contributions of Frederick Albert Cleveland"; Cleveland, "Revenues and Expenses."

50. Baker, "Uniform Municipal Accounting."

51. Previts and Brown, "Development of Government Accounting."

52. Powers, "Governmental Accounting for Efficiency."

53. U.S. Bureau of the Census, *Wealth, Debt, and Taxation. Special Reports of the Census Office*, 3–35, 131–216, 613–844, 953–974; U.S. Bureau of the Census, *Wealth, Debt, and Taxation, 1913*, vol. 2, pp. 11–60.

54. U.S. Bureau of the Census, *Wealth, Debt, and Taxation, 1913*, vol. 2, pp. 11–14.

55. U.S. Bureau of the Census, *Wealth, Debt, and Taxation. Special Reports of the Census Office*, 953–961; U.S. Bureau of the Census, *Wealth, Debt, and Taxation, 1913*, vol. 2, pp. 15–28.

56. Powers, "Governmental Accounting for Efficiency," 26.

57. Marwick, Mitchell & Co., "Municipal Accounting," 216.

58. Previts and Merino, *History of Accountancy*, 178.

59. Chase, "Brief History of the Movement," 39–40, emphasis in the original.

60. Hartwell, "Report of the Committee."

61. Figlewicz, Anderson, and Strupek, "Financial Accounting Concepts and Standards," 75.

62. McKinsey, "Municipal Accounting," 90–92.

63. Potts, "Evolution of Municipal Accounting," 523–534.

64. Powers, "Uniform Accounting in its Relation," 1904, 235–236.

65. Hackett, "Recent Developments," 122. See also Morecroft, Coffman, and Jensen, "T. Coleman Andrews," on Coleman Andrews' efforts in the early 1930s to reform and standardize accounting by Virginia's governments.

66. See, e.g., Holmes, Kistler, and Corsini, *Three Centuries of Accounting*, and Cushing, "Kuhnian Interpretation," 1989.

67. Colquhoun, "The State," 556.

68. Jones, *History of Financial Control Function*, 1992, 18–22.

69. Governmental Accounting Standards Board, *Why Governmental Accounting*, 29 (appendix C).

70. Figlewicz, Anderson, and Strupeck, "Evolution and Current State," 74; see also Remis, "Governmental Accounting Standards."

71. Bain comments on this in "Two Early American Treatises," 130. For an example of such work in economics, see Sylla, Legler, and Wallis, *Sources and Uses of Funds in State and Local Governments*.

72. Previts and Brown, "Development of Government Accounting," 134.

73. Edwards, *History of Accounting*, 2000, vol. 1, xxiii.

74. Sargiacomo and Gomes, "Accounting and Accountability."

75. Clow, "Suggestions for the Study," 457.

76. The predecessor organization to today's American Institute of Certified Public Accountants.

77. Previts and Merino, *History of Accountancy*, 97.

78. The following briefly review the history of these studies that began in the early twentieth century: Figlewicz, Anderson, and Strupeck, "Financial Accounting Concepts," 83–92; Holder, *Study of Selected Concepts*, chap. 2; Ingram and Robbins, *Financial Reporting Practices of Local Governments*; Jones et al., *Needs of Users*, 1–3; Kwiatkowski, "Infrastructure Assets"; Remis, "Governmental Accounting Standards"; Wilson, *Financial Reporting by State and Local Governments*, chap. 2.

79. Jones et al., *Needs of Users*.

80. Jones et al., *Needs of Users*, chap. 4. The major findings of this study were later supported by a second study by Ingram and Robbins, "Partial Validation of the GASB User Needs Survey."

81. Ingram and Robbins, *Financial Reporting Practices*, 79–80.

82. See bibliography.

83. Ingram and Robbins, *Financial Reporting Practices*.

7

The Talk

Management's Discussion and Analysis

The financial reports of a government should begin with Management's Discussion and Analysis (MD&A), according to the Governmental Accounting Standards Board (GASB). "MD&A should provide an objective and easily readable analysis of the government's financial activities based on currently known facts, decisions, or conditions," according to the GASB.[1] It is the one part of the report that normally occurs as a narrative.

What is the origin of this standard? Before there was a GASB, and before its predecessor standard-setting bodies, did governments in the United States have anything recognizable as a forerunner to today's MD&A?

Examination of New Mexico's and Arizona's financial reports over the forty-five years from the 1880s to 1930 suggests that nascent MD&A practices did exist, though national standards did not. Nonauthoritative standards for uniform government financial reporting appeared in the United States in the early years of the twentieth century, as part of Progressivism's drive for government reform. These standards were seldom incorporated into state law until later decades, and they did not require MD&A.

Most of this chapter consists of excerpts organized by *type* of narrative content in the New Mexico and Arizona reports. The excerpts illustrate the voices of the financial officers of a century or more ago, telling stories about the problems they and the people of the area faced. The length and frequency of MD&A sections are also covered. In the conclusion, I discuss the findings and compare them to today's standards. But first, we begin with a short description of today's MD&A standard.

MANAGEMENT'S DISCUSSION AND ANALYSIS TODAY

In 1999, the Governmental Accounting Standards Board issued Statement No. 34 (usually called "GASB 34"), "Basic Financial Statements—and Management's Discussion and Analysis—for State and Local Government."[2] Governments choosing to comply with GASB 34 needed to implement the guidance in the subsequent decade.

According to the standard, the MD&A should display condensed financial information for the current year and compare it to such information for the past year. The text should analyze the government's financial position, results of operations, and significant changes in its fund balances, capital assets, and long-term liabilities. Finally, the MD&A should describe any currently known information expected to significantly affect net assets, revenues, or expenses in the future.[3]

Previously, this narrative material had appeared in the letter of transmittal. Statement 34 moved it to a new, separate section of the financial report to be called "Management's Discussion and Analysis." The MD&A follows the letter of transmittal and precedes the basic financial statements.

The GASB required that the MD&A be written in an easy-to-read style. It may not include boilerplate language repeated year after year.[4]

For most of the standards it issues, the GASB considers users of government financial reports to include both the government itself (legislators and their staff) and outsiders such as financial professionals (bond raters, etc.) and the public.[5] In contrast, the new MD&A addresses an intended audience consisting of "those with neither knowledge of governmental accounting nor expertise in reading or analyzing financial statements," as Kravchuk and Voorhees point out[6]—the general public, in other words.

Auditors and accountants worry that some of these requirements are difficult to achieve with the required level of objectivity, so that preparing and auditing them is risky.[7] But the GASB believed the MD&A should be audited nevertheless, and that more subjective material could still be presented in the unaudited letter of transmittal, for which no standards have been written.

These are the GASB standards for MD&A as they exist today—a preliminary overview of the financial statements, written in an objective fashion aimed at a non-expert audience, in a format that is largely but not exclusively narrative.

FREQUENCY AND LENGTH OF
MD&A IN NEW MEXICO AND ARIZONA

I examined every readily available published report by a New Mexico or Arizona auditor, traveling auditor, treasurer, tax commission, and comptroller from the 1880s until 1930. Many reports are biennial and some are missing, so this constitutes a total of forty reports for New Mexico and forty-four for Arizona (see table 7.1). If a report had narrative text, I counted it as what is today called Management's Discussion and Analysis. I also noted the MD&A's length, specific content, and relation to a letter of transmittal.

Narrative text was just about as likely to appear in New Mexico reports as in Arizona reports. Two-thirds of the reports in both places had such proto-MD&A (twenty-seven out of forty reports for New Mexico; twenty-nine of forty-four Arizona reports).

However, Arizona officials wrote a lot more after statehood than their New Mexican counterparts did—272 pages versus 178 pages in total. The difference is mainly due to a loquacious first state auditor and first state tax commission in Arizona. The former's report had sixty-five pages of MD&A and the latter's had ninety. These numbers are so high that even when calculated as an average per report, Arizonans far out-talked the New Mexicans.

As a rule, the auditors wrote a lot more than the treasurers, and the "other" offices—state tax commissions, traveling auditors, and so forth—wrote the most of all. In reports containing any MD&A, Arizona treasurers wrote 2.6 pages on the average, the auditors wrote 9.2 pages, and the other entities wrote 23.6 pages.

But there were exceptions to the rule. The New Mexico auditors fell silent in 1909, reporting nothing but the numbers, and did not resume narratives for the next two decades. The state tax commissions and traveling auditors compensated, though. They often added ten or twenty pages of MD&A to their reports.

An exception in the opposite direction was the Arizona territorial auditors. They wrote almost half again what the "other" entities did, on the average. This is because the only other entities whose reports I read for the Territory of Arizona were the Board of Loan Commissioners and the bank comptroller, neither of whom wrote much. After statehood, the Tax Commission was formed; its MD&As resembled short books.

Every office grew more talkative after statehood (except the silent New Mexico state auditors). Even the terse treasurers of Arizona more than doubled what they had to say once they were working for a state. Perhaps the complexities of the two-master territorial system, in which the officials were reporting both to Congress and to local legislatures and citizens, had a tendency to silence financial officers.

Recall that today's GASB 34 requires the MD&A to be separate from the letter of transmittal. Letters of transmittal themselves are old. Very few of the reports I examined omitted them. Presaging today's requirement that the letters be separate from the MD&A, New Mexico's state tax commissions always separated the two. The traveling auditors usually, and the treasurers

Table 7.1. Narrative Text Similar to Management's Discussion and Analysis, 1880s–1930

	New Mexico				Arizona			
	Auditor	Treasurer	Other	Total	Auditor	Treasurer	Other	Total
No. of reports obtained								
territory	7	3	1	11	8	6	3	17
state	10	7	12	29	16	8	3	27
total	17	10	13	40	24	14	6	44
No. of reports with MD&A								
territory	6	2	1	9	8	2	2	12
state	2	4	12	18	10	3	4	17
total	8	6	13	27	18	5	6	29
No. of pages of MD&A, all years								
territory	30.5	3.5	5.5	39.5	38.5	3	6.5	48
state	7	8	162.5	177.5	127	10	135	272
total	37.5	11.5	168	217	165.5	13	141.5	320
Average pages of MD&A per report, all years								
territory	4.4	1.2	5.5	3.6	4.8	0.5	2.2	2.8
state	1.0	1.1	13.5	6.1	7.9	1.3	45.0	10.1
territory and state	2.2	1.2	12.9	5.4	6.9	0.9	23.6	7.3
Average pages of MD&A per report containing MD&A								
territory	5.1	1.8	5.5	4.4	4.8	1.5	3.3	4.0
state	3.5	2.0	13.5	9.9	12.7	3.3	33.8	16.0
territory and state	4.7	1.9	12.9	8.0	9.2	2.6	23.6	11.0

sometimes, followed suit. But New Mexico's auditors never separated the letter of transmittal from their discussions in the reports I examined. As for Arizona, only three of the forty-four reports had separate MD&As, one each for the auditor, the treasurer, and the state tax commission.

In short, for the most part, both New Mexico and Arizona reports presented MD&A as a continuation of the letters of transmittal. They generally did not separate the letter from the MD&A, in contrast to today's requirement.

EXCERPTS FROM MD&A IN NEW MEXICO AND ARIZONA

Today, the GASB mandates that the MD&A include condensed financial information. The government reports I studied often had such material in some form. The New Mexico auditor sometimes began his reports with facing pages summarizing receipts and disbursements, for instance. The Arizona treasurer had a table in 1917 showing the year-end balance in every fund.

However, it is the *narratives* that usually accompanied these tables that I am classifying as proto-MD&A for this study. Sometimes, such text was a simple and objective recitation of the facts. Much more often, it took the form of suggestions or requests, and they were seldom objective. These are the voices of New Mexico's and Arizona's financial officials. Excerpts follow, which I have grouped roughly by type of comment and by government.

Requests for More Resources

Throughout the study period, reporting officials used the MD&A to request more funds and personnel for their offices, always with some sort of justification. I begin with an example from the New Mexico auditor.

New Mexico

New Mexico Auditor Demetrio Perez noted in 1891 to 1892 that:

> The destruction by fire of the capitol building on the evening of the 12th day of May, 1892, made it an absolute necessity for the auditor and treasurer to procure suitable rooms for offices for the transaction of the public business and for the accommodation and custody of the public records.[8]

Perez went on to ask the legislature to appropriate $1,000 per year for maintaining these new offices.

The New Mexico traveling auditors of 1912, 1916, and 1918 all requested more staff to handle the job of auditing the various state and local government entities. In 1916, A. G. Whittier justified his request by attacking his predecessor:

> With no desire to criticise the self evident fact that the work of auditing the counties and state officers and institutions had been grossly neglected during the administration of the office of Traveling Auditor . . . Mr. Earnest [Whittier's predecessor], doubtless owing to lack of sufficient clerical help, this office must nevertheless point to the work so neglected by the former administration as the reason why more counties and state officers and institutions have not been audited during the present administration. . . . [V]astly more work has been done under the present administration, in twenty months, than was accomplished under Mr. Earnest's administration, with considerable special help, in thirty-nine months.[9]

Whittier provided a table comparing his output to that of Earnest. He also asked for more clerical help so he could speed up his work and so he could add the school districts and municipalities to his work load.

Arizona

In Arizona, Territorial Auditor Thomas Hughes requested in his 1891–1892 report that his salary be doubled:

> The increasing amount of business and correspondence connected with his office render it imperative that additional provision be made to conduct the same, the present salary of $1000 per annum, I have found inadequate to meet the expenses of clerical services and other requirements of the office. I therefore recommend that the salary be increased to $2000 per annum with a suitable allowance for office rent.[10]

A few years later, the auditor's salary was increased to $1,800, with a separate account to cover the $30 monthly rent.[11] In contrast, the treasurer continued at $1,000 through 1902, when Treasurer I. M. Christy's sole narrative text was a request for a raise:

> In connection herewith I would respectfully call your attention and also that of the members of the Legislature to the meager salary allowed the Territorial Treasurer, viz. One Thousand Dollars per year, which is not reasonable compensation for the labor and responsibility attached to the office.[12]

This request, too, was successful; the treasurer's pay soon rose to $2,500.[13]

Without doubt, the most eloquent plea for a raise came from the first state auditor, J. C. Callaghan, in 1912:

If the purpose of auditing the fiscal affairs of the State is not only to determine the accuracy of the written accounts, but also to make a careful and thorough investigation of the justness and honesty of all the transactions which comprise the State's business, if the Auditor is intended to be de-facto, the sentinel, so to speak, of the treasury, checking the financial transactions of all other departments, then the doubtful wisdom of hampering him in the performance of his functions by a penurious or insufficient appropriation cannot but be apparent.[14]

Lest the legislature rank the auditor's need no higher than the needs of other departments, Callaghan added:

While an insufficient appropriation for any other given department might and would limit that department within its scope or sphere, anything which tends to arbitrarily tie the hands of the accounting department, obviously opens the door to that extent, to possible waste and extravagance affecting the entire State.[15]

The argument worked like a charm. Callaghan's salary shot up from $2,625.84 for fiscal year 1912 to a total of $5,155.50 for 1913, when he was paid as both auditor and bank examiner. He also acquired a deputy auditor who was paid $2,400.[16]

Problems and Procedures

The bookkeeping and fiscal practices of every governmental entity in the state affected the work of the auditors and treasurers, who generally had to correct any problems they caused. Probably as a result, one of the most common types of MD&A was recommendations for changes in the fiscal procedures of the government. For the accounting historian, this is a fortuitous glimpse into the development of the "technologies of government," to use Miller's term.[17]

New Mexico

Problematic procedures in New Mexico ranged from the burning of warrants to county bookkeeping to the use of old technology.

Burning the Warrants

Customarily, New Mexico treasurers destroyed already paid warrants in an annual burning whose date was set by law. For years, the treasurers requested changes in this schedule.[18] In 1918, they gave the reason, asking that the warrants be burned less often "to permit their being kept in the files at least five years."[19]

Audits

The traveling auditors of New Mexico performed what would today be considered an audit, examining the books of counties and various state entities. In 1918, A. G. Whittier detailed his six-step method, which he considered "more or less identical with all accountants." Step 2 was "to check, from the books and records of original entry, every item of receipt and payment from the date of starting to and including the last date to which the examination is conducted."[20]

New Mexico law did not require the traveling auditor to resolve any discrepancies, but Whittier wrote that "public interest seemed to demand at the outset, and experience has proved in the past four years, that this office should undertake to make actual settlements with officials where differences are found."[21] Thus the traveling auditor's duties led them into active participation in the fiscal activities of the government.

As for the auditor himself, when former governor Miguel Otero took the post in 1927, he was not happy with the fact that the "auditor" really did not audit:

> Although called an Auditor, there are, strictly speaking, no auditing duties connected with the office. . . . As a matter of fact, the Auditor's office should not only be given full power and authority to control and audit the expenditures of public money, but, in addition, it should be entirely removed from politics, somewhat on the order of the office of the Comptroller-General of the United States.[22]

The Progressive dream was always to remove politics from government. Otero apparently shared the dream, though it sounds strange coming from a particularly successful politician and former governor.

County Bookkeeping

County bookkeeping improved in the years around statehood, according to New Mexico's traveling auditors. In 1910, county clerks began settling their accounts with the territory on a monthly instead of a quarterly basis.[23] In 1912, Traveling Auditor Howell Earnest reported that the counties had installed "a uniform and comprehensive system of accounting" and were using the associated forms that had been distributed to them. He predicted the next year's report would be more detailed and more efficiently prepared as a result.[24]

In 1915, the legislature required that all public books show the ending cash balance on a daily basis. Traveling Auditor Whittier noted in his 1916 report that although the state institutions already complied with this law, the statute "necessitated an entirely new system of accounting for county officials, and during the fourth fiscal year, forms were prescribed, and beginning December 1, 1916, are to be installed by all county officials."[25] In 1918, he reported the counties were now in compliance.[26]

Office Procedures and Technology

These were decades when modern financial procedures and new technology often appeared. Auditor Miguel Otero, arriving in January of 1927, "found the office run on a system of beekeeping [*sic*] which had possibly seen its best days some twenty-five years ago."[27] The State Board of Finance "came to the rescue" with funding.[28] By August of 1928, work routines had changed drastically:

> I am happy to report that a thoroughly up-to-date and simplified system of book-keeping was installed and is now in full operation in my office, and that of the State Treasurer as well. . . . The posting of accounts is now done on an electric posting machine . . . , doing away with the old and tedious system of posting all accounts by hand.[29]

New voucher procedures, continued Otero,

> would result in the saving of approximately $10,000 in notary fees alone, not to mention doing away with an endless amount of "red tape." . . . The old system of *issuing* warrants . . . by writing them out in longhand . . . is now replaced with a system of making warrants on the typewriter and preserving a carbon copy of each warrant so issued. This is not only vastly more simple, but avoids the mistakes which frequently happened through discrepancies between the warrants and the stubs. . . . [E]xcept in very rare cases, the work of issuing warrants is completely cleared by my office every day.[30]

Both Otero and the comptroller, Gilberto Mirabel, recommended bonding key individuals as a control measure—Otero for financial officials[31] and Mirabel for independent auditors.[32] Mirabel further argued that biennial appropriations ought to "be divided into two halves" so that an official could not use up all the money in the first year, leaving his successor without funds.[33]

The Motor Vehicle Department came under Mirabel's purview. He recommended that the statutes should be revised "along the lines of the uniform Motor Vehicle Code adopted by the National Automobile Association."[34] The Motor Vehicle Register should be abolished as it cost "over $4,000.00 a year and, so far as can be learned, this is the only State still printing such a register."[35]

Arizona

In Arizona, officials dealt with interim reports, mileage rates, and audit procedures, among other issues.

Monthly Reports

Arizona State Treasurer D. F. Johnson lauded his office's new monthly reports in 1917: "Additional work in this office prevented me from submitting this report within the time prescribed by statute, but the cumulative monthly report method now adopted will enable this office to make its annual report promptly at the close of the fiscal year."[36]

Report Format

The unfortunate auditor for the 1919 report, Jesse Boyce, had to deal with a new statute in which the legislature specified the format of his reports without, it appears, having consulted the auditor. Most of Boyce's MD&A is a testy explanation of why he cannot comply with the statute as written. Quoting a statutory requirement that he publish the ending balances in the various appropriations, he observes that:

> Here, the author of this Act confuses the duties of the Auditor with those of the Treasurer; it is the duty of the Auditor to issue warrants, and of the Treasurer to pay them. Naturally, any statement of expenditures taken from the Auditor's records deals only with the total amount of warrants issued.[37]

Standard Mileage

A few years later, Auditor R. H. Ramsey called for a standard state mileage rate because:

> considerable trouble is experienced in this office in the handling of expense claims for travel allowance where the individual uses a private car. . . . Our efforts have been to keep the allowance to an amount not to exceed the . . . expense if the trip were made by rail. However we have had adverse opinions from the office of the Attorney General on this. . . .[38]

Audits

Like his contemporary New Mexico counterpart, Ramsey wished the auditors could conduct audits. "I seriously doubt," he complained, "that the taxpayers and citizens of the State in general are aware of the fact that since statehood, with the exception of two or three special audits made by the legislative committees, no examination or audit of the sixty-eight departments of the State has ever been made."[39] Ramsey wanted to merge the State Examiner's and State Auditor's offices. The "combined personnel," he believed, could "perform the work with very little additional expense."[40]

Uniform Accounting Systems

Having attended national meetings of state financial officers, Ramsey was enthusiastic about the potential of uniform accounting systems "to provide a basis of comparison of per capita governmental costs as between all the States." He "respectfully recommend[ed] that the State of Arizona . . . make the departmental appropriations" so he could implement uniform systems.[41] At the time, though, this was probably a lost cause.

Serious Controversy

Poor fiscal procedures frequently embroiled the responsible officers in serious controversy, whether they sought it or not. Who, for instance, had the final authority to decide whether public funds could be disbursed in any given situation?

Such questions were not settled at the turn of the twentieth century. They illustrate Miller's point that the "calculative technologies of government" are intimately involved with power.[42] The financial officials of this period often discussed their exercise of power over public resources, whether by denying or disbursing funds, or by recommending such action.

New Mexico

New Mexico Territorial Auditor Trinidad Alarid reported in 1887 to 1888 that he had refused to disburse school funds:

[T]here is in the Territorial Treasury the sum of two thousand four hundred and thirty dollars ($2,430.00) collected from licenses on insurance agents, to go to the public school fund, but as the law does not provide its distribution, the money remains in the treasury. A law providing for the distribution is necessary and indispensable.[43]

His successor, Demetrio Perez, faced a worse problem. Unsure about what the property tax levied in part of the statutes was to be applied to, he asked the solicitor general for advice, pursuant to which he levied an additional millage rate to cover the territory's bond interest payments. County tax commissions and taxpayers disagreed with Perez, however. Many refused to collect or pay his new levy. Taken to court, the county boards and taxpayers won their case, making Perez's levy illegal and putting the territory in deficit.[44]

After that, Perez became more cautious. He kept an especially close eye on the courts. In the following biennium (1893–1894), when the Territorial Supreme Court attempted to authorize expenditures, Perez reported that:

> At the last regular session of the supreme court allowances were made by the said court to the sheriff and stenographer for services rendered to said court, the same being special services, and the Auditor was directed to pay said allowances out of the Territorial funds, and as no appropriation was made at the last session of the Legislature to meet these expenses, no warrants were drawn by me.[45]

Then there was the question of the treasurer. Did he have the independent authority to disburse money? New Mexico Auditor W. G. Sargent thought not, as he explained in his report of 1907 to 1908. Noting that his accounts and the treasurer's would not reconcile, he continued:

> The cause of this is found in the fact that the Treasurer, makes payments from several funds, without same going through this office, said payments not being reported to this office, until the annual burning.
>
> Under the present system the Superintendent of Insurance draws warrants on the Territorial Treasurer, in payment of his salary and the expenses of his office, payable out of the insurance fund.
>
> The Commissioner of Public Lands, pays his salary and the expenses of his office, out of the proceeds of Territorial Lands.
>
> I will strongly recommend that some legislation be enacted whereby, no Territorial monies be paid out, except, by warrant through this office.[46]

Such practices seriously complicated my task of determining the total expenditures of the governments.

Corruption—one of the banes of state and local governments during the 1920s and the target of Progressives across the country—came under State Auditor M. A. Otero, Jr.'s scrutiny in his 1927–1928 report. He recommended:

> That a law be passed requiring the officials having charge of the fiscal affairs of the State to give full and complete publicity . . . to any and all cases of irregularities in accounts which public officials or their agents file for payment by the State, either in the form of overcharges or "padding," or in attempts to make illegal and improper charges. . . .[47]

Otero believed strongly in the power of sunshine to cleanse government:

Perhaps the greatest weapon in the enforcement of the law has been by . . . publicity to all cases of what has popularly been termed "graft." This form of raiding the pubic treasury is probably as old as government itself and, of course, will never be completely eradicated until public opinion undergoes a radical change. However, it can be reduced to a minimum. . . . I am thoroughly convinced that publicity is a great deterant [*sic*] to those who are inclined to make "a good thing" out of a public office.[48]

This may have been less controversial than it sounds. Otero after all did not name names, but just proposed a change in procedure to reduce corruption, something that everyone condemned in theory but many embraced in practice.

More controversial perhaps was the problem raised by his successor, Auditor Victor Ulibarri. The State Board of Finance had approved "emergency expenditures for which no funds were appropriated." These were for heating plant repairs, dike reconstruction, and so forth. However, "the State Auditor is not supposed to draw warrants against a fund without a specific appropriation," so he had to ask the legislature to approve his paying them.[49]

Arizona officials often were bedeviled by the same conflict over who had the authority to spend money from the public purse, as the next example shows.

Arizona

Territorial Auditor Jonathan J. Hawkins noted in his 1887–1888 report that he could not say how much the counties had paid to the territory because:

The present law does not require the various county treasurers to report to this office. A law should be enacted requiring a duplicate statement of all moneys transmitted to the Treasurer to be sent to the Territorial Auditor by county officers or other persons having in charge Territorial moneys.[50]

This problem had still not been resolved at the beginning of the new century, when W. F. Nichols made the same recommendation.[51]

Recommendations in Good Times and Bad

Attuned to their governments' finances as they were, New Mexico and Arizona officials broadcast any remarkable good or bad news in the MD&As. In good times, they happily listed the benefits of prosperity to the governments. In bad times, they warned their readers of imminent dire consequences and the drastic corrections they thought were needed.

New Mexico

Territorial Auditor J. H. Vaughn reported a "highly satisfactory condition" in the 1903–1904 biennium. "All claims" were promptly paid, the bonded debt was reduced, and the casual deficit bonds were refinanced at a lower rate. "The credit of this Territory with eastern financial institutions is of the best," glowed Vaughn.[52]

In the next biennium, 1905–1906, Auditor William Sargent was equally happy: "It is very gratifying to state that the financial condition of the Territory is in fine condition, all bills against the Territory authorized by law, are promptly paid."[53]

On a few occasions, the government's fiscal house was so prosperous that a jubilant note crept into the report. According to the New Mexico traveling auditor in 1910, C. V. Safford:

> During the year ended June 30, 1910, from a financial standpoint, the Territory, the individual counties, and the territorial institutions were, as a whole successful and prosperous, and at the close of the year were in a condition which gives assurance of a capable and economical administration during the past and promises equally good results for the future. . . . All appropriations have been promptly paid, the territorial rate of taxation has been materially reduced, [and bonds] bearing low rates of interest, when offered for sale, have been eagerly sought for by the bond buyer.[54]

Bad times returned, of course. When the agricultural depression of the 1920s ravaged property values in New Mexico, the State Tax Commission noted that: "To say that the tax situation in New Mexico is, at this time, critical is but to repeat a statement used until it has become chronic."[55]

The Tax Commission said there was no way out except raising rates or "a number of our counties will be forced to a seven months school term, or even less."[56] Instead of cutting school terms, however, the schools continued to make expenditures. They just failed to disburse the money, according to the Tax Commission's 1925–1926 report: "Upon examination of the unpaid obligations legally incurred by the schools, it was found that at least one-half million dollars was unpaid, a great portion of this being salaries due the teachers of the State . . . and school districts failing to meet their interest payments."[57]

Arizona

Good times arrived in Arizona in the late 1890s. Auditor George W. Vickers noted in his 1897–1898 report that:

. . . the finances of the Territory are in better condition than they have been for years. With the floating debt bearing 10 per cent interest, funded into a bonded debt bearing 5 per cent, the burden will be easy to bear, and I can see no reason why, if only necessary appropriations are made by the Legislature, and the affairs of the Territory are administered in an economical way, the territory should not be on a cash basis within two years.[58]

During the hard times in agricultural lands of the early 1920s, Treasurer Raymond Earhart noted that a large amount of taxes were delinquent, so that he had issued tax anticipation bonds. However:

The law under which these bonds were issued will expire December 31, 1922, and unless a new law is authorized the issuance of Tax Anticipation Bonds can not be done and it will be necessary to go back to the days of registered warrants when thousands of registered Arizona warrants were scattered throughout the United States drawing interest at a greater rate than it would be necessary to pay on Tax Anticipation Bonds with a definite date of maturity.[59]

Broad-Ranging Commentary

On occasion, auditors strayed directly into the realm of public policy opinion.

New Mexico

In his 1905–1906 report, New Mexico Territorial Auditor W. G. Sargent opined that spending had gone too far:

The territorial institutions should be liberally maintained, but it occurs to this department that when the liberal manner in which these institutions were dealt with two years ago in the way of appropriations is taken into consideration, a happy medium between extravagance and parsimony should be struck and that the legislature will see the necessity of hewing close to the line in this respect.[60]

Arizona

In Arizona, the Territorial Board of Control chose not to issue a bond authorized for repairing the bridge across the Gila River several years before statehood. The old bridge was so dilapidated that it could not be repaired, according to the Board. Auditor Sims Ely asked the president of the Southern Pacific Railroad in Arizona, Epes Randolph, to look at the situation and Randolph recommended that the territory buy one of his old bridges. Ely strongly urged the legislature to levy a tax to do so in his 1907–1908 report.[61]

Rarely, a fiscal officer wrote a long essay that resembled a state-of-the-state speech. The best example of this type of report was that of Arizona's first state auditor, J. C. Callaghan. On the excuse that a statute required him "to submit 'such plans as he may deem expedient . . . for the better management and more perfect understanding of the fiscal affairs of the state,'"[62] Callaghan wrote a sixty-five-page essay in 1912.

Callaghan wrote dozens of pages extolling the excellence of Arizona and its state institutions, listing all the academic subjects and museum exhibits available at the state university. He recommended changes in the handling of bonds, caution in selling state lands, and a reapportionment of the tax burden from land and small businessmen to the mining industry, a change he said the mines welcomed eagerly.[63]

The territorial prison of Arizona was a constant drain on the public purse.[64] But Callaghan did not confine his comments on the prison to finances. In his most colorful passages, Callaghan discussed prison reform, a term he usually placed in quotation marks:

"Prison reform" has been held up to view in Arizona as the very pinnacle of progress by an administration pledged to progressive government. . . . To such an extent, however, have the rights of society now dwindled, that in our prisons calm business discipline is being replaced by maudlin sentiment and heroics. The inmates are apparently encouraged to think and believe, not that they have offended against the laws of God and man, but that they are, in reality, victims of a conspiracy formed by society. . . .[65]

An egregious example of misguided reform, he told his readers, concerned a murderer who taunted the authorities and then bet the jury they would sentence him to death:

The jury, however, with that leniency which characterizes Arizona juries, specifies only a prison life sentence. He is thus denied the visits of morbid women bearing gifts and flowers to a self-confessed degenerate, and becomes an inmate. . . . He soon makes his presence felt, and although admitting always his degeneracy, is, under present management, permitted and encouraged to satisfy his craving for writing and publishing "prison reform" matter. He becomes, de facto, the director of the prison policy. . . . Think of it![66]

Prison reform, and particularly the abolition of capital punishment, were very controversial topics in Arizona's first years.[67] While Callaghan scorned many reforms, he did passionately share one of the Progressive dreams for ending crime: eugenics.

The question as to whether the child's destiny is that of a useful citizen of the earth or a criminal is fundamentally, though not conclusively, determined at the instant of embryogony. . . .

The . . . paramount . . . problem is not the reform of the criminal, but *the prevention of crime*; . . . it . . . contemplates perhaps the sterilization of the proven vicious and incurably defective, medical attention toward abnormal and subnormal children, prenuptial medical examination, . . . and the voluntary or peremptory application of, the philosophy of eugenics. . . . The world is coming to need, not so much, more and many destructive warriors, but rather *well-bred, constructive* men and women, co-operating in the planet's work. . . .

Intelligent, thinking people, with but even a meager analytical turn of mind, cannot fail to grasp the fact that the endeavor to reform criminals is of absolute impotency and futility while society continues simultaneously to procreate and cultivate a new and increased crop of degenerates with each generation.[68]

This ode to the Progressive dream of perfecting mankind by controlling human breeding was the height of the opinionated prose printed in any of the financial reports of New Mexico, Arizona, or Nevada during the study period. Whether it was a product of the exuberance of statehood or just the outpouring of an idealist-turned-auditor, it was not repeated, even by Callaghan himself, in any other report.

Callaghan was criticized for his policy advice, as he might have expected. When he chose not to run for the auditor's office again, his swan song, a 1916 MD&A of only four pages, was quite defensive:

Conscience permits of no departure from duty and when fundamental principles of government are involved, there can be no compromise. These occurrences, however, are in and of the past, and as the writer lays down his pen, he does so with the unmistakable feeling, of which he is glad, that however much he may have differed officially with associates in the line of duty, he feels in his heart no personal animosity toward any man.[69]

CONCLUSIONS

Remember that this study is limited by being based on only two governments, and only some of the reports of those governments, albeit for over forty-five years. Whether the findings can be generalized to other American governments is a question that can only be answered by further research. Nevertheless, New Mexico and Arizona's financial reports provide a glimpse into what I assume were typical government practices of the late nineteenth and early twentieth centuries.

Bearing in mind this assumption and its limitations, then: To the first question of this chapter—did government financial reports of a century or more ago something that could be considered MD&A?—the answer is yes, usually. State and territorial officials in charge of fiscal operations have generally commented upon them in prose narratives for well over one hundred years. Today's MD&A requirement is not new, but has grown out of long-standing, generally accepted practice.

Secondly, statehood did not seem to have a major effect on the MD&A sections of New Mexico and Arizona reports, except in their length. Statehood narratives were longer, on the average. The difference was much greater in Arizona, but that was primarily because of a few anomalously long MD&As. Still, even in New Mexico, statehood MD&A averaged twice the length of territorial MD&A.

Thirdly, the modern resistance to the separation of the letter of transmittal from the MD&A may not spring entirely from fear of audits. The fact is MD&A was not traditionally separated from the transmittal letter. There was one letter, beginning with a formal announcement of transmittal, and continuing with whatever narrative comments the official in charge thought best to include. The many state and local governments of the United States may well not see the point of replacing such a long-established practice with the brand-new format required by today's GASB.

Fourthly, a remarkable feature of these MD&As of a century ago is that they were generally *not* objective. The auditors and treasurers had opinions and suggestions about the fiscal activities and condition of the governments they served, and more often than not, they expressed them. This is a striking difference from today's GASB requirement that the MD&A be objective.

The tone and content of the New Mexico and Arizona narratives of the 1880s to the 1920s clearly implied that their intended audience was government decision-makers, not the general public. Only occasionally did the writers seem to be addressing the public.[70] Instead, the writers were asking the legislatures for more money, or suggesting changes in procedure, or reporting on controversial problems, or suggesting future budgetary changes.

These facts suggest that the MD&A of early government financial reports played a different role a hundred years ago than it does today. Early MD&A was part of the policy-making process. Today's MD&A, on the other hand, is supposed to be policy description, strictly objective, and addressed largely to entities outside the government itself. I conclude that modern MD&A has lost a large part of the importance it once had.

Why has this change taken place? To speculate, perhaps it is for the same reason that today's report preparers and auditors do not want the MD&A to be audited. Fiscal policy is inherently political, and politics is hot. The Nevada controller of 1908 expressed just that view. He limited his MD&A to six lines, followed by this admonition: "As to making any further suggestions, I do not deem it advisable, as the members of the Legislature should be the best judges as to the reforms necessary to be made."[71]

Most of the New Mexico and Arizona officials of the five decades following 1880 had not learned that lesson, or did not agree with it. They did not leave fiscal politics to the politicians; they wanted to play in the decision-making waters. As managers of the governments' fiscal affairs, their discussions and analyses were well-informed, up-to-date, and often persuasive.

What is remarkable for our purposes is that the New Mexico and Arizona officials did not play their politics behind the scenes, as fiscal officials today may do. They put their opinions in official public reports. I conclude that the MD&A of the turn of the late nineteenth and early twentieth centuries was more important than the deliberately bland and restrained texts of today.

Finally, the colorful, opinionated, and knowledgeable MD&A of the late nineteenth and early twentieth centuries offers accounting historians an important source of information about both sides of Miller's concerns—the programmatic realm of political rationalities and the technologies of government. Political scientists and scholars of public administration, too, can see the genesis of policies and procedures in these officials' words.

In the next chapters, we will see how the issues raised in the MD&A played out in practice, beginning with an area then in crying need of reform—the property tax.

NOTES

1. Governmental Accounting Standards Board, *Statement 34*, par. 8.
2. Governmental Accounting Standards Board, *Statement 34*.
3. Governmental Accounting Standards Board, *Codification*, sec 2200.109.
4. Governmental Accounting Standards Board, *Codification*, sec. 2200.106.
5. Governmental Accounting Standards Board, "GASB and the User Community." http://www.gasb.org/jsp/GASB/Page/GASBSectionPage&cid=1176156741809 (accessed July 10, 2011).
6. Kravchuck and Voorhees, "New Governmental Financial," 6.
7. Governmental Accounting Standards Board, *Statement 34*, Appendix B, part II, par. 289–294.
8. NM Terr. Auditor, *Report*, 1891–1892.
9. NM Traveling Auditor, *Report*, 1916.
10. AZ Terr. Auditor, *Report*, 1891–1892, 6.
11. AZ Terr. Auditor, *Report*, 1897–1898, 59, 62.
12. AZ Terr. Treasurer, *Report*, 1902, 26.

13. AZ Terr. Auditor, *Report,* 1903–1904, 18–19.

14. AZ Auditor, *Report,* 1912, 4.

15. AZ Auditor, *Report,* 1912, 4.

16. AZ Auditor, *Report,* 1913, 11–12.

17. Miller, "Interrelations."

18. NM Terr. Treasurer, *Report,* 1903–1904, 5.

19. NM Treasurer, *Report,* 1918, 4.

20. NM Traveling Auditor, *Report,* 1918, 48.

21. NM Traveling Auditor, *Report,* 1918, 49.

22. NM Auditor, *Report,* 1928, 6.

23. NM Traveling Auditor, *Report,* 1910, 13.

24. NM Traveling Auditor, *Report,* 1912, 38.

25. NM Traveling Auditor, *Report,* 1916, 94.

26. NM Traveling Auditor, *Report,* 1918, 56.

27. NM Auditor, *Report,* 1927–1928, 3. Otero was formerly the territorial governor (Hornung, *Fullerton's Rangers*, 181).

28. NM Auditor, *Report,* 1927–1928, 3.

29. NM Auditor, *Report,* 1927–1928, 3.

30. NM Auditor, *Report,* 1927–1928, 4.

31. NM Auditor, *Report,* 1927–1928, 4.

32. NM Comptroller, *Report,* 1927–1928, 7.

33. NM Comptroller, *Report,* 1927–1928, 8.

34. NM Comptroller, *Report,* 1927–1928, 9.

35. NM Comptroller, *Report,* 1927–1928, 10.

36. AZ Treasurer, *Report,* 1917, 6.

37. AZ Auditor, *Report,* 1919, 4.

38. AZ Auditor, *Report,* 1923, 4.

39. AZ Auditor, *Report,* 1924, 4.

40. AZ Auditor, *Report,* 1924, 4.

41. AZ Auditor, *Report,* 1924, 4.

42. Miller, "Governing by Numbers."

43. NM Terr. Auditor, *Report,* 1887–1888, 2.

44. NM Terr. Auditor, *Report,* 1891–1892, 3–4.

45. NM Terr. Auditor, *Report,* 1893–1894, 9–10.

46. NM Terr. Auditor, *Report,* 1907–1908, 6.

47. NM Auditor, *Report,* 1927–1928, 5.

48. NM Auditor, *Report,* 1927–1928, 5.

49. NM Auditor, *Report,* 1929–1930, 3–4.

50. AZ Terr. Auditor, *Report,* 1887–1888, 7.

51. AZ Terr. Auditor, *Report,* 1901–1902, 5.

52. NM Terr. Auditor, *Report,* 1903–1904, 3, 5.

53. NM Terr. Auditor, *Report,* 1905–1906, 3.

54. NM Terr. Traveling Auditor, *Report,* 1910, 5.

55. NM State Tax Commission, *Report,* 1922–1924, 4.

56. NM State Tax Commission, *Report,* 1925–1926, 8.

57. NM State Tax Commission, *Report,* 1925–1926, 6.

58. AZ Terr. Auditor, *Report,* 1897–1898, 5.

59. Arizona, Treasurer, *Report,* 1922, 5.

60. NM Terr. Auditor, *Report,* 1905–1906, 5.

61. AZ Terr. Auditor, *Report,* 1907–1908, 9–10.

62. AZ Auditor, *Report,* 1912, 3.

63. AZ Auditor, *Report,* 1912, 28–47.

64. Wilson, *Crime & Punishment.*

65. AZ Auditor, *Report,* 1912, 51, 52.

66. AZ Auditor, *Report,* 1912, 58.

67. Hayostek, "Douglas Delegates," 358–360.

68. AZ Auditor, *Report,* 1912, 55, 56.

69. AZ Auditor, *Report,* 1916, 5.

70. Examples of addressing the public occur in AZ Auditor, *Report,* 1924, referring to the people and the legislature as the audience. Callaghan omitted part of an investigation he had made into a youth reformatory "out of regard for the permanent history of the State." AZ Auditor, *Report,* 1914, 6.

71. NV Controller, *Report,* 1908, 7.

8

Accountants at the Service of the State

Reforming Property Tax Administration

The property tax has caused problems in American communities since it arrived from England several centuries ago. "Reviled . . . as bad in principle and worse in practice . . . more poorly [administered] without question than any other major tax,"[1] it has been in a state of more or less perpetual reform throughout its history.

In 1912, when New Mexico and Arizona became states and the relative size of their governments soared, they simultaneously reformed their property tax systems to make them more transparent and efficient. They also began assessing property at 100 percent of its true value. Meanwhile, in neighboring Nevada, none of the above happened. Nevada had been a state for over four decades in 1912, the size of its government did not increase at that time, and its participation in Progressive reforms of the property tax was gradual and relatively limited.

I conclude that the accountants who brought their expertise to bear, often passionately, on full-value assessments[2] and other improvements in the administration of the property tax, also facilitated an increase in the size of the new state governments far greater than most citizens had anticipated when deciding on statehood. This level of change in the property tax could not have happened, I believe, in the absence of a dramatic change in government, in this case a change from territorial status to state.[3]

CONTEXT OF REFORM

Tax rates, assessments, and collections were perennial thorns in the fiscal policy field of this period.[4] Indeed, neither the problems nor the solutions for the property tax were unique to New Mexico and Arizona. The problems reached a crescendo in the Progressive era, causing changes (though no permanent solutions) in state after state in the decades around 1900.

Enduring criticisms of the property tax focus on problems with administering it.[5] Competitive underassessments by county tax officials attempting to shift tax burdens to other counties, unequal rates caused by political favoritism and assessor ignorance, arbitrariness in assessment, overassessment of absentee owners' property, and difficulties with locating and valuing personalty and intangibles—all were common problems in the nineteenth century.

Ohio experienced these problems in the early 1800s, as did Kansas in the middle of the century,[6] and Wisconsin,[7] Illinois, New York, and Georgia[8] in the late 1800s. "Everybody who has thought at all about the subject knows that the methods of assessment and taxation in the United States are irregular, unjust, and inefficient," remarked one observer at a national conference in 1907 on state and local taxation.[9] Accountants of the Progressive decades particularly wanted to reform municipal accounting and taxation, and a wave of reform efforts swept the country in the late 1800s and early 1900s.

The National Tax Association, one of many reform organizations set up in this period, spent a great deal of time in the first decade of the twentieth century criticizing the property tax.[10] The NTA began regular meetings on the tax in 1907.[11] The organization promoted efficiency, as tax reformers typically do.[12] Property assessment methods preoccupied the members, who argued constantly for making assessments fairer, more uniform, and more complete (i.e., covering more property). Specific proposals often involved creating powerful professional tax and assessment bureaucracies,[13] such as powerful state tax commissions.

Statewide boards of equalization appeared in the Midwest in the 1850s[14] to counter the local pressure to which county and municipal boards so frequently succumbed. Between 1880 and 1920 nearly every state also created statewide tax commissions to develop better tax procedures.[15]

How did these problems affect New Mexico, Arizona, and Nevada, and what solutions did they try? These are the questions I address next.

THE PROPERTY TAX AND ITS REFORMS
IN NEW MEXICO, ARIZONA, AND NEVADA

County sheriffs collected taxes through most of the territorial years in both New Mexico and Arizona.[16] Sheriffs received about 5 percent of the collections in addition to their law enforcement salaries, so the job was one of the most passionately sought government positions in the territories.

Often, however, taxes went uncollected, and the county commissioners, responsible for overseeing tax collections, simply ignored the problem.[17] This allowed dishonest sheriffs to add illegal income to their take. Sheriff Nowlin of Lincoln County, New Mexico, collected and pocketed overdue taxes on a regular basis. As the county had written off the receivables, no one knew of the crime until new counties were created in the sheriff's collection area in 1891. The collectors for the new counties demanded unpaid taxes from citizens and companies who irately waved receipts for their payments. Meanwhile, Nowlin had vanished.[18]

At least one sheriff in every county in territorial Arizona and New Mexico was accused of misbehavior with tax collections, according to historian Larry Ball.[19] In fact, it was alleged tax abuses by a sheriff that helped start the infamous Lincoln County War in 1878.[20] In Roswell in 1896, Sheriff Charles Perry absconded with over $7,600.[21] In 1905, Governor Otero removed three Bernalillo County officials, including the sheriff, for misappropriation of tax monies.[22]

As early as 1892, the New Mexico Territory attempted without much success to apply the property tax to all types of property, including personalty such as furniture, merchandise, and books, as well as intangibles such as accounts receivable and notes receivable.[23] The legislature of 1891–1892 also switched to semi-annual tax collections, which Auditor Demetrio Perez said caused average collections to be greater than in any previous year.[24]

The property assessor was usually the county clerk in the Territory of New Mexico. Auditor Perez recommended increasing the assessors' compensation[25] and stopping the practice of having the tax collectors pay the assessors' commissions directly. The state treasurer, he said, should pay the commissions upon approval by the auditor,[26] an elementary example of the separation of duties.

Governor Otero reported a classic case of competitive underassessments in 1899: many county commissions simply abated territorial taxes for the residents of their counties "without any pretense of authority or law for so doing."[27] An outcry in the 1890s finally caused the territory to put the county treasurer in charge of tax collections in 1900.[28]

The territory set up a board of equalization to ensure equal assessment outcomes. However, the board sometimes followed the lead of the county commissioners in making wide-ranging deductions from the taxpayers' obligations. In 1903, Governor Otero called for "the amplification of [the Board's] powers." He also recommended hiring traveling auditors to examine the operations of the local governments, including their taxing activities and other fiscal responsibilities. In 1905, the traveling auditor positions were created by the territorial assembly.[29]

In short, New Mexico tried a number of property tax reforms before state-hood. Too many reforms, in the opinion of at least one knowledgeable participant. Territorial Auditor W. G. Sargent believed there had been too many new procedures and not enough compliance with old ones:

> The problem of the best methods to be employed in attempting to get all of the taxable property on the assessment rolls is still unsolved, and will always remain so until the taxation system now in vogue in the Territory is more strictly enforced. It is respectfully suggested that frequent and radical changes in the system of the assessment and collection of taxes, is against public policy. When a system that is generally understood by the public, which in its operation, serves to equitably distribute the tax burden, and at the same time produces sufficient revenue to meet the demands, it should not be hastily discarded.[30]

But with statehood came more changes, including constitutional restraints, as discussed in chapter 2. And the people continued to tinker with the article on taxes during my study period. Article 8 was amended twice—extensively in 1914 and again in 1921.[31]

The incidence of taxation did in fact change with statehood, as some had hoped and others feared (see fig. 8.1).[32] Railroads did much worse at first. Just before statehood, they had been assessed at 24 percent of the total property valuations in New Mexico. That assessment jumped to one-third of total valuations in 1913. But after intense pressure, railroads' share fell back to 26 percent of the total by 1919.

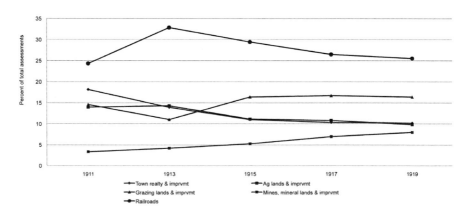

Figure 8.1. Percent of total property assessments by property class, New Mexico, 1911–1919. Source: Based on data from NM Special Revenue Commission, Report, appendix 31, p. 297.

Mines also suffered greater tax assessments upon statehood. Valued at a trivial 3 percent of the total before statehood, they steadily increased to 8 percent by 1919.

Ranchers were an odd case. Initially, they did very well. Grazing lands fell from 15 percent in 1911 to 11 percent of total valuations in 1913, a not unexpected break for such a powerful interest group. But then their valuations jumped back up to 16 percent in 1915, and stayed there through the end of the decade.

Farmers benefited from some tax relief, though not immediately. Their lands were valued at 14 percent of total property valuations in 1911 and 1913, but then fell to 10 percent by 1919.

New Mexico's city dwellers were the ones who did the best on the property tax front. They were the only group whose assessments declined throughout the 1910s. Urban real estate dropped from 18 percent of the total in 1911 to 14 percent in 1913. By the end of the decade, city land was only 10 percent of the state's total assessments for tax purposes.

The tax bureaucracy itself prospered with statehood in New Mexico. A state tax commission was created and within a few years, Governor McDonald called for it to have more power over assessments.[33] By 1919, the commission was in fact granted increased powers.[34]

In fact, both the tax commission and the tax assessors had their power and funding increased during this period.[35] The Tax Commission spent a total of just under $16,000 in fiscal year 1916.[36] Commissioners requested $35,000 for the next year.[37] By 1920, they were up to $40,000. But that was a depression year, and by 1924, the Commission was back down to just $29,000 for the year. Penury did not last long, though. Spending more than quadrupled four years later, to $122,000, and increased again to $147,000 in 1929.[38]

In search of more money during the nasty depression year of 1920, the state appointed a Special Revenue Commission to consider an income tax and the further reform of the property tax. The Commission declined to approve an income tax. Instead, it reached the Progressive good-government conclusion that improved, simplified, and efficient administration of existing taxes would make up the fiscal shortfalls.[39]

In particular, "a professional technician," with a centralized administration under a well-paid and more powerful tax commission, should replace the county assessors. The whole system, state and county, would cost about $50,000 more than the $135,000 it cost in 1920, according to the Revenue Commission.[40] Finally, the Commission proposed detailed means of increasing the share of taxes paid by the railroads and mines.

The legislature enacted many of the changes desired by the Commission, in a seventy-three-page revision of the tax and revenue laws. The new statutes

increased funds for assessments and created a "full-fledged state tax commission" with "broad powers." "All-told," concluded the National Tax Association in its 1921 bulletin, "the legislation of this state appears to be the most
important [of all the states] that has come to our attention."[41]

Thus, the tax reforms of New Mexico modernized the system, helped it
collect a great deal more money, and produced a much larger, better-paid tax
bureaucracy. The reforms also produced full-value assessments, as we will
see shortly.

Arizona

Arizona's experience with the property tax was similar to New Mexico's,
though a little harsher, as was Arizona's wont in those days. For one thing,
territorial sheriffs not only collected the property tax, but assessed the property, too.[42] That is, Arizona did not separate these duties, as New Mexico did
and as a rudimentary concern for internal controls would suggest.

Unequal assessments were commonplace—in the early 1890s, the Arizona
auditor found unimproved land assessed at "over $27.77 in one county in the
territory, and less than 24 cts. in another county."[43] The Arizona territorial
auditor criticized the situation in his 1883–1884 report:

> The law as it now stands makes the sheriff of each county *ex officio* assessor and
> tax-collector. The sheriff makes A, B and C his deputy-assessors, regardless of
> their fitness, simply because they are "dead-broke," and are out of employment,
> and, perhaps, helped elect the sheriff. Said deputies, with some rare exceptions,
> are wholly irresponsible and incompetent, they will list a tax-payer's property
> and assess it. If it is assessed too high in Mr. Tax-payer's opinion his recourse
> is before the board of supervisors . . . What can the board of supervisors know
> of the property of the tax-payer, the idea is simply absurd.[44]

Mine and railroad assessments were other sore points among tax authorities. The Board of Equalization among others argued in 1906 that justice demanded increasing the valuation of mines.[45] When it came time for the popular vote on statehood, Arizona railroads, mining companies, and some other
interests opposed statehood for fear it would bring them a higher tax burden.
It did.

Immediately upon statehood, the Atchison, Topeka and Santa Fe Railroad's assessment in Apache County shot up 76 percent.[46] The railroad passing through Tucson, previously valued at less than $200,000, was now valued
at $1,250,000.[47]

In 1916, a two-year effort began to better assess intangibles, a problem
that was not solved during the study period.[48] In 1914, the legislature added
merchandise taxes and more finely classified land taxes and telegraph assess-

ments.[49] The new telegraph tax particularly pleased the Commission, which took the view that the previous rate of 1 percent of gross revenue had been "the greatest farce in the entire revenue law." The new law brought in seven times the tax revenues.[50]

As for the powerful mines of Arizona, the first state auditor, firebrand J. C. Callaghan, sitting *ex officio* on the Board of Equalization, argued that land owners and small businesses "were paying very much more than their just proportion of taxes . . . due to the fact that the large corporate industries were bearing but a small part of their just proportion of the expense of government." Mines were the "most favored" of these industries.[51] Indignant tax commissioners in 1912 noted that all Arizonans "have known for some time that the United Verde Copper Company has been in politics for the last twenty years, solely, and only for the purpose of evading the payment of its just proportion of the State and county tax."[52]

So the mines' tax assessment jumped from 19 percent to 37 percent of the state total in 1913, and again to over half of the total—58 percent—by 1919 (see fig. 8.2). All other classes of property either fell or increased only a little. City real estate fell the most after statehood, from 26.5 percent of the late territorial total, to 15 percent in 1913 and down to just 9 percent by 1919.

These were such extreme changes that the young state legislature had to sit for two special sessions before confirming the increase for the mines. When the county boards decided collectively to cut mine assessments by half in August of 1912, J. C. Callaghan, who was both president of the State Board

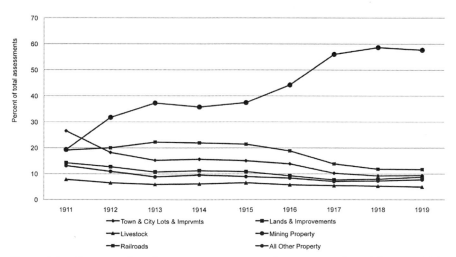

Figure 8.2. Percent of total property assessments by property class, Arizona, 1911–1919. Source: Based on data from AZ Tax Commission, Report, table 28.

of Equalization and state auditor, took the Yavapai County's supervisors to court to force them to obey the law.[53] The state authorities won their case in the state Supreme Court.[54]

But the Tax Commission was still not satisfied with mine taxation in those early years of statehood. Mining property "constitutes the greatest class of wealth in the West," declared the Commission in 1914, "and it seems the day must be near when it must pay its share of taxes . . . At one time or another it has used every means to resist any raise proposed and to dodge or beat the taxes laid. . . ."

Waxing more idealistic by the page, the Commission declared that:

All property in the State belongs to the State for the benefit of society. All natural resources are the heritage of the State and all other wealth is created by society, and society on that account has its claim upon it. The mines are being continually exhausted. It follows then that the wealth of the metalliferous mines is a heritage of the State and should be so regarded by the State, and therefore, the State is entitled to its just proportion of that wealth as it is made available for the uses of society.[55]

Even J. C. Callaghan thought this was excessive. He noted tartly:

When the people grasped the reins of government, [they] enacted great governmental changes, many of which were of a radical nature.

As is ever the case, a taste of power, long denied, provokes a lust for excess, and results in an arbitrary abuse thereof . . . much freak legislation has found its way into the statues . . . [that] establishes a reputation for Arizona as a state entertaining an antipathy toward capital . . . Capital and labor are essential, each to the other, and their true relationship is thorough harmony.[56]

On the practical front, by 1916, mining property was valued at $220 million, an increase of $60 million from the previous year. Under New Mexico or Nevada law, the valuation would have been just $81 million, according to one of the tax commissioners.[57] But the courts stepped in and reduced assessments in 1918,[58] and the tax rate was finally cut in 1922, following the depression of 1919 to 1921.[59]

Meanwhile, the Arizona Tax Commission grew rapidly in power. In 1912, the Commission argued it needed more authority and money to do its job properly, and the local Boards of Equalization, "crushed between the upper and nether mill stones," were abolished.[60] The Commission thought government could be made cheaper by eliminating the city assessors and centralizing all assessments. The Commission needed, in fact, a "free hand" to fix the state's tax and revenue problems.

They got it. The Tax Commission was endowed with "unrestricted powers," which it used to call "into an inquisitorial conference all the county assessors. . . ." The conference was an extraordinary success, according to the Commission: "History, as well as taxation, was in the making. . . . " at this conference. Commissioners managed to more than double the level of assessments for the new state.[61]

So powerful were commissioners that one of them, State Tax Commissioner Thomas Campbell, a Republican, was almost elected governor in 1916. The Democratic incumbent, George W. P. Hunt, refused to step down when the results came in with a thirty-vote majority for his opponent (out of more than 55,000 ballots cast).

This "political upheaval"—a Republican win at the top of the ballot in a year of Democratic sweeps in the other elections—was probably due in part to the increased mine assessments. Incumbent Governor Hunt feared that "the beasts of mining companies were out to defeat him at any cost" because of the increases.[62] Of course, the new state's revenues had jumped by 70 percent upon statehood, a leap that may have angered any number of groups besides the mining companies.

Hunt challenged the election results. In December of 1917, the state Supreme Court decided that he was right; he had actually won the election by forty-one votes.[63] The gubernatorial candidate from the Tax Commission had lost, but the Commission itself prospered—it was accorded an unlimited appropriation.

Nevada

Despite having been a state since the Civil War, Nevada seems to have had as many troubles with the property tax as its neighbors. An 1891 law required 100 percent valuations, but it was ignored.[64] Like his colleagues to the east, the Nevada controller of 1892, one R. L. Horton, complained of competitive underassessments by local governments: "The State rate [of taxation levied from a given county] is fixed at a per cent of the valuation of property in a county, [so] it is to the interest of each county to fix as low a valuation as possible, as thereby they lessen the amount they must pay the State."[65]

Horton praised the new State Board of Assessors and Equalization for its power to "equalize" tax assessments. This was "one of the most important powers conferred upon" the Board, and would "correct much injustice." "The Board should also be clothed with authority to add to the asessment [*sic*] roll" any unassessed property.[66]

Nevada frequently tried to improve its property tax system. But the 1903 controller's report still lamented the poor tax collection system, as did numerous other reports.

The first Tax Commission of Nevada met in 1913 and described the problems it faced, despite ongoing reforms:

> A State Board of Equalization, consisting of certain of the state officers acting in an ex officio capacity, was tried out here in the early '90s, but its action did not meet with popular approval. Later an effort was made to effect equalization by methods which would usurp in the slightest degree possible the powers theretofore enjoyed by the separate county governments. The State Board of Assessors was created by the Twentieth Session of the Legislature in 1901. It was composed of the several County Assessors . . . it made substantial increases in the assessed valuation of the railroads, and theoretically, in the assessed valuation of live stock. That some of the individual Assessors failed to keep faith with the board is clearly enough shown in the fact that, after years of attempted equalization by this method, no two counties were found to be assessing property on the same percentage of actual value. Two counties in 1912 had the bulk of their property assessed for more than 100 percent of its value, and one county at an average of not over 20 percent.[67]

In contrast to the abrupt and sizable changes in New Mexico and Arizona tax administration in 1912 and 1913, the Nevada Commission of 1913 made only "slight increases" in assessments. "[I]n 1914 somewhat sharp raises in the assessed valuation of certain classes of property were made" in Nevada. Angry taxpayers filed hundreds of lawsuits against the Commission that year.[68]

In 1915, the government backed down a little and gave to "the local taxing authorities . . . a larger voice in the matter of equalization." The tax commission assessed only the property of large companies, while the counties took back control of property within their borders. Nevertheless, the Commission judged the assessments that year to be the first in Nevada to produce roughly equalized assessments across the state.[69]

The 1917 legislature reorganized the tax commission.[70] Instead of being composed entirely of *ex officio* members, only the governor and a member of the Railroad Commission served *ex officio*. The other five commissioners were to be appointed by the governor to represent the five leading industries of the state: livestock, banking, business, mining, and land.

The reorganized Tax Commission met for the first time in April of 1917. It aggressively sought uniform valuations. But a subsequent "comparison of the county rolls disclosed little attention had been paid by Assessors to the recommendations made by the board in 1917 for the purpose of bringing about uniformity in the assessed valuations of different classes of property . . . particularly . . . lands."[71] Some counties increased the assessments more than 100 percent, while others decreased them. Also, complained the Commission, "[m]erchandise stocks throughout the State are very unevenly, and therefore, inequitably assessed."[72]

Nevada continued to tinker with its tax commission through the late 1920s.[73] But actual changes in tax collections were hard to come by. In 1920, the constitutional requirement of uniformity of taxation, which had come to be seen as "too rigid,"[74] and which the Tax Commission had been recommending should be abolished since its first report,[75] was dropped in favor of discriminating by class of property. This new view of reform was then becoming popular across the country.

The next year, 1921, was quieter. No particular changes were made, nor were there noteworthy improvements, according to Nevada's report to the National Tax Association.[76]

In short, while Nevada frequently reformed the property tax throughout the study period, there were no very dramatic effects around 1912 comparable to those in New Mexico and Arizona at statehood.

ASSESSMENTS AS A PERCENTAGE OF FULL VALUE

Fiscal officials across the country insisted that property be assessed at 100 percent of its full value in the late nineteenth and early twentieth centuries. John H. MacCracken, speaking at the first conference on state and local taxation in 1907, and New Mexico's Governor W. C. McDonald, writing in 1916, both called for 100 percent assessments.[77] The Nevada controller recommended that assessments be gradually increased to 100 percent.[78] New Mexico Governor Miguel Otero explained why in 1901[79] Full value assessments would allow New Mexico, then seeking statehood, to "appear to the world what we are in fact, as to our wealth and ability to pay our obligations."

Officials liked to point out that 100 percent valuations need have no effect on the amount of taxes citizens paid. The Nevada controller of 1906, for instance, insisted that the "object is to increase valuations and lower rates."

Of course, keeping the tax burden constant when valuations increased required lower tax rates. And lower tax rates usually required legislative action. Perhaps the officials hoped to offload the political heavy lifting onto the legislature by having it stand responsible for changing the actual tax burden. This would leave tax authorities free to change assessments without, in theory, tax consequences—and without becoming targets for the resultant public outcries.

But as loudly as officials proclaimed the virtues of 100 percent assessments, citizens proclaimed the need to keep lower percentage valuations. The Taxpayers' Association of New Mexico feared "the unhappy situation in other states where increased assessments had resulted in a somewhat more equitable valuation, but in taxes so vastly increased that none derived benefit from the change."[80] In Arizona, the first State Tax Commission received "many complaints from taxpayers . . . that the different bodies entrusted with making the annual tax levies did not *decrease* the levy in proportion as the valuation of property is raised." In fact, some counties *raised* the rates.[81]

That is, in both New Mexico and Arizona, increased assessments were *not* always matched by decreased rates. No wonder citizens so strongly opposed 100 percent assessments.

Given these opposing forces, the next question is: What percent of full value did the tax officials in New Mexico, Arizona, and Nevada actually report over time?

I needed to know the answer to that question for two reasons: to tell the story of the quality of financial information reported by these governments, and also to measure the size of the economy each year in New Mexico, Arizona, and Nevada. The fiscal ratio F-RevA measures government revenues as a share of the local economy, and it measures the economy by the annual property tax assessments.

So the accuracy of those values is crucial. Hundreds of territorial, state, and local officials, many on the frontier, gathered and recorded the information a century ago with greatly varying degrees of care and expertise. These sources of error are likely random and were therefore partly controlled by the use of many years' observations in three different states.

A more serious issue is that tax assessors often systematically misvalued property.[82] This is the problem that so enraged the accountant-reformers of the era. And this is what they attempted to rectify with their push for full-value assessments.

Location of the Data

Of all the financial data available on these governments, assessed property values were some of the most consistently reported. These were the only data collected annually on the size of state or territorial economies in the late nineteenth and early twentieth centuries, before 1915. The states collected information on the value of real and (some) personal property in order to levy the then-dominant property tax, which was intended to reach all wealth. The property tax supplied from 50 percent to 87 percent of the governments' revenues during my study period (see table 8.1).

Official totals of assessed property values were easy to locate for New Mexico, Arizona, and Nevada in almost every year I looked for. The information provided ranged from a single figure—the total assessed valuation for the

Table 8.1.　Percent of Total Receipts by Source and State, Selected Years

		Revenue Source		
	Property taxes	Business, income, poll, & occupational taxes; licenses	Subventions & grants	Interest, rent, enterprise earnings, fines, escheats, misc.
New Mexico				
1903	79.6	2.3	12.0	6.1
1913	69.9	5.7	13.5	10.9
1919	50.2	7.0	3.6	39.2
Arizona				
1903	86.8	4.1	4.4	4.7
1913	81.4	2.3	5.2	11.2
1919	70.7	6.3	4.4	18.6
Nevada				
1903	54.7	8.5	0.0	36.8
1913	62.0	8.9	0.3	28.8
1919	66.2	10.5	5.9	17.4

Sources: Calculations for 1903—U.S. Bureau of the Census, *Wealth, Debt, and Taxation 1913*, vol. 2, pt. 6, table 7; for 1913—ibid., table 6; for 1919—U.S. Bureau of the Census, *Financial Statistics of States, 1919*, table 3.

territory or state for a year[83]—to a seventeen-page series of tables detailing assessments by type of property for every county.[84]

Occasionally, a report contained a table listing total assessments for a number of years. More often, multiple sources gave different figures, and I had to make judgments about which to use. Then I combed tables and textual material for clues as to what percentage of true or full value was represented by the reported numbers. In most years, especially during the territorial period, the reported value was substantially lower than the full value.

The offices publishing assessment information varied. In Nevada, the most consistent of the three governments, assessments always appeared in the controller's report. Once the state tax commission was created in 1914, the data appeared in that body's reports, too. In Arizona, the reports of the auditor, the board of equalization, and, from 1912 on, the state tax commission contained property valuations. New Mexico was the least predictable state. Information on assessments appeared variously in the reports of the auditor, the treasurer, the traveling auditor, the board of equalization, and the state tax commission.

Results

Table 8.2 shows property assessment information for New Mexico, Arizona, and Nevada from the 1880s to 1930. Total *published* property assessments

Table 8.2. Published Assessments and Estimated Full Values of Property, New Mexico, Arizona, Nevada, 1880–1930

Year	New Mexico Published assessments	New Mexico Fraction of full value	New Mexico Estimated full value	Arizona Published assessments	Arizona Fraction of full value	Arizona Estimated full value	Nevada Published assessments Other prop	Nevada Published assessments Mines	Nevada Fraction of full value	Nevada Fraction of full value	Nevada Estimated full value
1880							$27,598,659	$4,496,739	40%	100%	$73,493,386
1881							28,367,239	2,542,372	40%	100%	73,460,468
1882							27,369,335	1,740,554	40%	100%	70,163,893
1883				$31,588,355	35%	$90,252,442	27,758,173	1,643,408	40%	100%	71,038,840
1884				30,227,766	35%	86,365,046	26,597,299	1,453,686	40%	100%	67,946,934
1885							26,463,289	939,336	40%	100%	67,097,559
1886							25,748,877	554,347	35%	100%	74,122,568
1887				26,173,506	35%	74,781,446	26,440,207	1,557,132	35%	100%	77,100,580
1888				25,913,015	35%	74,037,186	26,738,379	2,109,293	35%	100%	78,504,660
1889							26,629,681	1,285,494	35%	100%	77,370,297
1890	$43,227,686	20%	$216,138,430				24,663,385	686,710	35%	100%	71,153,523
1891	30,691,265	20%	153,456,325	28,270,466	35%	80,772,761	29,807,543	762,896	35%	100%	85,927,304
1892	41,602,198	20%	208,010,990	27,923,163	35%	79,780,464	31,096,341	222,215	35%	100%	89,068,904
1893	41,574,845	20%	207,874,225	28,486,183	35%	81,389,093	26,178,061	157,514	35%	100%	74,951,974
1894	39,090,502	20%	195,452,510	27,061,975	35%	77,319,928	23,628,720	181,295	25%	100%	94,696,177
1895	41,140,803	20%	205,704,015				23,555,722	167,740	25%	100%	94,390,629
1896	36,891,102	20%	184,455,510				23,106,134	352,335	25%	100%	92,776,871
1897	39,478,119	20%	197,390,595	30,693,209	35%	87,694,883	23,048,197	449,051	25%	100%	92,641,840
1898	38,808,041	20%	194,040,205	31,473,540	35%	89,924,400	23,187,211	330,034	25%	100%	93,078,879
1899				32,509,520	35%	92,884,344	23,566,458	126,251	25%	100%	94,392,085
1900				33,782,466	35%	96,521,331	24,180,857	105,900	25%	100%	96,829,328
1901				38,853,831	35%	111,010,947	28,096,792	294,462	35%	100%	80,571,009
1902	38,633,993	20%	193,169,965	39,083,178	35%	111,666,222	29,324,667	506,710	35%	100%	84,291,472
1903	39,596,952	20%	197,984,760	43,088,041	35%	123,108,687	32,707,464	454,220	35%	100%	93,904,116
1904	42,665,000	20%	213,325,000	45,079,431	35%	128,798,375	36,270,135	925,635	35%	100%	104,554,593

Year											
1906	43,245,746	20%	216,228,730	62,946,963	35%	179,848,464	65,084,766	6,901,516	45%,	100%	151,534,329
1907	48,509,097	20%	242,545,485	77,372,156	35%	221,063,303	73,856,142	3,154,109	45%,	100%	167,278,870
1908	52,526,295	20%	262,631,475	80,637,541	35%	230,392,976	73,825,601	5,784,601	45%	100%	169,841,492
1909	59,464,311	20%	297,321,555	82,684,063	35%	236,240,179	78,554,979	8,874,228	45%	100%	183,440,848
1910				86,126,226	35%	246,074,932					
1911	59,248,881	25%	236,995,523	98,032,709	35%	280,093,453	85,347,058	9,823,169	45%	100%	199,483,299
1912[a]	**72,457,454**	**33%**	**217,372,362**	**140,338,191**	**50%**	**280,676,382**	**92,354,221**	**8,732,859**	**50%,**	**100%**	**193,441,301**
1913	252,259,554	100%	252,259,554	375,862,414	100%	375,862,414	107,794,730	4,415,734	50%	100%	220,005,194
1914	271,902,119	100%	271,902,119	408,540,283	100%	408,540,283	132,923,505	3,681,544	60%	100%	225,220,719
1915	305,710,502	100%	305,710,502	422,102,389	100%	422,102,389	143,738,557	7,400,195	65%	100%	228,536,437
1916	330,387,523	100%	330,387,523	488,226,371	100%	488,226,371	159,610,557	14,860,569	70%	100%	242,875,651
1917	329,869,888	75%	439,826,517	699,245,000	100%	699,245,000	167,424,213	15,635,475	70%	100%	254,812,922
1918	357,062,509	75%	476,083,345	835,916,000	100%	835,916,000	188,901,638	9,091,462	70%	100%	278,950,945
1919	371,559,631	75%	495,412,841	856,791,000	100%	856,791,000	192,239,238	5,804,767	70%	100%	280,432,250
1920	403,046,652	75%	537,395,536	884,455,682	100%	884,455,682	208,844,302	4,577,096	65%	100%	325,876,022
1921	363,490,112	75%	484,653,483	830,536,582	100%	830,536,582	201,560,699	1,861,833	65%	100%	311,955,216
1922	329,898,508	67%	492,385,833	733,995,000	100%	733,995,000	195,835,427	2,801,035	65%	100%	304,086,308
1923	313,065,243	60% 90%b	468,910,613	733,994,556	100%	733,994,556	195,189,126	3,864,810	60%	100%	329,180,021
1924	309,808,236	60% 90%	458,751,118	699,142,997	100%	699,142,997	198,137,637	3,154,301	60%	100%	333,383,69
1925	311,661,655	70% 90%	412,318,969	652,444,309	100%	652,444,309	195,639,193	3,679,481	60%	100%	329,744,802
1926	313,561,903	70% 90%	414,929,703	653,163,397	100%	653,163,397	199,152,099	3,835,254	60%	100%	335,755,41
1927	315,373,405	60%	525,622,342	673,127,177	100%	673,127,177	198,491,211	4,579,660	60%	100%	335,398,346
1928	316,468,567	60%	527,447,612	681,736,018	100%	681,736,018	197,550,475	7,635,571	60%	100%	336,886,363
1929	312,210,679	60%	520,351,132	700,890,801	100%	700,890,801	204,891,023	12,046,109	60%	100%	353,531,148
1930	344,671,212	60%	574,452,020	714,945,809	100%	714,945,809	201,994,660	5,856,472	60%	100%	342,514,238

a Year of statehood for New Mexico and Arizona.

b Different classes of property were assessed at different percentages.

appear in the first column for each government. Column 2 in each group lists the percentage of true value that was reported in each year. It is based on the best information I could obtain from the records about what percentage of true value was published. This column is crucial to the study; I explain how I decided on these percentages in detail in the appendix. Column 3 inflates the published assessment values (column 1) up to the full value implied by the percentage in column 2.

New Mexico

The Territory of New Mexico assessed property at about 20 percent of its true value. On the eve of statehood, in 1911, this percentage began creeping up, and in 1912, it reached one-third of full value. This is because the tax basis for official property valuations was required by law to be "one third of the true value."[85]

From 1913 to 1916, the new State of New Mexico published assessments in its State Tax Commission reports that were said to be 100 percent of true property values. However, this full-value assessment was not the basis for taxation in 1913 or 1914. The 1915 legislature repealed the one-third statute and substituted "a full valuation" as the tax basis,[86] but this remained an aspiration, rather than the actual basis for tax levies.

This illustrates a problem with interpretation of the details of tax reform during this period. New Mexico reported 100 percent valuations, but probably did not use them for levying taxes. The assessment process seems to have improved enough by the first years of statehood that New Mexico could roughly estimate the full value of property within its borders, a great achievement in improving fiscal administration. But the state never used those numbers in a serious way to calculate taxes.

From 1916 through 1930, the percentage of property values published, as reported by New Mexico to the U.S. Census, declined from 100 percent to 75 percent and then to 60 percent (see Table 8.2).

In some years in the 1920s, different classes of property faced different rates, a maneuver that had once been considered anti-reform. Informally, this happened often. For instance, the State Tax Commission tabulated all land sales in the state in 1919 and estimated that valuations for tax purposes were about 56 percent of true value. In its 1917–1918 report, the Commission complained that agricultural land valuations "range from $18 per acre to more than $100 per acre on practically the same class of land."[87]

The assessment reform process continued over a number of years. But the first years of statehood were the first (and only) time during the study period that New Mexico published 100 percent valuations. It was an important step towards the professionalization of the assessment process.

Arizona

When Arizona was a territory, it published property valuations that were about 35 percent of full value. After it became a state, Arizona always reported its estimates of 100 percent property values to the U.S. Census, though it almost certainly never reached full-value assessments for *tax purposes* during the study period.

Progressive passions burned hotly in Arizona, and upon statehood these passions fired up the fiscal authorities. With enormous difficulty and against a popular uproar, they increased assessments to about 50 percent of true value in the first year, 1912.

Then came 1913.

The state tax commission was charged in 1913 with bringing assessed values up to 100 percent of true and making assessments uniform across the state.[88] The Commission described its experience as follows:

> The Commission opened the season of 1913 by an order to all assessors to assess all property at its full cash value. . . . The assessors carried out the orders, both in letter and in spirit. There was no rest either night or day from the issuance of these orders until the books were finally closed. It is a matter of geology that Arizona is a land of extinct volcanos [*sic*], but the Tax Commission was soon aware of the fact that geology was wrong.
>
> Telegrams, letter, resolutions and delegations poured in on the Commission. Town councils, boards of supervisors, boards of trade, chambers of commerce and associations met and resolved that it was all wrong. Newspapers poured out their vials vituperation [*sic*] figuratively showing their teeth and shaking their fists and saying in direct English, "We'll get you! Damn you." Corporations pawed the air. Classes tore their hair, individuals frothed at the mouth and all sent supplications to the throne of grace, or elsewhere, for the love of Mike to help them or they were ruined.
>
> "The pounding became so hard that the Commission and Assessors soon found themselves working and standing together as a unit and actually 'putting the thing over.'"[89]

Despite all this heat and excitement, the reforms did gradually produce less politicized property assessments. In fact, beginning in 1925, the amounts Arizona reported to the U.S. Bureau of the Census and the amounts it recorded in its own state tables for property values agreed.

Nevada

In Nevada's first few years of statehood, in the 1860s, mines were partly exempted from taxation. One observer remarked that if the state did tax mine proceeds, "there [would] be found no net proceeds . . . for 1000 years."[90]

Later, the law required mines to be assessed at 100 percent of true value, "value" usually meaning the mine proceeds net of costs of production. In practice, the mines negotiated the figures for proceeds with the taxing authorities. However, I have no information on the specific percentage of true value that was actually recorded for the mines. Therefore, table 8.2 shows the mines at the valuation Nevada claimed to be reporting—100 percent.

As for all other classes of property in Nevada, assessments hovered around 40 percent in the early 1880s. They declined thereafter through the end of the century. Beginning in 1900, they started rising again, finally reaching a high of about 70 percent in the late 1910s. The depression of 1919–1921 dropped the assessment values back down to 65 percent, and soon down to 60 percent, where they remained through the end of the study period.

Accuracy of the Estimates

How accurate are the numbers listed in column 3 of table 8.2? That is, how accurate are my estimates of the true value of assessed property in New Mexico, Arizona, and Nevada?

The quality of the data is a central issue of this paper, both in part 1, where I test a hypothesis based on these data, and in part 2, where I track the quality of the published financial reports. That is why I calculated the fiscal ratio with the gross national product as the denominator (F-GNP) as well as using property values for the denominator (F-RevA). The F-GNP series and F-RevA series are highly correlated and the change to statehood had similar effects on the two variables. This suggests that the estimates of assessment percentages I gleaned from reading official reports were reasonably accurate.

TAX OFFICIALS AT THE SERVICE OF LEVIATHAN

New Mexicans and Arizonans got a lot more accountability from their tax system upon statehood, as this chapter shows. But they also got a much more expensive government, as part 1 of the book shows. In fact, I believe, the improved tax system was the mechanism that *created* the more expensive government, at least in part.

Fiscal officials emphasized the need for efficiency and fairness in tax administration. For the most part, they preferred to ignore the issue of how much more money was being collected as efficiency improved.

New Mexico's Miguel Otero, writing as auditor in 1927 to 1928, said it clearly: "[W]ithout going into the question as to whether or not the State may be living beyond its means . . . one of the chief causes . . . of the present financial straits of the State consists in the unequal and decidedly unfair method of collecting taxes." But Otero's preferred solution was to hand the state a stick—state sale of property on which taxes were more than 90 days delinquent—that would not only discourage tax evasion but also raise state revenues.[91]

The truth is the fiscal officials more or less knew that a better tax system would bring much higher revenues for the government. Sometimes they said so. The New Mexico Tax Commission wrote admiringly in 1923 of Guadalupe County's reassessment, which corrected many problems springing from lack of adequate property records: "The tax roll has been cleared of innumerable errors which would have resulted in discrimination and injustice. The thorough reassessment of this county will bring larger revenues for State and County purposes."[92]

Fiscal officials differed in their opinions as to whether increased government spending was a good idea. Some of them were full-throated supporters of bigger government, like C. M. Zander, one of the first state tax commissioners of Arizona. Zander, an ardent admirer of Lloyd George's inheritance tax in England, informed the 7th Annual Arizona Tax Conference in 1919 that the new federal income tax was a wonderful and just thing, because before it:

> tremendous fortunes [were] created and handed down from generation to generation . . . which paid no taxes or tribute to federal, state or local governments. As a result we had upon the one hand a class of people restless under a smarting sense of deep injustice . . . and upon the other hand a class of people becoming more and more autocratic because they . . . less and less performed the greatest requirement of democracy, namely, the contribution from their wealth for purposes of democracy.[93]

Arizona's improved tax system had similar benefits, argued Zander, because it promoted both bigger government as well as a better society:

> Almost coincident with the advent of better equalization of taxes in Arizona has been a remarkable expansion of public expenditures,—and I want to say right here that it is not the policy of an enlightened people in this day to keep down public expenditures to the irreducible minimum. . . . If we distribute the burden of taxation fearlessly and equitably, the people . . . will make available the funds

necessary to develop all the material resources of the state. And more than that, the sense of justice superinduced by just taxation will be reflected in a near approach to democratic relations, in business, society and religion—fundamentals necessary before any people can become strong, enduring and contented. This is taxation. . . .[94]

On the other hand, J. C. Callaghan, also in Arizona, condemned the growth of government roundly. In 1914 he objected to the:

vast increased expenditure . . . without regard to . . . the actual needs of government [including an] enormous and unjustifiable increase in maintenance cost of the State Industrial School . . . the state is being administered under laws, and by means of appropriations, which permit reckless waste of public funds, and do not aim at economy of the taxpayers' money.[95]

In New Mexico, the tax commission of 1921–1922 reported that the combined state and local millage rates, which had been just 17.75 in 1916, had soared to 36.38 by 1921.[96] The Commission denounced the rise in strong terms:

This remarkable increase in the tax burden has, we feel, been entirely unjustified when we take into consideration the ability of those, who actually pay the taxes in New Mexico . . . We can no longer continue a policy which can not fail to result in drying up the sources of pubic revenues.[97]

The Commission noted that if all property were assessed at its full value, then:

the present average tax rate would produce nearly twice as much as is necessary now to meet even the heavy and sometimes extravagant expenditures being called for. However . . . the taxes to be paid under the existing rate would be prohibitive . . . there must be a sharp curtailment of governmental expenditures and a careful shaping of budgets so that the actual tax to be paid will not increase to such a degree as to make the taxes unbearable.[98]

Nevertheless, in the same report, these officials continued to insist on the full-value and more thorough assessments that they knew would raise more money, while hoping for lower tax rates.

Taxpayers knew that full-value assessments would bring higher tax bills, too. That's why they fought them so hard. Sotrey County, Nevada, for instance, where property values were rising dramatically in the 1880s, reduced its reported assessment by 20 percent.[99] In fact, Nevada taxpayers managed to prevent full-value assessments on most property throughout the study period.

Officials preferred to operate in the fond belief that taxpayers were not concerned with the total amount of the tax burden, but only with the fairness of who bore it. New Mexico's Tax Commission, writing in the mid-1920s just after a severe national depression, put it this way:

> It is our observation that the taxpayer is not so much concerned with the amount of taxes levied upon his particular property as with the question of whether he is carrying more than his portion of the aggregate or not.[100]

In fact, fiscal officials liked to see themselves as standing outside the political fray. People should move "away from the conception of tax administrator as a political office-holder and [see him] as a professional technician whose prosperity . . . depends entirely upon his skill, impartiality and industry," declared the Special Revenue Commission of New Mexico.[101]

To these simple technicians, the assessment "duty . . . is irksome and one that they would gladly be relieved from," claimed R. L. Horton, the Nevada Controller in 1892.[102]

No one should believe that fiscal officials had anything to do with politics or tax levels, declared Arizona's tax commissioners in 1916. Their Wisconsin colleagues, they wrote, expressed their own views so well that they quoted them at length:

> The subject of high taxes is one over which assessing officers have no control. . . . At no stage of the proceedings has the tax commission, assessors of incomes, or local assessors any word or voice in determining the amount of revenue to be raised or taxes to be levied . . . Our problem is exclusively one of equalization. . . . We can, therefore, establish a complete alibi against the charge of high taxes. . . . Nevertheless the responsibility is often laid at our door. . . . A jealous watchfulness of public expenditures is highly desirable, and I have no thought of criticising it or discouraging it. . . . We do not and should not complain of criticism of the work for which we are responsible, but it is both illogical and unfair to blame a department for conditions over which we have no control . . . We do not and should not appear either as advocates of or apologists for high taxes. . . . No department of the public service is more directly interested in moderate public expenditures than the tax department.[103]

Among the three commissioners espousing these views of themselves as simple technicians without a political thought in their heads were C. M. Zander, who wrote the ode to higher taxes and socialism quoted earlier, and T. E. Campbell, who was at that very moment defending his claim to have won the gubernatorial election in court. Simple, impartial technicians they were not.

Again and again, the fiscal officials of New Mexico and Arizona, whether they disavowed or embraced larger government, advised their governments on how to collect more money. The Arizona auditor of 1883–1884 advised the Thirteenth Legislature, later known as "the Thieving Thirteenth" for its outrageous spending, to raise taxes to cover the territory's high costs.[104] The 1916 Arizona tax commission report cited above promoted higher taxes on the grounds that the people wanted things that required them.[105] The New Mexico comptroller of 1927–1928 advocated a nationally uniform gas tax so as to protect New Mexico's dealers near state lines from tax competition from the neighboring states.[106]

The Arizona auditor a decade later thought tax rates were already "as high as can be fixed without seriously impeding business enterprises." His solution was to levy a new tax on every occupation in Arizona, from merchants to mills and from gambling tables to ten pin alleys. Business license taxes, too, should be imposed on most businesses, especially retail liquor and gambling since "these occupations are the cause of most of the expense incurred by the administration of our laws."[107]

Of course, everyone's taxes soared after statehood. Measured in absolute dollars, the New Mexican government's revenues grew from $831,000 (1911) to $1,695,000 (1913), while Arizona's collections rose from $1,014,000 to $1,719,000. Someone had to pay for that. But an interesting fact is that the change in the incidence of taxation with statehood was similar in both the subject states. The group that bore a declining share of the taxes in both states was urban property owners, while the group that bore the greatest percentage increase was mines.

CONCLUSIONS

Out of the three governments I studied, reformers managed to achieve 100 percent assessments, as well as enormous other improvements in the property tax system, in the two places that became states during the study period—New Mexico and Arizona. But then, within a few years, New Mexican taxpayers managed to rid themselves of the 100 percent valuations. A constitutional amendment subsequent to statehood made it crystal clear: "The percentage of value against which tax rates are assessed shall not exceed thirty-three and one-third per cent."[108] Arizonans did not drop the 100 percent valuations, but they did not use them for tax purposes.

Progressives saw in efficient government and administration by experts a way to end the partisanship, corruption, and ineptness of so many municipal governments of their era. Ethridge argues that the Progressive passion for efficient government also had the effect of countering the state of semi-gridlock deliberately designed by the American founders, enabling the rise of larger governments.[109] "Taxation is politics," as Radaelli[110] says, and many U.S. accountants took a stand with the Progressives, who generally saw "progress" as including a much larger role for governments than had been known in the nineteenth century.

So it is tempting to conclude that Progressivism accounted for the soaring costs of government in New Mexico and Arizona. But Nevada's government did not dramatically increase its spending at that time, nor did it dramatically reform its tax administration.

In New Mexico and Arizona, the Progressive reform wave happened to coincide with statehood. Together, the two produced dramatic improvements in the "accounting technologies of government," which, as Miller points out, "alter the capacities of organizations and power."[111] The improvements in New Mexico's and Arizona's main source of revenues, the property tax, helped unleash huge increases in the size of their governments. Accountants also garnered positions of unprecedented power in the new states.

The long and short of property tax reform in New Mexico and Arizona is this: tax and other fiscal officials greatly improved the system, making it more honest, efficient, and transparent. These changes helped collect a lot more money from the people, as the officials knew it would. In effect, whatever their individual views on the size of government, fiscal officials' agreement on the need for better tax administration placed them on the side of growth for the new states' governments.

NOTES

1. Aaron, "Observations on Property Tax," 153. See also Fisher, *Worst Tax?*, 122, describing the property tax as widely accepted and widely criticized.

2. Aaron, "Observations on Property Tax," 153, notes that the concept of "true value" is meaningless to assessors. Nevertheless, the terms "true value" and "full value" and "100 percent assessments" will be used in this paper to indicate what assessors estimated the 100 percent assessment value would be for practical purposes. Officials at the time wrote of 100 percent valuations.

3. In other places, war has enabled dramatic changes in tax administration, as discussed in chapter 6.

4. For a discussion of these widespread problems in the late nineteenth century, see Higgens–Evenson, *Price of Progress*, chap. 1. Toomey, "Prelude to Statehood," 45–53, discusses the same problems in Tennessee in the late eighteenth century, and Moore, "Local and State Governments," 1982, mentions similar issues in Mississippi in the early nineteenth century.

5. Oates, *Property Taxation.*

6. Fisher, *The Worst Tax?*

7. Mehrotra, "Forging Fiscal Reform."

8. McPherson, "State and Local Taxation."

9. Blackmon, *State and Local Taxation*.

10. Fisher, *The Worst Tax?;* Mehrotra, "Producing Tax Knowledge."

11. Fisher, *The Worst Tax?*

12. Radaelli, "Taxation Research."

13. Mehrotra, "Forging Fiscal Reform," 94, 103.

14. Fisher, *The Worst Tax?*

15. Webber and Wildavsky, *History of Taxation.*

16. Ball, *Desert Lawmen*, 246–249, 263.

17. Ball, *Desert Lawmen*, 262.

18. Ball, *Desert Lawmen*, 259–260.

19. Ball, *Desert Lawmen*, 258.

20. Ball, *Desert Lawmen*, 242–245, 259; Larson, *Forgotten Frontier*, 123–152.

21. Larson, *Forgotten Frontier*, 82.

22. Otero, *My Nine Years*, 240–243.

23. NM Terr. Auditor, *Report*, 1891–1892.

24. NM Terr. Auditor, *Report,* 1893–1894, 5–6.

25. NM Terr. Auditor, *Report,* 1893–1894, 12–13.

26. NM Terr. Auditor, *Report,* 1893–1894, 16.

27. Otero, *My Nine Years,* 361.

28. Ball, *Desert Lawmen,* 263.

29. Otero, *My Nine Years,* 84, 88.

30. NM Terr. Auditor, *Report,* 1905–1906, 3.

31. Folmar, *Piecemeal Amendment*, 27.

32. NM Special Revenue Commission, *Report,* 1920, 297.

33. McDonald, "Tax Problem," 24.

34. *Bulletin of the National Tax Association*, 200.

35. "New Mexico," 1917, 137.

36. NM State Tax Commission, *Report,* 1915–1916.

37. NM State Tax Commission, *Report,* 1915–1916.

38. NM State Tax Commission, *Report*, 1929–1930.

39. NM Special Revenue Commission, 7, 19.

40. NM Special Revenue Commission, 26–32.

41. "New Mexico," 1921, 235–236.

42. Ball, *Desert Lawmen.*

43. AZ Terr. Auditor, *Report,* 1891–1892, 5.

44. AZ Terr. Auditor, *Report,* 1883–1884, 47.

45. AZ Terr. Board of Equalization, *Proceedings*, 1906, 2.

46. AZ State Tax Commission, *Report,* 1912, 11.

47. AZ State Tax Commission, *Report,* 1914, 19.

48. AZ State Tax Commission, *Report,* 1918, 9–10. There had actually been legislation to tax intangibles at least as early as 1913, according to the 1914 State Tax Commission (p. 7).

49. AZ State Tax Commission, *Report,* 1914, 13.

50. AZ State Tax Commission, *Report,* 1914, 25. The Commission still wrote enthusiastically about the higher tax on telegraphs in its 1916 report (p. 8).

51. AZ Auditor, *Report,* 1912, 39.

52. AZ State Tax Commission, *Report,* 1912, 34.

53. AZ State Tax Commission, *Report,* 1912, 36–37.

54. AZ State Tax Commission, *Report,* 1912, 49.

55. AZ State Tax Commission, *Report,* 1914, 41, 43. One of the tax commissioners, C. M. Zander, was a great admirer of Lloyd George's leveling theory of taxation. Zander, "Tax Progress in Arizona."

56. AZ Auditor, *Report,* 1914, 14–15.

57. Zander, "Assessment of Mining Property."

58. Zander, "1918 Valuations," 80–81.

59. Fletcher, "Budget and State Taxes," 113–115.

60. AZ State Tax Commission, *Report,* 1912, 15.

61. AZ State Tax Commission, *Report,* 1914, 11.

62. Krenkel, "Disputed Arizona," 62.

63. Krenkel, "Disputed Arizona."

64. NV Controller, *Report,* 1902.

65. NV Controller, *Report,* 1892, 14. See also AZ State Tax Commission, *Report,* 1912, 16; and NV Controller, *Report,* 1888, 18–19.

66. NV Controller, *Report,* 1892, 13, 14.

67. NV State Tax Commission, *Report,* 1913–1914, 3.

68. NV State Tax Commission, *Report,* 1915–1916, 5.

69. NV State Tax Commission, *Report,* 1915–1916, 5.

70. NV State Tax Commission, *Report,* 1917–1918, 5.

71. NV State Tax Commission, *Report,* 1917–1918, 6.

72. NV State Tax Commission, *Report,* 1917–1918, 10.

73. NV State Tax Commission, *Report,* 1929–1930.

74. Adams, "Essentials to Orderly Progress," 42.

75. NV State Tax Commission, *Report,* 1913, 65.

76. "Nevada," 234.

77. McDonald, "Tax Problem," 24. Also MacCracken, "Taxation of City Real Estate," 386.

78. NV Controller, *Report,* 1915, 31.

79. Hornung, *Fullerton's Rangers,* 48.

80. James, "Review of the Tax Levies," 1.

81. NM Tax Commission, *Report,* 1912, 19. Emphasis in the original.

82. The Bureau of the Census did not believe, in the early twentieth century, that this source of error materially affected "the total for the nation or for the state." U.S. Bureau of the Census, *Wealth, Debt, and Taxation,* 6. See also discussion of the census method for estimating the true value of real property in the same source, 8–11.

83. E.g., NM Terr. Traveling Auditor, *Report,* 1910, 19.

84. NM Traveling Auditor, *Report,* 1912, 18–34. See also AZ State Tax Commission, *Report,* 1930, tab. 28, which discloses assessments by type of property, 1900–1930.

85. NM Special Revenue Commission, *Report,* 10, 297.
86. James, "Review of the Tax Levies," 1.
87. NM State Tax Commission, *Report,* 1916–1918, 7.
88. AZ State Tax Commission, *Report,* 1914, 7.
89. AZ State Tax Commission, *Report,* 1914, 10–11.
90. Benson, The American Property Tax, 46.
91. NM Auditor, *Report,* 1927–1928, 4–5.
92. NM State Tax Commission, *Report,* 1921–1922, 1.
93. Zander, "Tax Progress in Arizona," 13.
94. Zander, "Tax Progress in Arizona," 14–15.
95. AZ Auditor, *Report,* 1914, 10–12.
96. NM State Tax Commission, *Report,* 1921–1922, 115.
97. NM State Tax Commission, *Report,* 1921–1922, 6.
98. NM State Tax Commission, *Report,* 1921–1922, 8.
99. NV Controller, *Report,* 1888.
100. NM State Tax Commission, *Report,* 1922–1923–1924, 6.
101. NM Special Revenue Commission, *Report,* 27.
102. NV Controller, *Report,* 1892, 14.
103. AZ Tax Commission, *Report,* 1916, p 25.
104. AZ Auditor, *Report,* 1883–1884, 6 and 48–49.
105. AZ Tax Commission, *Report,* 1916, 30, 31, and *inter alia.*
106. NM Comptroller, *Report,* 1927–1928, 11.
107. AZ Auditor, *Report,* 1891–1892, 4.
108. NM Constitution, art. 8, § 1.
109. Ethridge, *Case for Gridlock.*
110. Radaelli, "Taxation Research," 84.
111. Miller, "Governing by Numbers," 379.

9

Funds, Assets, Liabilities, Fiscal Years, and Report Timing

Four accounting elements of particular interest in government accounting are 1) funds, 2) how and whether assets and liabilities are reported, 3) the fiscal years used, and 4) the timing of the reports. This chapter traces the development of these elements, beginning with the ancient practice of fund accounting.

FUNDS

Probably the most basic and oldest accounting practice characteristic of governments is fund accounting. Potts traces it to the English Magna Carta (1215 A.D.), which restricted taxes to those legislated by the Parliament. Earlier still, the Roman empire sometimes obliged a city to devote a given part of its collections to defensive wall maintenance, a practice Potts sees as an early version of fund accounting.[1]

To this day, fund accounting is ubiquitous among governments.[2] Certainly, funds long pre-date the 1880s and were used by New Mexico, Arizona, and Nevada throughout the study period.

The number of funds used by the governments of New Mexico and Arizona grew dramatically after statehood, presumably as local special interests flexed their political muscles. New Mexico introduced the Penitentiary Sewerage and Plumbing Fund, the University Saline Fund, and the Agricultural Deficiency Fund.[3] Arizona had such newcomers as the Sulphur Springs Valley Dry Farming Fund, the Plant Introduction Fund, and the Apiary Inspection Fund.[4]

An exact count of the growth is difficult to make because "funds" and "accounts" were not always clearly distinguished and not all funds were reported, especially in the early years. Furthermore, the number of funds probably increased slowly as time passed in both places.

Nevertheless, statehood clearly brought an explosion in the numbers. New Mexico reported on about eight to twenty funds from the 1880s through 1911, as did Arizona in the 1890s. By 1913 to 1914, just after statehood, the New Mexico auditor was detailing between 113 and 140 funds; by 1916, his Arizona counterpart listed 60 to 65. These numbers would be much larger if some of the accounts within the general funds were also counted as funds.

Such proliferation produces confusion. The reader has trouble understanding what the government is doing when its activities are so extensively subdivided. Even before statehood, there was some feeling that there were too many funds for easy comprehension. The New Mexico traveling auditor, in fact, tried to abandon them in 1910, as he wrote in his report that year:

> To convey a more definite idea of the sources from which receipts are derived and purposes for which public moneys were expended, this statement has been compiled without reference to the various funds and accounts as carried upon the books of the territorial treasurer and auditor. Expenditures of like character, as well as receipts from similar sources, have been condensed into a single item.[5]

But this foray into revolutionizing public sector accounting consisted in practice of simply grouping the fund titles by general function—a modest change that kept fund accounting untouched.

Funds Before Statehood

In the territorial years of the late nineteenth century, New Mexico and Arizona presented uninformative lists of the activity in each fund. In New Mexico's 1897–1898 report, for example, the fund statements listed all the transactions by date. The auditor described the transactions simply as tax receipts, "warrants destroyed," or interfund transfers in and out. He summed the debits, credits, and fund balances biennially, not annually.[6]

In Arizona a decade earlier, the auditor's fund statements were even less informative: a list of warrants and their payees. Occasionally a fund was credited for the annual appropriation, from which the sum of the warrants was subtracted to yield an "unexpended balance."[7] Even as the twentieth century began, Arizona's auditors continued to produce the sort of report Frederick Clow called "worthless"[8]—a list of warrants that ran, in 1907 and 1908, for 170 pages.

Funds Around Statehood

Fund presentation greatly improved in both New Mexico and Arizona around statehood. The interminable old lists of individual transactions vanished and more concise presentations appeared.

The New Mexico traveling auditor tried grouping funds by function in 1910, as mentioned above. Just after statehood, the auditor and treasurer introduced tables of fund abstracts.[9] These excellent tables showed beginning and ending balances, and the sums of receipts, warrants, and transfers to and from each fund.

About the same time, Arizona officials also improved fund presentations. The auditor drew up three lists in 1915. One showed the sources and sums of revenues in each fund. Another showed the increase or decrease in each fund's revenues by source since the previous year, and a third listed the fund increases or decreases in total expenditures since 1914.[10]

The treasurer had tables of fund abstracts similar to the auditor's. He also printed the fund statements; the only additional information these provided concerned the sources of receipts.[11]

Still lacking from all these early statehood reports were details of the purposes of expenditures. But this soon changed, as we see next.

Funds After Statehood

Over the decades following statehood, the new states gradually adopted more efficient fund reporting. The New Mexico auditor, in the mid-1920s, introduced what he called a "classification of payments" to summarize the fund information.[12]

Former governor Miguel Otero became the state auditor in January of 1927.[13] He expanded on the classification idea in his 1927–1928 report, grouping all funds under one of fifteen general headings ("Executive Department," "Protection to Person and Property," and so on).[14] There were even control accounts. For example, all the charitable institution funds were grouped under one item called "Charitable Institutions (Control Account)."[15] This is the same solution adopted by the traveling auditor seventeen years earlier and in fact may have been copied from that office.

Otero, who had paid close attention to New Mexico fiscal policy since territorial days, also introduced an excellent "analysis of accounts." This ran for fifty-eight pages in the 1927–1928 report and provided just the sort of information needed by decision-makers. The section for the Girls' Welfare Home, for instance, explained disbursements as being for "Groceries and Provisions" ($4,802), "Repairs Buildings and Machinery" ($656), "Rewards for return of escapes" ($45), and so forth.[16] Otero's successor kept the fund groupings but unfortunately dropped the analysis of accounts.

For each function reported in 1928, a list of the sources of receipts and the objects of disbursements was provided in a statement more than fifty pages long. For example, the cattle indemnity fund received $1,510.50 from brand application fees and spent $11,425 on health inspectors' salaries. Interestingly, expenditures of the governor's office were not analyzed because they were not subject to audit, and highway expenditures were omitted because that statement was "too large to be used in this report." Accounts in this analysis were categorized into fifty-six functions, while the fund abstracts were grouped more broadly into sixteen categories.[17]

Arizona also summarized fund information in the 1920s. Most funds were put under the General Fund umbrella; the remainder were consolidated into a smaller, more comprehensible number of accounts.[18]

Despite Arizona's general post-statehood improvement, problems continued throughout the study period. For instance, the 1918 auditor's report included a statement listing the funds with their appropriations, expenditures, and balances. But the statement failed to total the columns, leaving the interested reader a choice between ignorance and adding up ten pages of figures himself.[19]

In 1919, the same statement appeared, this time with totals and, for all funds except the general fund, the useful addition of fund receipts. No explanation for the omission of receipts from the general fund only is offered. The auditor's accompanying discussion objected strongly to the statutory requirements for particular types and forms of reports.[20] Perhaps this is why some of the statements during this period have odd characteristics.

Arizona law also required the use of particular funds, a provision the exasperated auditor of 1924, R. H. Ramsey, plead to have abolished:

> The present system . . . is valueless and should be discontinued for the reason that the law defining the various funds is so ambiguous that a number of items could be properly charged to either of at least three of the funds with the result that the department heads invariably charge such items against the fund in which they have the greatest surplus, thereby destroying the statistical value of the distribution of expenditures and frequently differing from the interpretation of the law as made by the State Auditor.[21]

Overall, by the end of the study period, both of the subject states were using more modern accounts and had added some degree of analysis of funds. The New Mexico audit report had appropriations, suspense, and control accounts, and provided excellent details of the purposes of expenditures from each fund.[22] The Arizona auditor listed purposes of expenditures for many of the funds and added appropriations to the table of fund abstracts.[23]

The Politics of Funds

As one of the oldest of government accounting practices, funds tell many a story. Like other governments then and now, both New Mexico and Arizona maintained general funds where most spending occurred. But the territorial and state "institutions," (insane asylum, university, prison, etc.) had special, separate funds—indicating the size and importance of these institutions.

In Arizona, a Board of Control was in charge of the various institutions and the auditor sat on the Board *ex officio*. Throughout the study period, the auditors identified problems with the institutions and recommended or implemented changes in government policy.

For example, Arizona Auditor John Hawkins noted that the Territorial Prison had cost over $100,000 in 1887 and 1888. The territory needed to "curtail this enormous drain" by requiring the United States "to pay the Territory for keeping their prisoners."[24] The costs were even higher in 1891 and 1892, when his successor, Thomas Hughes, noted there was "no means whereby this institution can be made self sustaining or even partially so in its present location."[25]

In 1907 and 1908, Arizona Auditor Sims Ely explained at length why little of the planned construction had yet happened at the asylum hospital, the prison, and the industrial school. The Board of Control had hesitated because the recent financial depression had made the amounts to be received from tax levies uncertain. Then an inmate of the insane asylum had attacked and severely injured the superintendent, so that his advice on the hospital was delayed, while the donors of the site for the new prison had failed for some time "to furnish a satisfactory title to the land."[26]

One of the most troublesome of the Board's duties was overseeing the Arizona Industrial School (a youth reformatory). Auditor Ely reported that the $17,500 appropriation for the industrial school:

> will, in all probability, remain unexpended [because] the school building is situated on sterile soil, which is unfit for any purpose of cultivation. Unquestionably the school should be on, or within easy reach of a farm whereon the inmates could be employed and taught the various lines of husbandry and housekeeping.[27]

Furthermore, the main building was so unsafe that no more money should be spent on adjacent buildings. The Board and the auditor awaited the further directions of the legislature.

The first auditor for the State of Arizona was a firebrand, J. C. Callaghan. One of the many things that infuriated Callaghan was outside interference in the personnel appointed to run the Industrial School.[28]

Complaints about the Industrial School's superintendent, Frank Brown, "were well founded," according to Callaghan's 1913 audit report. The Secretary of the Board of Control "had found a deplorable degeneration of discipline, lax stands of morality upon the part of the Superintendent, and a condition obtaining which threatened the morale of the inmates."[29]

Superintendent Brown was replaced by A. L. Harper, but "his ideas as to the necessity of corporal punishment being out of harmony with the administration," he was also dismissed.[30] Callaghan regretted the dismissal of Harper, "a young man of high integrity and strict morals" who practiced sound economy, because he was replaced by W. M. Whipple, an extravagant manager who increased the school's costs by 72 percent.

Callaghan believed that the root problem at the Industrial School was the Board of Control itself. The members of this body should be elected, he argued, "so as to be answerable to the people of the State." Increased accountability was urgently needed because the Board had failed to remedy some dire problems at the Industrial School:

> The location of the institution, isolated as it is, makes it possible to conceal from the public for a considerable period of time conditions which should be exposed and immediately remedied.
>
> The necessity for segregation of the sexes in institutions of this character is obvious, and provision should be made for the care of the girls in an entirely separate institution from that at Fort Grant.[31]

Callaghan added ominously that he had "conducted an investigation at the institution, the report of which is not incorporated in this official document out of regard for the permanent history of the State."[32]

The tone of importance in these excerpts is realistic. Both the Industrial School and the auditor's office did very well out of statehood. Arizona spent $25,000 on the school in 1908, shortly before statehood. By 1915, spending had tripled to $75,000. The auditor's office did even better in percentage terms. The territory spent $6,000 on audit personnel and other expenses in 1908, while the state spent $19,000 in 1915, a 217 percent increase.[33] In comparison, prison funding increased only 42 percent from 1908 to 1915 and the treasurer's office only 70 percent. Library funding dropped by 9 percent.[34]

ASSETS

Classification of accounts, on which fund accounting arguably is based, is an old practice in the public sector, possibly predating its appearance in the private sector. Applying the idea to balance sheets, however, is another question.

Classification of private sector balance sheets appeared quite late in the United States. Normand and Wootton, in their study of the reporting of current assets on U.S. company balance sheets, note that: "Immediately after the Civil War there was little need for classified balance sheets. By 1940, it was impossible not to have them."[35]

As for public sector balance sheets, no classification appeared in any balance sheet for New Mexico or Arizona in my study period (though funds served some classification purposes). In fact, New Mexico and Arizona produced only rudimentary balance sheets, and few of those, from the 1880s to 1930.[36]

But even without balance sheets, the treasurers reported one type of asset fairly faithfully: cash.[37]

Cash and Investment Bonds

The adherence to accounting for cash is probably a hold-over from the old charge-discharge origins of government accounting. Charge-discharge accounting dates back at least to medieval manorial estates. A steward or bailiff in charge of a bishop or lord's property accounted for his stewardship through the charge-discharge system.[38] The bishop or lord charged his subordinate with the proceeds of his property. The steward discharged the obligation by accounting for the expenses and turning over the profits. Charge-discharge methods carried over to government accounting, where they lingered for centuries, as New Mexico and Arizona procedures demonstrate.

New Mexico and Arizona officials normally reported both the amounts and whereabouts of cash, implying the discharge of official responsibility for cash collections. For example, the New Mexico treasurer's cash balance with the territory in 1895 and 1896 consisted of $43,306 "cash on hand in bank" and $440 of "warrants paid since last destruction."

The treasurer also listed which banks held which territorial funds. Thirty years later, the treasurer distinguished between that part of the fund balances held in cash and that held in securities.[39]

New Mexico's auditors were concerned with accounting for cash, as well. In his 1891–1892 report, Auditor Demetrio Perez reported a loss to the Territory of $6,654.67 due to the failure of the bank in Raton. The county sued the bank's assignee and suggested settling for 25 cents on the dollar, but apparently the loss of government funds was such a hot potato that Perez preferred "to leave the matter entirely in the hands of the Legislative Assembly."[40]

Bank instability caused many problems for the territorial governments. In 1892 and 1893, Perez reported that creditors were irate because two Albuquerque banks had been suspended, making the territorial cash they held unavailable.[41] The treasurer reported details of the incident, too.

In Arizona, the 1897–1898 treasurer reported a balance of cash on hand of $351,139.98. Ten years later, the Arizona books disclosed the territorial cash deposits held by particular banks.[42] By 1929, the auditor routinely reconciled his cash balance with the treasurer's. That year, the reconciliation showed a difference of $1.1 million due to warrants issued by the auditor but outstanding from the treasurer's office.[43]

The only other type of asset reported with any frequency was investment bonds held. After statehood, officials often reported investment bonds held by the various funds or institutions. For example, the 1926 New Mexican auditor showed $2.1 million held in investment accounts by governmental institutions such as the Agricultural College, the penitentiary, and the water reservoirs.[44]

Assets other than cash and securities were seldom disclosed. However, occasional efforts were made, as the next section shows.

Fixed and Other Assets

For over one hundred years, English and American accountants have debated whether and how governments should display capital assets and depreciation on their balance sheets.[45] Especially controversial is whether a government should disclose its infrastructure assets—bridges, roads, and the like.

A majority of users of governmental financial statements want such disclosure. In the 1980s, over two-thirds of local governments in the United States disclosed general fixed assets, but less than half disclosed infrastructure assets.[46] Only recently has U.S. GAAP required that government-wide financial statements disclose infrastructure assets and depreciate them.[47] Many governments have objected to doing this, and the extent to which pre-twentieth century governments did so has not been much studied.

An early version of this debate raged in the United States about the time that New Mexico and Arizona became states. Their responses were mixed.

New Mexico

New Mexico created the office of traveling auditor in the late territorial period partly to check on the workings of the various territorial and local offices.[48] The traveling auditor made a strong start by listing and attempting to value the territory's real property in 1910.[49] Statutes permitted him to require that state officers inventory their assets, as well. In 1917, he did so.

The traveling auditor considered the first year's compliance effort of mediocre quality. Still, it was good enough to let him print a schedule of assets, from furniture and fixtures to buildings, roads, and bridges. Total state assets were valued at just under $15.5 million, although the official offered no explanation of the basis of valuation.[50]

Arizona

The first state auditor of Arizona, J. C. Callaghan, described the state lands and the buildings of various state institutions in general terms in his 1912 report. However, Callaghan did not attempt to value any of this property. Instead, he recommended that "a complete inventory be taken of State property in each department and institution."[51]

The recommendation apparently bore fruit. The legislature of 1919 required "an itemized balance sheet for the State as of June 30th, 1919."[52] By then there was a new auditor, Jesse Boyce, and he reacted testily to the requirement:

> A balance sheet is a statement of assets and liabilities. There is nothing in the records of this Department to show that any appraisement and inventory has ever been made of the assets of the State. Such an inventory would be a work of considerable magnitude, and would, I believe, in order to make it authoritative, require special legislative action and certainly a special appropriation for that purpose.[53]

Such a bill was introduced in the Senate, but no favorable action ensued.[54]

Boyce may not have known that the value of county property had been recorded in the territorial treasurer's balance sheets for the counties almost twenty-five years earlier.[55] Some of this 1895–1896 information might have been usable for a 1919 inventory of state property. Of course, the information may have been lost, or the reports discontinued in the intervening years. In any case, what the 1895–1896 treasurer had printed was minimal—a single line summing "County Property" for each county.

Arizona officials occasionally tried to include some fixed assets in later years. The audit report of 1924 had entries for "capital investments" in the fund abstracts; these appear to have been for furniture, fixtures, and equipment.[56]

Assets: Conclusion

In comparison to the subject states, Nevada's controller reported on state assets at least as early as 1897, and made no significant improvements around 1912. It would appear that something about statehood induced better reporting on physical assets. Overall, however, property, plant, and equipment rarely appeared in the statements I examined. Depreciation was never recorded.[57]

LIABILITIES

Bonds

Today, the American public is alarmed by the bonded debt of its state and local governments, and demands information about it. Several decades ago, in the 1980s, a large majority of financial statement users favored bond disclosures, and an overwhelming majority of local governments—75 percent of counties, 95 percent of cities—printed schedules of outstanding bonds and debt service requirements.[58]

New Mexicans and Arizonans of the late nineteenth and early twentieth centuries were alarmed by their governments' debts, as well. Throughout the study period, almost the only liability reported by New Mexico and Arizona was bonded debt, and they reported it consistently. At least one office in New Mexico and Arizona disclosed bonded debt and bond transactions in most years from the 1880s to the 1920s.

Even more consistent, unfortunately, was the erroneous conflating of bond transactions with revenues and expenditures. Cash from bond issues and bond sales was always counted as revenue, while outlays for bond redemptions and bond purchases counted as expenditures.[59] However, the style and content of reporting varied widely, as the following sections demonstrate.

New Mexico

As early as the 1887–1888 report, New Mexico's territorial auditors printed brief statements of outstanding bonds—principal, redemption date, and interest rate.[60] They added bond issue dates a decade later.[61]

Usually, however, it was the territorial treasurer and the traveling auditor who provided the best bond information. The treasurer's 1897–1898 report, for instance, revealed the amounts outstanding, the relevant statutes, the places of payment, the interest due dates, and the provisions for repayment (e.g., "annual tax after twenty years sufficient to pay bonds at maturity").[62]

After statehood, in 1917–1918, the New Mexico treasurer also printed brief tables of bonds issued and paid by year.[63] This information, showing actual as opposed to scheduled activity, permitted the reader to eliminate these items from statements that conflated revenues and expenditures with bond transactions. Unfortunately, the treasurer dropped this item in 1929 and 1930.

New Mexico's treasurers continued to disclose more bond information than the auditors through the end of the study period. By the late 1920s, the disparity had become extreme. The auditor no longer had any schedule of bonds at all; bond transactions were simply mentioned in their related funds as they occurred. The treasurer's report for 1928, in contrast, had two debt statements: one showing the state's bonded indebtedness, and one listing outstanding debentures and certificates of indebtedness.[64]

Arizona

Unlike New Mexico, the Arizona auditor's coverage of bonded debt was as good (or as poor) as the treasurer's in most years. In 1883 and 1884, the only reference the auditor made to the subject was a brief textual mention of a bond sale.[65] The 1887–1888 report was better, showing the bonded debt by institution and statute, as well as the principal, due dates, and the interest rate and amount due annually.[66]

The 1895–1896 treasurer's report was much briefer but in some ways more informative: it displayed the bonds, their periods, rates, and amounts, and added the total to the territorial floating debt (mostly outstanding warrants) and the county and city debt. The grand total was called "total liability direct and indirect," thus acknowledging the territory's contingent liability for the debts of its subordinate units.[67]

By the late territorial period, Arizona's auditors and treasurers had developed the bonded debt disclosure style they were to use through the 1920s.[68] This was a list of the major bonds issued by unit of government, date of issue, interest rate, and period. Note that these did not provide as much information as had the New Mexico treasurer in 1897 and 1898.

Bond Politics

The chief statistician for the U.S. Bureau of the Census for many years was one LeGrand Powers. His experiences in collecting state and local government fiscal data made a passionate fiscal reformer and prolific author of him. In 1916, he penned an article for the *New Mexico Tax Review* on state and local bonds.[69]

Powers classified bonded debt as the good, the bad, and the middling. Bonds for revenue-producing infrastructure (what today would be called "enterprise-type activities") were "in all respects municipal blessings." Bonds for current non-revenue-producing operations or for boondoggles like railroads that were never built were "never blessings but are always drags if not positive curses." Bonds for non-revenue-producing fixed assets such as paving and school houses were good if the bond life was less than the useful life of the asset. Otherwise, they were "unmitigated curses upon the community incurring them, as the peons' debts are for them and their children."[70]

Repayment and interest costs, of course, were very sore points in the territories. New Mexico Treasurer Samuel Eldodt faced a situation in 1897 and 1898, the solution to which would require the territory to raise new funds:

> I respectfully call your attention to the importance of providing additional funds for the Interest Fund, which is now in arrears to the extent of $40,000, and will be, at the close of the present fiscal year . . . to the extent of $55,000. . . .
>
> About $25,000 of this arrearage existed two years ago, and the attention of the last legislature was called to the necessity of making some provision for its payment, but no action was taken . . . I have paid the coupons promptly at their maturity, in all cases, but to do so I have had to borrow from other funds, when conditions permitted, and when this was not possible, I have borrowed under the provisions of Sec. 2607 Compiled Laws. . . . To lay a tax for this purpose will require about three mills of taxation, and will not produce the amount in full, for over a year, and as taxation is already heavy, I suggest the propriety of a short-time bond issue, say ten-year 6 per cent bonds with option to the territory to redeem at any time after one year from their date, and with the provision for an annual tax beginning in 1899, sufficient to pay all the bonds by the time of their maturity.[71]

In other words, Eldodt advised doing just what LeGrand Powers saw as a curse: issuing ten-year bonds to pay off current interest on previously issued bonds.

The issue of contingent liabilities—that is, debt which the New Mexico or Arizona governments had not issued but might have to repay anyway—was crucial. The territorial and state governments were potentially responsible for their subordinate units' debts (as the national government often was for the territories' debts). That is why they occasionally reported on such debt in their financial reports. Fiscal officials sometimes urged better control of the counties for this reason.

Arizona Treasurer T. E. Farish, for example, wanted the legislature to crack down on irresponsible counties in 1895–1896:

> Under the Congressional funding act of 1890, the territory has become security on county and municipal bonds to the extent of $1,374,899.57, and it seems that further liberality in this direction is unwise. The city of Prescott and the city of Tombstone have neither of them responded to my demand for the semi-annual interest due from these municipalities, so the Territory will have to advance it.
>
> I recommend that such portion of the Act of 1891 as relates to the funding of other than Territorial securities be repealed, and that Treasurers of counties and towns be required under heavy penalties to place the interest due the Territory in the Territorial treasury not later than the 25th of June and 25th of December of each year.[72]

The most notorious of Arizona's contingent liabilities were the Pima County railroad bonds. Back in the free-spending days of 1883, the territorial legislature had authorized the county to issue $150,000 of bonds to help the Arizona Narrow Gauge Railroad Company. Pima issued the bonds the next year.

Accounts differ as to whether the railroad was partly built and then abandoned to rust and sold for scrap,[73] or never built at all.[74] Certainly it was never used. Pima County then repudiated its debt, claiming that it had never asked for the railroad in the first place.[75]

Prolonged litigation followed. The Arizona district court sided against the bondholders. The bonds were unenforceable, said the court, because they had been authorized by a body (the territorial legislature) which had in fact no authority to approve bonds under the Organic Act by which Congress created the territory. Litigation eventually reached the U.S. Supreme Court, which ordered that the bondholders be paid.[76] Congress validated the payment of the bonds, the case was returned to Arizona, and the territorial Supreme Court ordered the territory to assume the debt.[77]

The Loan Commissioners spent a year on the case, and in March of 1903, exchanged territorial bonds of $318,275.29 plus $1,515.94 interest for the worthless bonds held by Pima County's creditors.[78] "An exceedingly malodorous and disgraceful" transaction, sniffed the first state auditor in 1912, which was "perpetrated upon the taxpayers of Pima county by its then county officials in 'aid' of a fraudulent railroad."[79]

Of course, in the end, the fraud was perpetrated on all the taxpayers of Arizona, which is why the territory's contingent liabilities for its local governments' debts were important enough to rate occasional mention in the fiscal reports of the time.

Nevada

As for Nevada, so much better in some ways than New Mexico and Arizona, the controller actually began recording bond discounts and premiums in the late 1920s.

This is not to say that Nevada evaded all the bond problems that so plague governments, particularly the easy spending they facilitate. The Nevada Tax Commission of 1923 to 1924 commented that:

> The issuance of bonds has become almost a habit and clouds of them have been issued by counties, cities and school districts. Warnings have been issued from time to time against the increase of expenditures in this respect, but taxpayers seem to have regarded these well intended reminders as mere pretenses, and

have taken advantage of the law more freely on bond issues than they have on tax levies.[80]

Floating Debt and Other Liabilities

The governments of this period generally paid their obligations with warrants. The warrants sometimes circulated as currency before being presented to the state for payment. Thus, New Mexico and Arizona often had large outstanding short-term debt. These sums were reported almost as often as was the bonded debt, usually under the title "floating debt" or "outstanding warrants."[81]

Many problems arose from the use of warrants as short-term debt. In 1897 and 1898, Arizona Auditor George W. Vickers urged that the prison salaries and other accounts be paid monthly, as were the other institutions' accounts, instead of quarterly.[82] In 1899 and 1900, he repeated the suggestion and urged that the custom of paying the prison's expenses with 7 percent warrants be halted: "A law should be passed making an annual levy of a tax sufficient to cover all cost of its maintenance; this I consider very important, and is absolutely necessary to enable the Territory to conduct this part of its business on a cash basis, and discontinue the issuance of interest bearing warrants.[83]

Other liabilities were very occasionally mentioned in the statements I examined. Once, in 1895 and 1896, the Arizona territorial treasurer disclosed a legal liability among other items making up "floating debt."[84] Arizona also sometimes reported accounts payable in the 1920s. For instance, in the 1929 auditor's report, a line in the fund abstracts showed "unexpended balances and accounts payable carried forward." Schedule 1 included a brief summary of accounts payable by account. Also disclosed were the "encumbered accounts payable" in the statement of expenditures. Rarely, a note payable appeared in the financial reports.

In general, however, New Mexico's and Arizona's reporting of liabilities from the 1880s to the 1920s was limited to bonded debt and outstanding warrants. These were reported in various styles and were generally more detailed in New Mexico but more consistent in style in Arizona.

FISCAL YEARS

In 1931, at the end of the study period, New Mexico, Arizona, and Nevada all ended their fiscal years on June 30. June 30 has become a popular year-ending date in the public sector; in 1989, about half of local governments in the

United States used that day.[85] But it was not always so. Arizona switched to June 30 in 1899; New Mexico followed suit in 1925, as did Nevada in 1931.

The timing of this change to June 30 is interesting. Professional accountants in the early twentieth century concertedly urged businesses to drop their calendar years in favor of the natural business year—i.e., to choose a year-ending date that made sense from a business point of view. The purpose was to ease the incredible rush of business from January to March for professional accounting firms. Large businesses resisted, as the tax laws favored the calendar year. But many businesses complied; whereas in 1933 only 14 percent of taxpaying businesses used the natural business year, by 1958, almost half did so.[86]

State and territorial financial officials may have responded to the call, too, as the experiences of New Mexico, Arizona, and Nevada below suggest.

New Mexico

New Mexico's fiscal year was peripatetic. In 1887 and 1888, the fiscal year was pretty much the calendar year—it ended on December 15. From then until 1897, it typically ended on one of the first days of March.

Ending irregularly on "one of the first days of March" caused problems. In his 1897–1898 report, Auditor Marcelino Garcia recommended a change:

I beg to report that there is now due the clerks and other territorial officers a portion of their salaries, from the 1st to the 6th day of March, 1898, for the reason of the 49th fiscal year beginning on the 7th day of March, 1898, while the 48th fiscal year commenced on the 1st day of March, 1897, and some provision should be made for the payment to these officials for the period of six days, so due, and I would respectfully suggest, to avoid these discrepancies of dates in the fiscal years, that the law should be amended so that fiscal years commence on the 1st day of the month, without any regard to the day of the week.[87]

Possibly as a result, most New Mexico government offices observed a November 30 year-end after Garcia's report.

Some offices, however, did not, notably the traveling auditor's. In 1910, this official reported on "territorial finances for the fiscal year ended May 31 . . . and on county finances . . . for the fiscal year ended June 30."[88] The counties, in other words, observed a June 30 year-end. By 1913, the traveling auditor conformed to the November 30 year-end for his report on state finances in general, but used the calendar year for state institutions such as the university.

New Mexico had another timing oddity. In the nineteenth century, reporting years were not the same as fiscal years. Financial statements before 1897 used November 30 year-ends to report on fiscal years that ended on one of the first days of March. Each biennial report covered the last quarter of one fiscal year (December–February), all of the next fiscal year (March–February), and the first three quarters of the year after that (March–November). This complication continued until 1897, when the fiscal year was changed to match the report year.

These endless discrepancies among offices and over time made it impossible to reconcile the New Mexico auditor's reports to those of the treasurer, as the assistant attorney to the U.S. Secretary of the Interior complained in 1908.[89] Fortunately, by 1916, within a few years of statehood, all offices were using the November 30 year-end. This lasted for about a decade, until the 1925 switch to June 30.

Arizona

Arizona had a much more stable fiscal year than New Mexico's hodge-podge experience. In the nineteenth century, Arizona used the calendar year, ending on December 31. In 1899, the territory changed to June 30.

The change was troublesome. For several years, the treasurer included the subsequent six months in each report, apparently at the behest of the legislature. That is, reports covered a fiscal year from July 1 to June 30, and then added information on the first six months, July to December, of the next fiscal year. The calendar year thus lingered for awhile in Arizona, even after the official fiscal year had changed.

More trouble showed up in the treasurer's report in the first year after the change. The 1899–1900 report contained numerous timing problems. Many "overdraft" entries appeared in one fund and were then transferred to another, sometimes in the same fiscal year and sometimes not. Two months of the new fiscal year 1900 receipts were apparently included in 1899 receipts.[90] These problems had vanished by the next report (1901–1902).

Nevada

Nevada used the calendar year throughout the study period. Only in 1931 did it change to a June 30 year-end.

Fiscal Years: Conclusion

Thus, all three states once used the calendar year, and all three changed to June 30 by the end of the study period. If the movement for the natural business year actually dates back to the late nineteenth century, then it may be that all three of these governments made the change to June 30 in response to that movement.

TIMING OF FINANCIAL REPORTS

Users naturally prefer that governments publish their reports as soon as possible after the end of the fiscal year. In 1979, Ernst & Whinney studied timeliness in one hundred cities in 1979. Over half had their audit field work completed from two to four months after year-end, while 21 percent had audit dates of more than five months after year-end. Ernst & Whinney interpreted these dates as the earliest on which the financials could have been published.[91]

But little historiographical attention has been paid to how prompt American governments a century ago were with their reporting. I found that New Mexico and Arizona may have become less prompt over time. The length of the delays varied enormously.[92]

New Mexico's reports became less timely after the change to a June 30 closing in 1925. Before 1925, the November 30 closing was generally followed by a report within thirty days, according to the dates on the transmittal letters. After 1925, two to five months elapsed before statements were issued. The first biennial report (1925–1926) for the new fiscal year did not appear until the following April.[93]

In Arizona's early period, when the fiscal year was the calendar year, report dates varied from December 31 to March 1, a range of two months. When the fiscal year closed on June 30, reports generally appeared in October or November, although a few came out in July and one as late as the following February 1.[94]

Just as Nevada's fiscal year was more stable than New Mexico's and Arizona's, so was the timing of its reports. The transmittal letters suggest they were routinely issued before the end of January, less than a month after year-end.

In contrast, cities of that time may have been less prompt. An auditor in 1899 deplored the habit of "many of our larger municipalities" of delaying the publication of annual financial statements for as much as a year.[95] The frontier governments of Nevada, New Mexico, and Arizona in the early twentieth century seem to have produced more timely financial reports on the average than did major cities either then or a half-century later.

In the next chapter, I focus on the revenues and expenditures of New Mexico and Arizona, and on some elements closely related to spending.

NOTES

1. Potts, "Some Highlights in the Evolution," 58–59.
2. Ernst & Whinney, *How Cities Can Improve*, 45, Table 3–1.
3. NM Auditor, *Report*, 1914, 16, 17, 19.
4. AZ Auditor, *Report*, 1916, iv, vi, vii.
5. NM Terr. Traveling Auditor, *Report*, 1910, 6.
6. NM Terr. Auditor, *Report,* 1897–1898.
7. AZ Terr. Auditor, *Report*, 1887–1888.
8. Clow, "Suggestions for the Study."
9. NM Auditor, *Report*, 1915–1916; NM Treasurer, *Report,* 1917–1918.
10. AZ Auditor, *Report*, 1915.
11. AZ Treasurer, *Report*, 1915.
12. NM Auditor, *Report*, 1924, 39–46, 78–84.
13. NM Auditor, *Report*, 1927–1928, 3.
14. NM Auditor, *Report*, 1927–1928, 14–23.
15. NM Auditor, *Report*, 1927–1928, 20.
16. NM Auditor, *Report*, 1927–1928, 70.
17. NM Auditor, *Report*, 1927–1928, 37–94, 51–52, 70.
18. E.g., AZ Auditor, *Report*, 1924, statement 2; "Arizona Budgetary Reform."
19. AZ Auditor, *Report*, 1918, statement 2.
20. AZ Auditor, *Report*, 1919, statement 2 and pp. 3–7.
21. AZ Auditor, *Report*, 1924, 3.
22. E.g., NM Auditor, *Report*, 1928.
23. AZ Auditor, *Report*, 1929.
24. AZ Terr. Auditor, *Report*, 1887–1888, 3.
25. AZ Terr. Auditor, *Report*, 1891–1892, 5.
26. AZ Terr. Auditor, *Report*, 1907–1908, 4.
27. AZ Terr. Auditor, *Report*, 1907–1908, 5
28. E.g., AZ Auditor, *Report*, 1912, 15.
29. AZ Auditor, *Report*, 1913, 4. For more about this school, see Lynch, *Sunbelt Justice*.
30. AZ Auditor, *Report*, 1914, 5.
31. AZ Auditor, *Report*, 1914, 6.
32. AZ Auditor, *Report*, 1914, 6.
33. AZ Auditor, *Report*, 1908 and 1915. Note some of the spending was from the special funds and other spending was from the General Fund.
34. AZ Auditor, *Report*, 1908 and 1915.
35. Normand and Wootton, "Recognition and Valuation," 64.
36. See, e.g., the "trial balance" in AZ Terr. Treasurer, *Report*, 1895–1896, 24. In 1914, the Arizona treasurer produced what he called "balance sheets" for 1913 and 1914; the statements contained only assets, and few of those except cash. See also the "balance sheet" (a list of fund balances) in AZ Treasurer, *Report,* 1915, 6.
37. For two early examples, see AZ Terr. Treasurer, *Report*, 1895–1896, 24; and a list of banks holding territorial funds in NM Terr. Treasurer, *Report,* 1895–1896, 8.

38. Oldroyd and Dobie, "Bookkeeping," 101. See also Coombs and Edwards, "Record Keeping in Municipal Corporations."

39. NM Treasurer, *Report,* 1923–1924, 17.

40. NM Auditor, *Report,* 1891–1892, 5–6.

41. NM Auditor, *Report,* 1892–1893, 4.

42. AZ Terr. Treasurer, *Report,* 1907–1908, 15.

43. NM Terr. Treasurer, *Report,* 1895–1896, 13, 8; NM Treasurer, *Report,* 1923–1924, 17; AZ Terr. Treasurer, *Report,* 1897–1898, 5; AZ Auditor, *Report,* 1907–1908, 15; AZ Auditor, *Report,* 1929, statement 6, p. 100.

44. NM Auditor, *Report,* 1925–1926, 36. See also NM Treasurer, *Report,* 1917–1918, 27; NM Treasurer, *Report,* 1928, 38–46.

45. Potts, "Brief History of Property," 1982.

46. Jones et al., *Needs of Users,* 65; Ingram and Robbins, *Financial Reporting Practices,* 49.

47. Governmental Accounting Standards Board, statement 34.

48. Otero, *My Nine Years,* 84, 88–89.

49. NM Terr. Traveling Auditor, *Report,* 1910, 9–11.

50. NM Traveling Auditor, *Report,* 1918, 48, 59, 65.

51. AZ Auditor, *Report,* 1912, 37–39, 11–28, 67.

52. AZ Auditor, *Report,* 1919, 5–6.

53. AZ Auditor, *Report,* 1919, 6.

54. AZ Auditor, *Report,* 1919, 6.

55. AZ Terr. Treasurer, *Report,* 1895–1896, 25–27.

56. AZ Auditor, *Report,* 1924, e.g., 25.

57. Depreciation was fairly widely discussed in the United States at this time.

58. Jones et al., *Needs of Users,* 51; Ingram and Robbins, *Financial Reporting Practices,* 56.

59. See "Revenues and Expenditures" in the next chapter for more detail.

60. NM Terr. Auditor, *Report,* 1887–1888, statement I.

61. NM Terr. Auditor, *Report,* 1897–1898, statement 37.

62. NM Terr. Auditor, *Report,* 1887–1888, statement I; NM Terr. Auditor, *Report, Marcelino Garcia,* 1897–1898, statement 37; NM Terr. Treasurer, *Report,* 1896–1898, sched. 10.

63. E.g., NM Treasurer, *Report,* 1917–1918, foldout following p. 17.

64. NM Treasurer, *Report,* 1928, 47.

65. AZ Terr. Auditor, *Report,* 1883–1884, 7.

66. AZ Terr. Auditor, *Report,* 1887–1888, 32–35.

67. AZ Terr. Auditor, *Report,* 1883–1884, 7; AZ Terr. Auditor, *Report,* 1887–1888, 32–35 ; AZ Terr. Treasurer, *Report,* 1895–1896, 23.

68. Compare the territorial statement on p. 28 of AZ Terr. Auditor, *Report,* 1907–1908, to the state's statement on pp. 92–93 of AZ Auditor, *Report,* 1929.

69. Powers, "Public Indebtedness."

70. Powers, "Public Indebtedness," 28–29.

71. NM Terr. Treasurer, *Report,* 1897–1898, 6.

72. AZ Terr. Treasurer, *Report,* 1895–1896, 3.

73. Report of Governor to U.S. Secretary of the Interior, May 12, 1909, *Terr. Pap.: AZ.*

74. AZ Auditor, *Report*, 1912, 32.

75. Report of Governor to U.S. Secretary of the Interior, May 12, 1909, *Terr. Pap.: AZ.*

76. *Utter v. Franklin* 172 US 420.

77. AZ Terr. Board of Loan Commissioners, *Report*, December 31, 1904, pp. 193–195 in AZ Terr. Auditor, Treasurer, and Board of Loan Commissioners, *Report*, 1903–1904. Also Report of Governor to U.S. Secretary of the Interior, May 12, 1909, *Terr. Pap.: AZ.*

78. AZ Terr. Board of Loan Commissioners, *Report*, December 31, 1904, pp. 193–195 in AZ Terr. Auditor, Treasurer, and Board of Loan Commissioners, *Report*, 1903–1904.

79. AZ Auditor, *Report*, 1912, 32.

80. NV State Tax Commission, *Report*, 1923–1924, 6.

81. See, e.g., NM Terr. Auditor, *Report,* 1887–1888, 7; AZ Auditor, *Report,* 1929, 90.

82. AZ Terr. Auditor, *Report*, 1897–1898, 5.

83. AZ Terr. Auditor, *Report*, 1899–1900, 7.

84. AZ Auditor, *Report,* 1929, 32, 52, 50; AZ Terr. Treasurer, *Report*, 1895–1896, 23.

85. American Institute of Certified Public Accountants, *Local Governmental Accounting Trends,* 1.41.

86. Doron, "The American Institute of Accountants."

87. NM Terr. Auditor, *Report*, 1897–1898, 6.

88. NM Terr. Traveling Auditor, *Report*, 1910, cover.

89. James J. Parker, assistant attorney to the Secretary of the Interior, memorandum to Secretary, October 3, 1908, in *Terr. Pap.: NM*, reel 10.

90. AZ Terr. Treasurer, *Report,* 1899–1900, 13, 18, 19, 22.

91. Ernst & Whinney, *How Cities Can Improve*, 40. See also a study of major American cities in the 1970s finding that 61 percent issued their annual reports more than 90 days after the fiscal year ended. Coopers & Lybrand, *Statistical Supplement*, tables 2–11.

92. Note that a few of the report dates are questionable. The Arizona auditor's report of 1883–1884 is dated December 31, 1884, purports to cover the calendar year, and includes warrants issued on December 31. It seems unlikely that the report could have been issued on the same day as the last transactions of the period.

93. The timing of the treasurer's reports is unknown. All of them are undated from 1925 on, except the first. The treasurer claims to have issued that report on the last day of the fiscal year covered, June 30. This seems unlikely.

94. E.g., AZ Terr. Treasurer, *Report*, 1899–1900, AZ Terr. Auditor, *Report*, 1901–1903. The reports the treasurer was required to make on the six–month period subsequent to any given report (e.g., the six months ending December 31, 1902, which appeared at the end of the 1901–1902 report), came out slowly; in some cases as late as the following June.

95. Crosby, "Financial Control," 153.

10

Interfund Transfers, Federal Subsidies, Revenues and Expenditures, Tax Rates, and Budgets

Today, governments routinely reveal their revenues by source and their expenditures by function.[1] But in the late nineteenth century, they did not. Indeed, in my study, it was not always possible even to answer a much simpler question: What were the *total* revenues and expenditures of New Mexico, Arizona, or Nevada in any given year?

A few years after statehood, the New Mexico Tax Association began publishing a newsletter. In the first issue, the editors contemptuously dismissed the financial reports then produced by their government. "Reports there are," they admitted, "and tons of them." But the reports contain:

> Not a word as to how much the county commissioners cost, or the assessor . . . or even the schools. And the reports we have nowhere bring together the whole total of . . . revenues and . . . expenditures . . . What is the cost of the state government and of each of its departments?[2]

The Association planned to collect its own statistics on "what the state and its subdivisions are purchasing with the public funds" because their governments' existing reports didn't answer the question.

These difficulties in determining real governmental revenues and expenditures were not unusual in the Progressive decades. Sylla, Legler, and Wallis found that "revenues" included some or all loans in various states of that period.[3] Contemporaries, too, understood the inaccuracies of cash-basis accounting. In 1878, E. S. Mills criticized the cash basis then prevailing in municipal accounts.[4] The U.S. Bureau of the Census discussed the problem at length in 1915, noting that warrants issued more accurately measure the current costs of government than do warrants paid in subsequent periods

151

and that a lack of depreciation information caused current expenses to be understated.[5]

How well New Mexico, Arizona, and Nevada reported the additions to and subtractions from the public purse is the main subject of this chapter. But several closely related topics are also covered—interfund transfers, federal subsidies, tax rates, and budgets. Together, the quality of their presentation in the financial statements determined how easily the question above could be answered.

Interfund transfers, which pestered me for most of the study period, complicate the questions of both revenues and expenditures. I discuss transfers first in this chapter. Federal subsidies come next—never properly identified and a thorn in my side throughout. Then comes the main focus of the chapter—how the governments stated revenues and expenditures, and whether they clearly stated the difference between the two (usually, they did not). A quick look at the presentation of tax rates follows, and some insights into the history of budgeting end the chapter.

INTERFUND TRANSFERS

Governments often shift money about among funds. Today, it is assumed as a matter of course that interfund transfers are not included in the overall expenditures or revenues, because that would double-count the transferred monies.

However, the Territories of New Mexico and Arizona made no mention of transfers at all—although they occurred—until the late 1880s. Even then, the presentation was confusing and often incomplete. For this reason, the reader of the financial statements could not be sure what the numbers meant. Did they correctly report revenues and expenditures? Or did they include revenues plus transfers into a fund and expenditures plus transfers out?

Interfund Transfers Before Statehood

The New Mexico auditor disclosed interfund transfers beginning in 1891. But he did not always sum them. He dropped the separate disclosure altogether in the last territorial years, from 1907 to 1912. In fact, in 1912, the fund abstracts explicitly commingled receipts with transfers and payments with transfers.[6] A reader wishing to find receipts or expenditures totals net of transfer activity had to total the transfers and then eliminate them himself.

The territorial treasurer did better. He summed the transfers by fund and even, in 1903–1904, disclosed them in the quarterly schedules. Still, the reader had to eliminate them from the totals himself.

In Arizona, the 1887 auditor made minimal disclosures of interfund transfers. They remained very unclearly presented, however, and were sometimes absent through 1912. As in New Mexico, the treasurer did better. But he gave no summary information on transfers and it was unclear whether receipt and expenditure totals were net of interfund transfers or not.

The Arizona State Tax Commission, struggling to make policy in the state's first years, complained of just this problem:

> The defect in appropriations is that they include agency and trust transactions between the state and its minor political subdivisions and cover substantial amounts representing mere book transfers which are neither levied, collected nor expended for state purposes. To illustrate: when a new university or normal school building is required, the legislature makes an appropriation for the purpose and the money when collected is credited to the general fund, but when required for actual use is transferred to the university or normal school fund as the case may be, thus appearing as a receipt and disbursement of both funds. Obviously the receipt occurs when the money is collected by taxation or otherwise and disbursement when the money is paid out for actual construction . . . According to a report of state finances . . . , the amount of these transfers appearing on the state books alone for 1913 was over $3,000,000 and the transfers between the state, the counties and their municipal subdivisions, including school districts, exceeded $30,000,000. These transfers from one fund to another do not represent either taxes or expenditures in the proper sense.[7]

In other words, the distinction between transactions with third parties (taxpayers, construction companies) on the one hand, and money movement among government funds on the other hand, was perfectly clear to early twentieth-century policymakers. The wanton conflation of the two exasperated them as much as it did me a century later.

Changes at Statehood and Later

The old territorial practice of overstating receipts and expenditures by the amount of the transfers among funds finally ended within a few years of statehood. Indeed, the main improvement in New Mexico's 1913 fund abstracts was the separation of transfers from revenues and expenditures.[8] The Arizona auditor and treasurer identified at least some of the transfers by fund in the same year.[9]

By 1916, both new states were regularly and clearly identifying such transactions.[10] The Arizona auditor actually eliminated transfers from total revenues and expenditures that year,[11] and the presentation continued to improve for years afterwards.[12]

Interfund Transfers: Conclusion

Unlike the subject states, Nevada provided clear statements of its interfund transfers in 1888 and continued throughout the study period. This suggests that being a state had something to do with clearer identification of interfund transfers. Perhaps states had less incentive to create fiscal illusions than did territories. Or perhaps legislators just refused to put up with such an unnecessarily confusing error, and state fiscal officers had to heed them attentively, as territorial officials did not.

FEDERAL SUBSIDIES

From the nation's beginning, the U.S. government has subsidized territories in ways that it does not subsidize states. The difference has declined over time, but the territories of Arizona and New Mexico still enjoyed some subsidies that vanished after 1912. For my purposes, the subsidies confused the issue, because I needed to know what New Mexico's and Arizona's own-source revenues were.

"Own-source revenues" are the monies a government levies and collects itself, from the residents of its own jurisdiction. Subsidies from the federal government are not included. Knowing what own-source revenues are is crucial for local government budgeting, and crucial to answering my question: What relative fiscal burden did New Mexicans and Arizonans bear before and after 1912?

Unfortunately, no state or territorial report during the study period segregated, summed, and eliminated all the receipts from the United States to arrive at a single figure for the own-source revenues of the government involved. The best reports identified the U.S. treasurer as the source of line item amounts in the fund abstracts or similar schedules. From such information, the reader who wants to know own-source revenues may list and sum the U.S. subsidies and subtract them from total revenues.

An example of relatively good presentation occurred in New Mexico from 1919 to 1926. The auditors published a helpful "Receipts by Sources to Funds" table. A 1921 entry for the Common Schools 5 percent Fund noted the source as "Pro. [proceeds] U.S. Land Sales U.S. Treas."[13] Another schedule showed what the counties collected by source. One source was called "Federal Aid," although the relationship between the federal subsidies in the county tables and those in the fund receipts table was not clear.[14] This sort of information allowed me to calculate my measure of own-source revenues, Rev A.

In Arizona the auditor usually ignored federal subsidies altogether. The treasurer did better, enumerating all or some of the federal subsidies at the turn of the century. But he did not eliminate their totals from revenues to show own-source receipts. Unfortunately, he abandoned most of his interest in federal subsidies several years after statehood, providing only spotty and confusing coverage.

In short, U.S. subsidies were not identified as such in most of the reports I examined. Instead, "Agricultural College" or "Lever Agricultural Extension" was listed; the reader needs to know that these were federally subsidized programs. Even comparing the state reports to the U.S. Treasury's *Receipts and Expenditures* records was not helpful, because many of the items in the federal records did not appear as federal subsidies in the territorial or state records.

In fact, some U.S. transfers were never booked by the recipient governments at all, as best as I can tell. The New Mexico territorial legislators', governors', and secretaries' compensation, which federal *Receipts and Expenditures* records show to have been sent to the territory,[15] do not appear as either receipts or expenditures in the auditor's or the treasurer's reports. That is, the territories (and perhaps the young states) behaved as mere pass-through agents, who needed no records of the monies they passed along. But on other occasions they did record these subsidies, leaving the interested reader quite confused.

There was a slight improvement over time in reporting federal subsidies in both New Mexico and Arizona. No information at all appeared in several of the earliest reports, while the later ones usually had some information. There were years without improvements, however. Some reports were a little worse than those of previous years.

It is not only twenty-first-century researchers who wish to distinguish between own-source and total state revenues. The contemporary U.S. Bureau of the Census also wanted to know. The Census Bureau insisted that the states and territories identify the "subventions and grants"—primarily U.S. transfers—that were included in their revenues.

Other contemporaries wanted to know these figures, too. Territorial opponents and supporters of statehood alike frequently bemoaned the reduction in federal transfers that would accompany the change in status from territory to state. But despite this interest, distinguishing between locally derived and federally derived monies was simply not an important concern of the fiscal officers of New Mexico, Arizona, or Nevada during the study period.

Such are the confusions of interfund transfers and federal subsidies. I now turn to the revenues and expenditures themselves.

REVENUES AND EXPENDITURES

The reporting of receipts and expenditures by New Mexico and Arizona improved dramatically in the half century between the 1880s and 1930. Officials made small and steady progress over most of the period, but around 1912 the reports took a large jump for the better in both places.

However, some problems recurred frequently and persisted until the 1920s. Revenues and expenditures were reported on a cash basis. But they were often materially overstated because they included interfund transfers (see "Interfund Transfers" above) and bond transactions.

The governments generally counted as revenue both the proceeds of a bond issue and the taxes collected to redeem the bond. Then they counted as expenditures both the disbursements on statutory programs as well as the redemption of the bond. To discover how much a government was actually collecting or spending in a year, the reader usually had to identify transactions involving bonds and certificates of indebtedness and eliminate them from the receipts and expenditures totals.

This mistake was understood by at least some of the responsible parties. In Nevada, for example, the Tax Commission of 1913–1914 rebuked the controller for reporting bond purchases as expenditures, a mistake which "left every one concerned very much in the dark as to the true condition of the State's finances." The Commission explained the error of counting bond purchases as expenses:

> [I]t is perfectly obvious to any one at all familiar with accounting that this inclusion is erroneous . . . An expense is not incurred until an obligation is created. . . . The purchase of a bond . . . simply changes the form of an asset . . . when [an obligation is created, the money] then, and not until then, becomes a legitimate entry against the State's operating expense.[16]

As late as 1929, the Nevada controller mentioned that the inclusion of bond activity made receipts and disbursements spuriously appear higher than ever before in the state.[17] But he did not correct the fault in his attached financial statements.

New Mexico

In New Mexico, the 1887–1888 auditor's report did not disclose total receipts and expenditures at all. It did include statements for the general fund and several other funds, each containing minimal notes on the sources of receipts (e.g. "property and license taxes," "amount received during the year"). Schedules P and Q contained lists, almost certainly incomplete, of amounts paid out for purposes that were identified in general terms (e.g., "Paid to the Sisters of Charity, Santa Fe Industrial School for Orphans . . . $4,043.55").[18]

Ten years later, the New Mexico auditor's report had improved a little. The 1897–1898 biennial report began with thirty-six fund statements, presumably a complete list. These contained better information on the sources of receipts (e.g., "clerk's fees to date," "transfer territorial purposes"), followed by the fund balances.

The 1897–1898 report also disclosed, for each of the (partial or whole) fiscal years, the type, amount, and sums of receipts from each collecting officer, and the amounts and totals of warrants issued by purpose for each fund (e.g., "Pay of interpreters, 32d Legislative Assembly").[19]

Unfortunately, this was the period when New Mexican reports covered a period different from the fiscal year—beginning with the last half of year one, covering all of year two, and ending with the first half of year three (see "Fiscal Years" in chap. 9). To calculate totals for the first or third years, the reader must consult two reports.

The lingering charge-discharge nature of these late nineteenth-century records[20] is evidenced in both the auditor's and the treasurer's reports. The auditor included two schedules that listed by fund the "warrants . . . as presented by Samuel Eldodt territorial treasurer, and burned in the presence of the governor and territorial auditor of New Mexico."[21] In the treasurer's report, schedule 8 showed the treasurer's own account, debited with the amounts for which he was required to account and credited with the warrants he had destroyed and his ending balance.[22]

The New Mexico treasurer, too, showed improvements in his 1897–1898 report. On facing pages at the beginning of the report were two brief tables summarizing revenues by major source and expenditures by major function for each fiscal year. Reverting to the awkward three-period presentation, the treasurer then printed fund abstracts: a table listing the funds followed by columns for the beginning balance, receipts, transfers in, transfers out, payments, and ending balance of each fund.[23] This fund abstract proved to be a popular statement for the next three decades in New Mexico and, to some extent, in Arizona. However, transfers were not separately disclosed in some years.

Soon after statehood, New Mexico's reports improved noticeably. Following the treasurer's earlier example, the auditor in 1915 and 1916 included for the first time an initial summary table of receipts by source and expenditures by fund as well as fund abstracts that disclosed transfers. The treasurer for his part added a new feature in 1917 and 1918: a table of bonds issued by year that permitted the user more easily to identify bond transactions to be eliminated from revenue and expenditure totals.[24]

At this same time, the auditor began printing a series of tables showing county tax remittances by county and by the year of the tax levy being remitted. The traveling auditor's report for the same biennium disclosed collections and disbursements by county, as did the treasurer's 1917–1918 report. Thus, the reports of the early state period paid close attention, for the first time, to the funds collected from and spent by subordinate governments.[25]

In short, New Mexico reported revenues and expenditures better as the study period progressed. Revenues reporting improved markedly just after statehood, while expenditures were not well-disclosed until the late 1920s. Statehood brought closer attention to the receipts from counties.

Arizona

Like New Mexico, Arizona's financial reports in the 1880s were not nearly as informative as they were in the 1920s. Expenditures in the auditors' reports were just lists of warrants and their payees in each fund. Only biennial totals were given for the general fund and the school fund—no annual totals. General fund spending was listed by account, but no information on revenues was offered at all, except tax assessments.

The auditor did refer to the treasurer's report as having disclosed revenues in 1883–1884, but I did not locate the latter report.[26] As late as 1908, the auditor still offered no information on revenues, though he did group general fund warrants (expenditures) by purpose in that year.

The Arizona treasurer was supplying a little more information than the auditor by 1895–1896. He began with a statement summarizing receipts by source and disbursements by fund for the biennium. Then came the fund statements, each of which disclosed interfund transfers, biennial receipts by county, and unspecified disbursements by year (e.g., "warrants paid 1896"). To determine revenues or expenditures, I had to reconcile the summary statement's gross totals with the fund statements, and subtract the individual bond and interfund activity items that were listed (but not totaled!) in each fund.[27]

As the twentieth century began, Arizona's auditors continued to produce long, uninformative lists of warrants. It is true that this list was preceded in 1907 and 1908 by a statement of warrants on the general fund that were summed by purpose, so a little improvement had been made since the 1880s. The auditor still offered no information on revenues.[28]

The treasurer, in his 1903–1904 report, also began with the same table he had used in earlier years—a brief list of all receipts by source and all expenditures by fund. By now he had separated the lists by fiscal years instead of just giving biennial totals, a great improvement. On the other hand, he appended a schedule titled "distributed as follows" whose relationship to the disbursements is unclear. "Disbursements" and "distributions" were in different amounts to the same funds, and totaled the same amount for all funds together.[29] To understand the relationship of fund "disbursements" to fund "distributions," the reader must consult the individual fund statements that follow.

After statehood, both auditor's and treasurer's reports improved markedly in Arizona. The Arizona state auditor's first report, in 1912, included initial summaries of revenues and expenditures. This was a first for the auditor, though the treasurer had printed such summaries since territorial days. These summaries facilitated the work of readers wanting to know the annual surplus or deficit, although the figures still included amounts such as bond and interfund transfer activity that had to be eliminated.

By 1915, the auditor's long list of warrants had disappeared, as had his disinterest in revenues. Instead, he had a brief list of funds disclosing revenues by source and interfund transfers. At the end, a gross total was drawn, interfund transfers were summed, and a total for receipts net of transfer activity was shown. Another schedule gave the changes in revenues by fund and source from 1914 to 1915; yet another did the same for expenditures.[30]

The auditor's 1915 report included information from the treasurer's office: receipts and disbursements by fund and a reconciliation of the treasurer's warrants paid to the auditor's warrants issued. Because the treasurer sometimes disbursed monies without warrants, the auditor also published the "disbursements made by state treasurer in addition to payment of auditor's warrants." These off-the-auditor's-books transactions included interest paid on state debt, bond redemptions, and the disbursement of federal subsidies.[31]

In 1923, the Arizona auditor added a non-mandated statement to his annual report: a schedule of the distribution of monies by purpose, both in gross sums and in amounts net of non-tax receipts.[32] This statement proved so popular that it survived through the rest of the decade, and eventually came to include a pie chart of percentages expended on various functions. By 1929, the abstract of funds had also improved, disclosing interfund transfers and eliminating them from receipt and expenditure totals.[33]

As for the treasurer's office, post-statehood improvements included a schedule of fund abstracts similar to those used in New Mexico—a list of funds with columns for the balances, receipts, and expenditures. The treasurer, however, failed to disclose interfund transfers in 1915 and also provided minimal details on disbursements ("warrants paid" or "coupons paid").[34]

Nevada

Recall that the Nevada government had a much longer experience of statehood than Arizona and New Mexico. Throughout the study period, the quality of Nevada's reporting of revenues and expenditures was better than that of New Mexico and Arizona, and it improved gradually over time. However, the Nevada reports did not display a particularly large improvement around 1912, as did those of New Mexico and Arizona just after they became states.

In 1888, the Nevada controller's first statement, "Receipts into the Several Funds," disclosed and totaled receipts by source and fund, their apportionment by fund, and the total of interfund transfers due to financing activity (e.g., interest on Nevada bonds, sale of U.S. bonds to the university fund). Two other statements offered, for each year since 1865, total expenditures by function and total receipts by source. Column headings included the sale and redemption of bonds, enabling the reader to calculate receipts or expenditures net of bond activity, although these amounts were included in the grand totals.[35] Nevada controllers published these two statements through the 1920s, achieving a sustained uniformity in reporting unknown to New Mexico or Arizona.

Improvements over time were steady but not spectacular. In 1913–1914, the Tax Commission, called for better information about receipts and expenditures and the introduction of a new accounting system.[36] Perhaps in response, the 1915 Nevada controller printed a table in T-account style with receipts by source on the left, disbursements by function on the right, and totals and a balance at the bottom. Bond activity was displayed but not eliminated from the totals. Presumably interfund transfers were eliminated, however, given that the controller's office had been eliminating such activity for decades by that time.[37]

Finally, in the 1920s, the controller introduced several modern revenue and expenditure recognition techniques. The 1922 report distinguished bond purchases from the bond premiums paid.[38] In 1929, the list of revenues included lines for the amortization of "accrued interest purchased," bond discounts, and bond premiums.[39] In 1930, disbursements included "bond purchases (par value less discount)."[40]

DIFFERENCES BETWEEN REVENUES AND EXPENDITURES

Comparing the costs of government to its benefits has been a goal of government-watchers for a long time. Williams believes identifiable performance and productivity measurement of government activities was a Progressive achievement, beginning at the New York Bureau of Municipal Research.[41]

The goals were to hold government accountable, improve its productivity, and end its wastefulness.[42] The means were gathering and reporting the data and using it to manage more effectively.

In 1912, William Prendergast, comptroller of New York City, declared in a special issue of the *Annals of the American Academy of Political and Social Science*: "To enable [elected officials] to direct the activities of government intelligently and economically, it is essential that they should have constantly before them the facts and figures bearing upon current operations. It is only through proper accounting methods that these facts can be had."[43] A 1914 *Journal of Accountancy* article advocated creating governmental profit and loss statements to measure the value versus the cost of the public sector.[44] William notes that while "today these developments may seem trivial," they "were the cutting edge of government reform in the first years of the twentieth century."[45]

Basic to fiscal performance measurement is the comparison of revenues to expenditures. The "surplus" or "deficit" gives an idea whether enhanced performance might be affordable, and in the 1980s, almost all local governments in the United States published that number.[46] About 97 percent of readers who were surveyed in the 1980s wanted such disclosure.[47]

Early twentieth-century users were probably interested, too, in light of the fact that the New Mexico, Arizona, and Nevada reports of the time often (but not always) mentioned it. Their disclosure of the annual difference between revenues and expenditures varied from excellent to non-existent. Sometimes the disclosure was clear—a schedule at the beginning of the report with the relevant amount explicitly labeled. In other years, the amount was reasonably easy to determine—an initial summary tables of revenues and expenditures, for instance, with totals displayed on facing pages and amounts requiring elimination easily identified.

On the other hand, disclosure of the annual surplus or deficit was often unclear: both revenues and expenditures were disclosed and totaled, but displayed in separate places and containing items that should be eliminated but were hard to identify. Occasionally, there was no disclosure; either revenues or expenditures were absent, incomplete, or so confusingly presented that the difference could not be calculated. This occurred more often during the territorial than the state period.

Early territorial officials often mentioned the annual "surplus" or "deficit" in their textual remarks. The New Mexico auditor of 1887–1888 stated that "the expenditures exceeded the receipts by $155,631.09" for the biennium. Closer reading of the text reveals that this deficit was for the general fund only.[48] The Arizona auditor discussed the issue in the text of his 1883–1884 report, too.[49] In fact, the auditor's reports for Arizona continued this practice until 1907–1908.

Whether the numbers in such textual remarks included interfund transfers or U.S. subsidies or bond transactions was seldom explained. Sometimes they referred only to the general fund. Sometimes the official was referring to appropriations, not actual receipts or disbursements.

More useful than text discussion were numerical schedules, tables, or accounts. In the years just before 1900 or just afterwards, some officials in both territories adopted the practice of printing facing-page summaries of revenues and expenditures with annual totals.[50]

The New Mexico treasurer provided a moderately clear presentation of the difference between revenues and expenditures by the late 1890s. The first schedules in the 1897–1898 report were facing-page summaries of revenues and expenditures with annual totals. By 1909, the auditor was presenting similar facing summaries at the beginning of his reports.

Meanwhile, the Arizona treasurer had similar initial tables summarizing and totaling receipts and disbursements in his 1901–1902 report. The Arizona auditor, like his counterpart in New Mexico, was slow to adopt the practice, but his first state report, in 1912, did include initial summaries of revenues and expenditures. This type of presentation, used in both states for awhile, enabled the reader to estimate the surplus or deficit by subtracting two figures. In almost every case, however, the sums included amounts requiring elimination, such as bond transactions and interfund transfers. That is, the reader had to investigate further in the reports to avoid reaching a spurious conclusion.[51]

Unfortunately, neither New Mexico nor Arizona consistently improved its disclosure of the annual budget balance. For instance, the Arizona auditor in 1915 and the New Mexico auditor in 1920 both dropped the initial face-to-face tables. The curious reader had to consult the fund abstracts, the bottom line of which summed receipts, warrants, and interfund transfers. From this bottom line, and not forgetting to identify and eliminate the bond sales that were included in revenues, a simple calculation provided the difference between revenues and expenditures.

Presentations similar to that just described appeared through the whole decade of the 1920s in New Mexico. New Mexico made no further progress on reporting the annual surplus/deficit through the end of the study period in 1930.

In Arizona in 1923, on the other hand, the auditor began recapitulating his fund abstracts, net of interfund transfers, in a three-line statement ending with the "excess of expenditures over revenues."[52] This statement of the annual difference was buried in the middle of a long set of schedules and included bond transactions, but was at least reported consistently for the rest of the decade.

TAX RATES

A clear statement of statutory tax rates is of obvious interest to legislator and citizen readers of governmental financial statements. About 88 percent of all user groups wanted to see this information in the 1980s. A subsequent survey of local government practices found that a similarly large percentage of governments did in fact report tax rates.[53]

New Mexican territorial officials only disclosed tax rates irregularly, vaguely, and incompletely in most years. However, just before statehood, these items improved markedly. The 1909–1911 auditor's report contained a table of tax rates and amounts remitted by county for each year. A breakdown of the tax levy by millage rate for each general purpose followed—for example, 0.00005 mills for the Insane Asylum bonds sinking fund.

Soon afterwards, the first traveling auditor for the State of New Mexico reported the tax millage rate by fund and the revenue expected for each fund, as well as the revenue expected from other sources (e.g., auto licenses). By the 1920s, the state tax commission routinely provided tables showing the tax rates by level of government and by particular county for multiple years.[54]

In the Arizona Territory, officials disclosed tax rates more consistently than did their New Mexican counterparts. The 1891–1892 auditor, for example, reported, by county, the statutory tax rates for the support of each fund along with the expected revenues for each.[55] This form of reporting tax rates continued through statehood (albeit with lapses in some years, such as 1907–1908.)

After statehood in 1912, Arizona's new tax commission began publishing detailed tax rate information. The 1924 report had a foldout sheet showing state, county, and total tax rates by county by year from 1913 to 1924.[56] Perhaps because of this, the auditor and the treasurer had dropped their coverage by 1919.

BUDGETS

Although some elements of budgeting appear in antiquity, nothing resembling modern budgeting appeared in the United States until the late nineteenth century, according to Marquette and Fleischman.[57] Led not by private enterprise, but by state and local governments, budgeting blossomed from nothing to necessity over the few decades of Progressivism. The National Municipal League and the bureaus of municipal research, especially the New York Bureau, were prominent early advocates.[58]

At the turn of the century, an important member of the New York Bureau had never heard the term "budget."[59] By 1911, it was a much-discussed topic in municipal accounting.[60] By 1918, accounting theorist William Paton declared that "the most important function of municipal accounts is the furnishing of the material for the preparation of the budget."[61] Just a few years later, management accounting theorist James O. McKinsey wrote an entire book on the subject. He declared budgets indispensable for the coordination of revenues and expenditures.[62] Public sector budgeting was "universal" by the 1920s.[63]

More precise timing of the first government budgets in the United States is hard to come by. Potts finds no evidence of government budgetary accounting in this country before the twentieth century.[64] Supporting Potts, Allen claimed that New York only began budgeting in 1906.[65]

Contradicting Potts, Marquette and Fleischman note that there was some discussion of budgeting before 1900.[66] In their support, Clow argued in 1896 that cities were the only governments in the U.S. that "prepare[d] genuine budgets"—the states and national government did not have to, because they either raised taxes or ran deficits as necessary.[67]

Examination of the financial statements of New Mexico and Arizona suggests that budgeting at the state level began a decade or two earlier than it did at the municipal level. In fact, early evidence of budgeting in the territories of New Mexico and Arizona shows the practice in a stage of rapid development.

New Mexico

Before the word "budget" caught on in the United States, "estimates" was the preferred term. In New Mexico, the 1891–1892 auditor presented a seventeen-line "Estimate of Expenses" for the next year. Each line showed the expected requirements for a fund, but no total was drawn for all the funds together.

In 1893 and 1894, the "Estimate of Expenses" was much better developed than the one in the previous report. It ran to two pages, included a grand total, and explained the basis of some of the estimates.

These early budgets were probably required by statute. In his 1898–1899 report, the auditor noted that the law required "[d]etailed estimates of the probable expenditures to be defrayed from the treasury during the two ensuing years."[68]

By the early 1900s, such nascent budgets had disappeared from the reports of the New Mexico auditor, treasurer, and traveling auditor. However, they did not disappear from all New Mexican reports—other governmental entities published budgetary information.

The lead article in the first bulletin of the Taxpayers' Association of New Mexico, in 1916, strongly recommended "that some sort of a budget plan be put in use by our counties and municipalities [because] the most notable feature of the work of 1915 was the obvious lack of close figuring in the making of levies."[69] The suggestion bore fruit. The Special Revenue Commission of 1920 devoted an entire chapter to "The Budget, Bond Control and Tax Limitations." The Commission explained how the state's local governments had been required to prepare budgets since 1915 using forms supplied by the tax commission. In places, the chapter referred to "budget estimates," an interesting combination of the old term "estimate" with the new "budget."[70]

The chapter also discussed in detail the huge effort then underway to comply with a 1919 statute requiring a state budget. This first budget law fell short of its goals and in 1920 or 1921, New Mexico passed major changes to its fiscal statutes, according to the National Tax Association's roundup of state tax news. The legislation included a budget law "to be prepared by the Governor, which definitely controls the legislative appropriations."[71]

Budgets continued to be a focus and a target for improvements throughout my study period. The State Tax Commission of 1925–1926 titled a section of its report "Budget".[72] The Comptroller of 1927–1928 recommended splitting the biennial budgets into two equal parts so that the manager in the first year could not drain the entire appropriation, leaving his successor without funds.[73]

Arizona

The Territory of Arizona took its first steps toward budgeting at least as early as 1887–1888, when the auditor included a two-paragraph section titled "Estimates." The auditor concluded the section as follows:

> I therefore estimate the amount of revenue required to defray the current expenses of the Territory including the payment of the said interest for the years 1889 and 1890, at $320,000. And the probable amount of revenue derivable from the various sources for said years of 1889–90 should aggregate that sum.[74]

By 1912, the first state report included a much better developed budget, although it was still not called by that name. The "Statement of General Fund Requirements" and the "Approximate Revenues Required for all Purposes" estimated the expenses of the next biennium in detail. The following year, the auditor had a foldout spreadsheet detailing approximate assessed valuations, expected revenues, and proposed appropriations by line item.

The year 1913 was the last time the budget appeared in the auditor's report. A statute that year required a budget to be presented to the legislature and apparently after that the auditor prepared and printed the budgets separately from the annual reports.[75]

By 1922, Arizona had a Budget Secretary, who reported on major budget reforms to the National Tax Association. The Arizona legislature had also passed a new fiscal code that "repeal[ed] one hundred seventy-nine continuing and special appropriations." For departments that had multiple such appropriations, "the sky was the limit." Since they asked for no appropriations each year, the legislature gave them "practically no thought." The new fiscal code thus restrained their previously free-spending ways.[76]

The 1924 auditor, R. H. Ramsey, recommended changes to the accounting system that would support improved budget processes:

> I suggest that the appropriations for the maintenance of the various departments be made under not more than two headings, viz: Salaries and Wages and Operation, thus making it possible for the Auditor to set up a system of cost accounting and distribution of expense which would be of great value in the comparison of costs as between the various departments and between different fiscal years for the same department. Such a system of uniform cost accounting and distribution of expense should be of assistance to the legislature in passing the biennial appropriation bill.[77]

Nevada

The Nevada legislature of 1920 was the first to work from an executive budget, according to the Bulletin of the National Tax Association. The legislature used it to cut planned spending in that depression year by $40,000.[78]

The secretary of the state tax commission praised the improvements the law created. Previous legislatures, working without budgets, ignored appropriations until the last day of the session, when they were passed with:

> many incongruities, without adequate consideration, and with little relation to the financial condition of the state. [In 1921] Governor Boyle presented the legislature with a complete and easily comprehended statement of the state's finances . . . the result of a vast amount of . . . investigation such as never before been given to the state's affairs . . . That any state should longer continue without [a budget] is evidence of a lack of ordinary business sagacity.[79]

The 1921 legislature, using the new budget, actually increased the final appropriations slightly over Boyles' recommendation.

Budgeting continued to be a great success, according to the 1925 controller, George Cole. He reported that:

our fiscal program has balanced more closely than in any other year of our state history. There is a difference of but one and one-half per cent between receipts and disbursements; and of two and one-half per cent between income and expenses. This condition proves the merit of the budget system, and indicates careful legislative calculation and efficient administrative management.[80]

Budgets: Conclusion

More than a decade before the twentieth century dawned, the Territories of New Mexico and Arizona had begun using simple budgets. This is before most scholars see evidence of budgeting by U.S. municipalities.

Note also that all three governments markedly increased their reliance on budgeting as a process in the early 1920s. This may have been due to the post-war recession in 1918 and 1919 and the nasty subsequent depression of 1920 and 1921. It was probably not a function of statehood.

NOTES

1. Ingram and Robbins, *Financial Reporting Practices*, 50.
2. "Statistical Survey of Government Costs in New Mexico."
3. Sylla, Legler, and Wallis, *Sources and Uses of Funds in State and Local Governments*, 8–9.
4. Potts, "Evolution of Municipal Accounting," 49–51.
5. U.S. Bureau of the Census, *Financial Statistics of States, 1915*, 13, 14.
6. NM Auditor, *Report*, 1912, 11–16.
7. AZ State Tax Commission, *Report*, 1916, 26.
8. NM Auditor, *Report*, 1914, 14–19.
9. AZ Auditor, *Report*, 1913, 17–18, 23–24. AZ Treasurer, *Report*, 1913, see individual funds statements.
10. NM Auditor, *Report*, 1915–1916, 16–21, 35–40; AZ Auditor, *Report*, 1916, 8–9, 23–24.
11. NM Auditor, *Report*, 1915–1916, 27.
12. E.g., NM Auditor, *Report*, 1923–1924, 15.
13. NM Auditor, *Report*, 1921–1922, 32.
14. NM Auditor, *Report*, 1921–1922, 5–19, 32.
15. E.g., U.S. Congress, House, *Receipts and Expenditures*, 56th Cong., 1st sess., December 4, 1899, Serial Set 3937, doc. 36, p. 23.
16. NV Tax Commission, *Report*, 1913–1914, 8.
17. NV Controller, *Report*, 1929, 3.
18. NM Terr. Auditor, *Report*, 1887–1888.
19. NM Terr. Auditor, *Report*, 1897–1898, 54.

20. Ball, *Desert Lawmen*, 253.

21. NM Terr. Auditor, *Report*, 1897–1898, 60, 61.

22. NM Terr. Treasurer, *Report*, 1897–1898, 20–21.

23. NM Terr. Treasurer, *Report*, 1897–1898.

24. NM Auditor, *Report*, 1915–1916, 5–9, 16–21, 35–40; NM Treasurer, *Report*, 1917–1918, 17.

25. NM Auditor, *Report*, 1915–1916, 11–15, 29–34; NM Traveling Auditor, *Report*, April 1, 1915–November 30, 1916, 50–76; NM Treasurer, *Report*, 1917–1918, 10–14.

26. AZ Terr. Auditor, 1884, 6; AZ Terr. Auditor, 1887–1888.

27. AZ Terr. Treasurer, *Report*, 1895–1896.

28. AZ Terr. Auditor, *Report*, 1907–1908.

29. AZ Terr. Treasurer, *Report*, 1904, 141–143.

30. AZ Auditor, *Report*, 1915. See also discussion under "Funds" in chap. 9.

31. AZ Auditor, *Report*, 1915, vi, xviii–xxii.

32. AZ Auditor, *Report*, 1923, schedule 3.

33. AZ Auditor, *Report*, 1929, statement 3. Note that statement 1, which contains the fund statements, also eliminates transfers. However, statement 2 only identifies the interfund transfers and does not eliminate them from the totals.

34. AZ Treasurer, *Report*, 1915, 8–9, 13.

35. NV Controller, *Report*, 1888, statements C, N, O.

36. NV Tax Commission, *Report*, 1913–1914, 7–10.

37. NV Controller, *Report*, 1915, 6–7.

38. NV Controller, *Report*, 1922, 7.

39. NV Controller, *Report*, 1929, 6

40. NV Controller, *Report*, 1930, 7.

41. Williams, "Measuring Government," 644.

42. Williams, "Measuring Government," 644–649. For contemporary examples of the strong interest in performance, see Cleveland, "Need for Coordinating Municipal," 1912; Prendergast, "Efficiency through Accounting," 1912; Taussig, "Results Obtainable through Reorganization," 1912; Treleven, "Milwaukee Bureau of Economy," 1912; Walton, "Application to a Municipality," 1912.

43. Prendergast, "Efficiency through Accounting," 43.

44. Tanner, "Governmental Profit and Loss," 265 *et passim*.

45. Tanner, "Governmental Profit and Loss," 645.

46. Ingram and Robbins, *Financial Reporting Practices*, 50.

47. Jones, *Needs of Users*, 1985, 57.

48. NM Terr. Auditor, *Report*, 1887–1888, 1.

49. AZ Terr. Auditor, *Report*, 1884, 6.

50. NM Terr. Treasurer, *Report*, 1897–1898, 4–5; AZ Terr. Treasurer, *Report*, 1901–1902, 2–3.

51. NM Terr. Treasurer, *Report*, 1897–1898, 4–5; NM Terr. Auditor, *Report*, 1909–1910–1911, 6–9; AZ Terr. Treasurer, *Report*, 1901–1902, 2–3; AZ Auditor, *Report*, 1912, iii–iv.

52. AZ Auditor, *Report*, 1923, 48.

53. Jones, *Needs of Users*, 55; Ingram and Robbins, *Financial Reporting Practices*, 55.

54. NM Terr. Auditor, *Report*, 1909–1910–1911, 16–19; NM Traveling Auditor, *Report*, 1912, 8, 10. An example of state tax commission disclosure is in NM State Tax Commission, *Report*, 1921–1922, 115.

55. AZ Terr. Auditor, *Report*, 1891–1892, 38–39.

56. AZ State Tax Commission, *Report*, 1924, tab. 23.

57. Marquette and Fleischman, "Government/Business Synergy," 124. See Potts, "Evolution of Budgetary Accounting Theory," for late-nineteenth-century developments in budgeting outside the United States, including a description of failed attempts to link budgetary and actual accounts. Outside the United States, there is evidence for earlier budgeting. See Forrester, "Aspects of French Accounting," p. 5, who discusses a 1786 requirement in France for public expense estimates by account.

58. Marquette and Fleischman, "Government/Business Synergy," 126–128; Rubin, "Who Invented Budgeting in the United States?"

59. Marquette and Fleischman, "Government/Business Synergy," 125–126.

60. Marquette and Fleischman, "Government/Business Synergy."

61. Paton and Stevenson, *Principles of Accounting*, 627.

62. McKinsey, *Budgetary Control*, 1922; "Municipal Accounting," 83.

63. Marquette and Fleischman, "Government/Business Synergy," 141.

64. Potts, "The Evolution of Budgetary Accounting Theory."

65. Allen, "The Budget as an Instrument."

66. Marquette and Fleischman, "Government/Business Synergy."

67. Clow, "Suggestions for the Study," 458–459.

68. NM Terr. Auditor, *Report*, 1891–1892, schedule 1, 38–39; NM Terr. Auditor, *Report*, 1893–1894, schedule A, 57–59; NM Terr. Auditor, *Report*, 1897–1898, 3.

69. James, "Review of the Tax Levies," 10.

70. NM Special Revenue Commission, *Report*, 1920, 173.

71. "New Mexico," 1921.

72. NM State Tax Commission, *Report*, 1925–1926, 19–20.

73. NM Comptroller, *Report*, 1927–1928, 8.

74. AZ Terr. Auditor, *Report*, 1887–1988, 6.

75. AZ Auditor, *Report*, 1912, 29–33; AZ Auditor, *Report*, 1913, foldout table "Comparative Detailed Statement of Approximate Assessed Valuation, Tax Levy and Approximate Appropriation for the Fiscal Years 1913–1914 and 1914–1915"; AZ Auditor, *Report*, 1918, 3.

76. "Arizona Budgetary Reform," 276.

77. AZ Auditor, *Report*, 1924, 4.

78. "Nevada."

79. Fletcher, "Budget and State Taxes in Nevada," 114–115.

80. NV Controller, *Report*, 1925, 5.

11

The Elements of Accountability

The most fundamental fact about these governments' financial statements was that they existed. These three frontier governments—two of them only territories until 1912—literally practiced public accountability by publishing their accounts almost without fail for decade after decade around the turn of the twentieth century.

There were, as Frederick Clow said at the time, "tons of . . . statements."[1] Even Arizona's Fourteenth Legislature, which in 1887 refused on the grounds of expense to publish a journal of its own proceedings because of the nationally notorious overspending of its predecessor, the "Thieving Thirteenth," nevertheless funded the publication of the territory's accounts. Indeed, all of the governments in this study created more than one fiscal office and had each office produce annual or biennial reports.

But part 2 demonstrates more than this most basic fact of accountability. It shows that over the half-century from the 1880s to 1930, financial reporting by New Mexico, Arizona, and Nevada improved dramatically in *quality*. Reports became longer, more detailed, more complete, and a little more analytical. In short, they became more informative.

Furthermore, the study casts light on *why* the improvements occurred—on whether statehood affects how a government accounts for its fiscal behavior, whether there are signs that Progressive reforms reached the frontier West, and whether the governments learned better financial reporting with experience. Examination of New Mexico, Arizona, and Nevada financial statements suggests the answer to all three questions is yes.

STATEHOOD

Around statehood, in or just after 1912, quite a few changes occurred in the financial reports of New Mexico and Arizona. The number of funds the governments used exploded, along with spending. New Mexico and Arizona both began classifying or consolidating the funds into functional categories, which improved comprehensibility. They dropped the territorial practice of printing long lists of individual warrants and fund transactions. The frequency and length of textual narrative (a forerunner of today's management discussion and analysis) doubled. Fixed asset disclosure improved significantly.

Much clearer identification of interfund transfers appeared with statehood, too, ameliorating (but not quite ending) the territorial practice of overstating receipts and expenditures by the amount of the transfers among funds. New Mexico's auditors began printing initial summaries of receipts and expenditures as well as fund abstracts that included interfund transfers. The treasurer began printing a table of bonds issued by year, making their elimination from revenues easier. Receipts from the counties were disclosed in more detail than they had been in territorial days.

In Arizona, early state reports presented much improved information on revenues by source, a set of fund abstracts, and a better accounting for treasurer's disbursements that had not gone through the auditor's books. The Arizona state auditor began printing an introductory summary of revenues and expenditures in his reports.

In both states, a declaration of the surplus or deficit became more common (though not consistent) after statehood. The new constitutions of both states imposed myriad fiscal restraints on their governments.

As for taxes, New Mexico improved its reporting of tax rates dramatically just before statehood. Arizona followed suit immediately after 1912, publishing very detailed tax rate information. Both states began publishing 100 percent valuations of property, and both shifted the incidence of taxation from urban property owners to mines.

Finally, fiscal officials' own remuneration and powers took a significant jump at statehood. New Mexico's traveling auditors acquired more staff and the new state tax commission was given a lot more power and money in the first six or seven years after 1912. In Arizona, the state tax commission was endowed with "unrestricted powers" and the local Boards of Equalization were abolished. One of the tax commissioners, Thomas Campbell, was almost elected governor in 1916.

As for the Arizona auditor, he wrote the longest management discussion and analysis of any official in the three governments in fifty years, full of recommendations for the legislature. For instance, he recommended more spending on the Industrial School, which the legislature accepted, increasing its funding from $25,000 in 1908 to $75,000 in 1915. His own salary was increased for 1913, and he was given a well-paid deputy auditor. Between 1908 and 1915, total state spending on the auditor and his staff and office more than tripled, from $6,000 to $19,000.

These findings fit Waymire and Basu's punctuated equilibrium pattern for how accounting changes over time. Substituting statehood for the economic crises they examine, and governments for the private sector firms they study, I conclude that statehood did act as a punctuator of the accounting equilibrium in New Mexico and Arizona. It interrupted a history of slow, incremental change with numerous dramatic improvements in the years immediately around 1912.

In contrast, Nevada, which did not become a state during the study period, did not initiate such dramatic changes around 1912 as did the other two states.

PROGRESSIVISM AND EXPERIENCE

The default mode for financial reporting by all three governments, aside from the effects of statehood, was one of numerous incremental changes throughout the study period, in areas from funds to fiscal years. These changes were a product of general experience or of Progressive reforms.

For example, in the 1920s, New Mexico and to some extent Arizona began using new account types such as appropriations, suspense, and control accounts. The reporting of revenues and expenditures improved slowly in all three states throughout the study period. New Mexico introduced the disclosure of the sources of receipts in the nineteenth century and the Arizona auditor began reporting receipts at the same time. Bond reporting gradually improved over the years in both states.

Well after 1912, in the late 1920s, the Nevada controller began recording bond discounts and premiums and Arizona finally began eliminating interfund transfers, instead of just listing them. All three states changed their fiscal year end dates to June 30 at one time or another during the study period, and all three slowly improved the transparency of the property assessment process.

Budgeting, too, was born and blossomed independently of statehood. Budgeting was an important part of Progressive efforts to improve municipal accounting, and prior literature finds it swept the country from 1900 to 1920. But this study finds that at the higher level of territorial government, both New Mexico and Arizona had introduced budgets at least a decade earlier. The process was so well-developed by the second decade of the new century that budgetary reports moved out of the auditors' and treasurers' reports altogether.

Then, around 1920, New Mexico, Arizona, and Nevada all made huge improvements in their budgeting process. Perhaps the needs of territorial and state governments for a budgetary process were so exigent, especially following a serious economic shock like the depression of 1919, that they tended to develop budgets before smaller local governments.

CONSTANTS

Not every quality or element of fiscal reporting by these governments changed. Some things stayed the same, for better or worse.

A good example is the funds themselves. Fund accounting was a constant during my study period, and in fact continues to this day. Throughout the study period, all the governments displayed a concern for disclosing the whereabouts and disposition of the cash they took in. Bond disclosures and assessed property values also appeared in some form almost every year.

On the negative side, subsidies from the United States were never systematically identified and eliminated from receipts so as to identify total own-source revenues. Bond activity was conflated with receipts and expenditures throughout the period. Depreciation for fixed assets and infrastructure was not recorded in any of the reports examined, nor did any report contain classified balance sheets; there were very few balance sheets of any sort.

CONCLUSION

To summarize, statehood makes quite a difference in the quality of a government's financial reporting. The states of New Mexico and Arizona had better reports than their predecessor territories, and the state of Nevada had better reports than the territories of New Mexico and Arizona.

The Northwest Ordinance process, which created subordinate territorial governments on the grounds that evolutionary development is needed before a government is ready for the sovereign status of statehood, had consequences for the territories other than the political consequences usually discussed. New Mexico and Arizona behaved less accountably to their citizens as territories than they did as states and than did the neighboring state of Nevada.

The longevity of a government seems to make a difference, too. All three governments improved their financial reporting over time. Furthermore, the quality of reporting by the new states never caught up, in many respects, with the quality of reports in the much older state of Nevada.

On the other hand, the frontier status of the governments in this study does not seem to have been very important. Progressive-era changes in public sector accounting that swept the eastern United States also swept these desert territories and states. Similarly, the deficiencies in the financial statements of Arizona and New Mexico resembled the deficiencies of public sector reporting in other parts of the United States at the time.

Next, in the last chapter of the book, I link the developments in government financial reporting reported in part 2 to the fiscal dynamics of statehood reported in part 1.

NOTE

1. Clow, "Study of Municipal Finance," 457.

Conclusion

Statehood and Accountability, Leviathan and Accountants

It is a little-discussed but common phenomenon in American history that large numbers of citizens in the territories oppose statehood for fear it will fiscally unleash their governments. They argue that they and their neighbors are too poor to support a state government, which they believe will be far more expensive than the territory.

Statehood supporters, including most historians, believe that these fears are exaggerated. They argue that spending will only increase to provide a few necessary improvements and to replace lost federal subsidies—for legislators' and executive officials' salaries and expenses, for instance. Furthermore, they expect statehood itself to boost the local economy enough that any increased costs will not be burdensome.

However, no prior research has systematically studied the costs of statehood. One reason for this research gap is that almost all American states entered the union before World War I, a time when generally accepted government accounting principles were in a stage of informal development. Researchers curious about the fiscal effects of territory-to-state transitions must sift through old financial reports of widely varying condition and quality, which are based on very diverse accounting and reporting techniques.

Difficult as they are to work with, many financial reports of the territories and early states do still exist, especially for states that entered the union in the late nineteenth and early twentieth centuries. This study took advantage of both the existence of these archival documents and their inconsistent quality to investigate two questions:

Question 1: Does statehood increase the fiscal burden of government?
Question 2: Does statehood improve a government's accounting for its use
   of the public purse?

Part 1 of this book presents evidence supporting my claim that the answer to question 1 is yes—there is a Leviathan dynamic in statehood. Part 2 shows evidence for a significant increase in accountability by the governments involved.

Below, I summarize these two lines of evidence. After that, I tie the two ideas together, to argue that increased accountability is one of the the *means* by which statehood unleashes Leviathan.

QUESTION 1: STATEHOOD AND LEVIATHAN

When a territory of the United States becomes a state, many things change in the new government. Notably, the state has far more fiscal sovereignty than did the predecessor territory. Territories' taxing and spending powers are subject to close federal supervision, but this ends upon statehood. Federal supervision during the territorial years creates endless arguments between the two levels of government. These tensions hasten the desires of territorial politicians to acquire the independent powers of statehood.

This feature of federalism offers an opportunity to test Brennan and Buchanan's Leviathan theory of government. In this theory, which falls within the public choice paradigm, the government is treated as a self-interested actor in the making of public policy. Government's goal in this paradigm, independent of other actors' goals, is to grow in size and power. Statehood opponents in American territories implicitly endorse a Leviathan dynamic of statehood when they argue that a state will use its greater powers to increase substantially its fiscal "bite" from the local society's wealth.

In contrast, statehood supporters implicitly endorse the more traditional public interest view of government. In this view, government is a neutral or benevolent reflector of the interests of the public, so a state should cost only a modest amount more than a territory.

A Leviathan dynamic of statehood, if it exists, implies that the cost of government varies directly with its level of sovereignty (see fig. 1.1). I chose two states to test this hypothesis: New Mexico and Arizona, both of which entered the union in 1912. The control is Nevada, a western neighbor that had joined the union many years earlier (1864). I examined the published financial reports of all three governments from the 1880s to 1930 to determine the cost of government and the quality of the financial statements.

The cost of government relative to the size of the local economy (F-RevA) and the cost relative to the national economy (F-GNP) were measured to control for changes in the local economy and national trends. By hypothesis, the graphs of F were expected to show an abrupt increase in slope in the two subject states sometime around the year of statehood, 1912 (see fig. 1.2). In contrast, the graph of F in Nevada was not expected to show a similar jump at that time.

In all three states, the graphs of the fiscal burden behaved just as predicted. In New Mexico and Arizona, the F ratio rose sharply immediately after 1912. In Nevada, F showed no significant change around 1912 (cf. figs. 5.1 and 5.2). Descriptive statistics confirm what the graphs display: between 1911 and 1913, the main F ratio jumped from 0.35 percent to 0.67 percent in New Mexico and from 0.36 percent to 0.46 percent in Arizona.

Regression analysis supports these results. SOVEREIGNTY (which distinguishes the years through 1912 from the years after it) accounted for over 90 percent of the variation in the fiscal price of the New Mexican government and 58 percent in Arizona. The passage of time may have had a modest positive effect in New Mexico and a modest negative effect in Arizona, but in both cases the effect of SOVEREIGNTY was much greater. A regional variable using the Nevada residual variation had no significant effect on F in either subject state. In Nevada, the pre- and post-1912 division created by SOVEREIGNTY had no significant effect on F.

Regression analysis for F-GNP produced similar results as the regression models for the main F ratio: SOVEREIGNTY explains almost all the variation in F-GNP for New Mexico and Arizona, but has no significant effect in Nevada.

In short, the study results support the Leviathan hypothesis and strongly support the naysayers in New Mexico and Arizona. In both places, state government was much more expensive than territorial government. The increase was not a simple function of rising wealth, because the government's receipts increased much more than the economy did. It was not a purely nominal increase due to inflation, because it showed up in a relative fiscal measure as well as in absolute dollars. The increase was not a coincidence occurring in just one state, because it happened in both New Mexico and Arizona. It was not a spurious observation based on inaccurate data or poor calculations because it appeared in numerous measures of the government's fiscal size.

The increases in New Mexico and Arizona did not result from regional or national economic trends, because equations controlling for those trends still show the effect, and the effect did not occur in the control state, Nevada. For the same reason, the increases did not result from emulation of the federal government's forthcoming increased tax power under the 16th amendment to the U.S. Constitution. New Mexico, Arizona, and Nevada all voted for the 16th amendment, and New Mexico in fact provided the last vote necessary for the amendment's national ratification, in early 1913, but it was only in New Mexico and Arizona that tax collections increased significantly just after 1912.[1] Nevada, equally aware of the federal tax innovation, did not increase its relative tax burden at that time.

The statehood bump was not transitory. Compared to territorial levels, the mean of F in the first seven years of statehood rose from 0.33 percent to 0.69 percent in New Mexico and from 0.38 percent to 0.52 percent in Arizona. Meanwhile, the mean of Nevada's F remained at 0.55 percent in the periods both before and after 1912.

Someone had to pay, after all, for New Mexico's Elephant Butte Water Users Association. And someone did pay—the fund's spending soared by 69 percent from 1910 to 1913. The Eradication Indemnity Fund, too, increased expenditures by 61 percent. The schools did particularly well. The Spanish American Normal School fund shot up from $4,500 in 1910 to $8,000 in 1913, while the Normal University of Las Vegas fund spent $30,000 in 1913, up from only $20,400 just three years earlier.

To be sure, the first decades of the twentieth century brought increased costs of government everywhere. For instance, from 1915 to 1925, F-RevA in Nevada increased 47 percent; in absolute dollars, the increase was 112 percent. As the Nevada controller of 1925 remarked,

> there have been many new fields of service entered by the State since 1915; and these, together with the increase of general costs, so well known to every consumer, have been covered by an increase of 10 percent in the state tax rate and a raise of 32 percent in the state tax roll.[2]

The Good Roads movement, to take another example, sparked a nation-wide explosion in state-level spending, and this was reflected in the western states (see fig. A.1 in the appendix). But this growth, like the growth men-tioned by the Nevada controller, occurred *after* the entry of New Mexico and Arizona into the union and *after* the growth spurt their governments experi-enced upon statehood.

The simplest explanation for these findings is that the change from terri-tory to state caused an increase in the relative price of government. And after all, that is what territorial opponents of statehood have predicted throughout American history. It is also what the Leviathan model of government pre-dicts: when an increase in sovereignty unleashes a government's power, the price the people pay for the government soars. There is a Leviathan dynamic in statehood.

QUESTION 2: STATEHOOD AND ACCOUNTABILITY

This study opens a window on a world accounting historians know little about—how American sub-national governments of the late nineteenth and early twentieth centuries accounted for their use of the people's funds. The data set consists of the reports of New Mexico, Arizona, and Nevada financial officials from the 1880s to 1930. To structure the work, I recorded observations of a set of financial elements drawn from a 1987 study of the financial reporting practices of local governments conducted for the Governmental Accounting Standards Board.

Two general observations may be made concerning the nineteenth century's public sector financial records. First, it is remarkable how copious they are. This suggests that American state and local governments were widely expected to be financially accountable to the people who supported them, a point ignored by dissatisfied Progressive reformers. Second, the effectiveness with which the governments met their public accountability obligations varied from excellent to scandalous over the whole century.

As for specific drivers of change, statehood, Progressivism, and sheer experience all seem to have improved the territories' and states' financial reporting. But the greatest of these was statehood. Statehood punctuated the financial reporting equilibrium and ratcheted it up several notches.

When New Mexico and Arizona became states in 1912, their financial reports took a leap in transparency and efficiency. Their textual narratives became much longer and more informative, they began publishing 100 percent property value assessments, they dropped the tedious old lists of individual transactions, they vastly improved the summary and analysis of revenues and expenditures (including the annual deficit or surplus), they made more serious efforts to inventory and value fixed assets, they began identifying interfund transfers, and they reported tax rates and receipts in much more detail.

Such momentous changes did not occur in Nevada at that time. I conclude that something about statehood caused much better financial reporting.

In addition to these large statehood-associated changes, all three governments gradually improved their accounting, as their experience dictated or as the good government reforms of Progressivism suggested. Progressive reforms from the more settled parts of the country did reach the frontier West. Other improvements seem to have resulted from simple experience—small corrections made gradually over time.

There were also elements of these financial reports that did not change significantly during the study period. Fund accounting, a focus on the whereabouts and disposition of cash, and the disclosure of some information on bonds issued and property values assessed were constants. On the other hand, subsidies from the federal government and bond transactions were conflated with revenues throughout the period and depreciation was never reported.

As for Nevada, the control state, analysis of this half-century of financial reports shows that the quality of its reporting was always better, in a number of respects, than that of the subject governments. Furthermore, the states of

New Mexico and Arizona issued better reports than did their predecessor territories. That is, state governments accounted for their handling of the public purse better than territorial governments did, despite the fact that territories faced far greater reporting obligations to the federal government than did states.

In short, to the extent it is possible to generalize from these documents, statehood matters to the quality of financial reporting, and, to a lesser extent, so do the longevity of a government and the accounting reform efforts of citizen groups. The greater the sovereignty of the government, the longer its experience, and the greater the popular efforts to improve its public accounting, the higher the quality of its published reports.

Thus, examination of these reports tells many stories. But perhaps the most notable story is that accountability itself was a constant. Without fail throughout the half century from the 1880s to 1930, these frontier governments published detailed accounts of their handling of the public purse. Regardless of how disorganized or new a government was, how dismal or scandalous the fiscal situation, or how differently a new official or legislature thought the information should be presented, the fiscal conduct of the New Mexico, Arizona, and Nevada governments was recorded in detail and published for its citizens in nearly every year or biennial period.

Apparently, frontier Americans of a century ago would have agreed with today's GASB that "[a]ccountability requires governments to answer to the citizenry—to justify the raising of public resources and the purposes for which they are used."[3]

SYNTHESIS: FISCAL SIZE AND FINANCIAL REPORTING QUALITY

Statehood presumably brought many benefits to New Mexico and Arizona. This is what statehood supporters expected when they voted to enter the Union. But the governments, in assuming the sovereign powers of states, also took much bigger bites from the pockets of the people than most voters must have expected, both in absolute dollars and relative to the size of the new states' economies.

Similarly, the myriad fiscal officials of those years created innumerable improvements in the public accountability and transparency of the New Mexico and Arizona governments. How could they not? They could hardly have ignored the opportunities they had to reform the pitiful financial reports typical of the 1870s.

Yet these experts also benefited personally. Their salaries and powers and numbers multiplied upon statehood. Whatever their personal politics—

whether they were for or against Progressive ideas about bigger government—they were part of Leviathan, and they grew with it.

More, they helped it grow. They improved tax collections, rendered the public accounts far clearer, provided much more detailed and useful information to budget makers, and surely soothed some of the fears of suspicious citizens. They made young state governments just stretching their new fiscal muscles stronger, more knowledgeable, and less vulnerable to citizens' accusations of shady financial dealings. This is the same story Brewer told for eighteenth-century England, and similar to Ezzamel's story about ancient Egypt.[4]

Or, as public choice theory might put it, a government with new powers puts its thumb on the scales in its own favor, being simultaneously a player among other players on the public policy field, the umpire, and the accounting expert.

The fact is, accountability is a tricky thing. No accountant would argue against efficiency, transparency, and honesty in public administration. Nor would any, I imagine, argue against seizing the opportunity of statehood to implement dramatic improvements in financial reporting that have long been needed. Yet, whether particular fiscal officials like it or not, these changes also feed Leviathan.

In the end, accountability and accounting are intimately involved with money and power. In the context of government, at least, such a mélange is unlikely ever to be entirely apolitical or even disinterested.

LIMITATIONS, CONTRIBUTIONS, AND FURTHER WORK

My conclusions should be taken with some grains of salt, because the study design (like all designs) has limitations. First, I draw my information primarily from the reports of territorial and state financial officials. The point of view is that of insiders, people who worked for the governments involved. Furthermore, county receipts and expenditures were not examined, so that the total fiscal burden is unknown. People in other parts of the governments, or outside them, may offer information that would change my conclusions.

Secondly, the financial reports I examined are not exhaustive. I tried to obtain at least one officer's report—usually the auditor's, the treasurer's, or the controller's—for every year from the early 1880s to 1930 for each state. However, if data were not easily obtainable for some years, I made no extraordinary attempt to locate them. Nor did I examine ledgers, books of original entry, and legislative reports. Therefore, I can only report for certain the presence of a practice, but not its absence, since it may have appeared in documents I did not locate.

Thirdly, the sample of subject states was neither random nor large enough in number to make it possible to generalize the results to other states with a measurable degree of probability. Therefore, although the study design ruled out a number of known alternative explanations of the results, unrecognized variables could also explain the government's jump in fiscal size and the improvements in its financial reporting practices.

Fourthly, the study covers only three governments and only one half-century. Perhaps other times and places had different experiences.

This study makes several contributions to fiscal and accounting scholarship despite its limitations. It investigates an institutional change that is fundamental to the U.S. experience: statehood. It provides previously unavailable, usable, and reasonably accurate data on the fiscal behavior of three governments from the 1880s to 1930. Systematic descriptions of the financial reporting practices of several state and territorial governments from that era are also provided. Both of these data sets can be used by scholars investigating quite different questions from those I address.

This study also adds to the relatively limited scholarly accounting literature that treats fiscal policy and accounting practices as endogenous rather than exogenous variables. Most tax policy research investigates the effects rather than the causes of the policy. As for other accounting research, the recent American Accounting Association president William Kinney defined the "domain of accounting scholarship" as "*knowledge of the . . . effects of alternative standardized business measurement and reporting structures.*"[5] The fact that Kinney ignored the possibilities of studying the *causes* of accounting structures suggests that this is an under-explored area of accounting scholarship.

But a great deal of further work could be done.

For example, if it is true that change in a government's degree of sovereignty is directly related to change in the fiscal "price" it charges the local economy, as my model hypothesizes, then a government whose sovereignty *declines* should also experience a decline in its F ratio. Texas would be an excellent test. Texas was an independent nation before it became a state, so its sovereignty decreased when it entered the union. Texans of the 1840s believed the cost of government would also drop; would study of the accounts confirm their belief and support my hypothesis?

Any number of other questions could be investigated. For instance, could it be that the nineteenth-century accounts of the first thirteen states differ in quality by their original status as a proprietary or a royal colony? An alternative hypothesis is that states with well-established, powerful commercial economies kept better fiscal records. Perhaps in Louisiana, Massachusetts, and New York, antebellum government accounting was better than the accounting in Kentucky, North Carolina, or Vermont.

These are only a few of an enormous number of questions that could be answered with more study of how generally accepted government accounting practices evolved in the United States in the centuries before official standards appeared. Official standards facilitate historiography because they "leave documentary traces," as a former president of the American Accounting Association, Shyam Sunder, noted. He pointed out that it is tempting "to identify the history of accounting with the organized efforts to produce written rules."[6] Accounting historians, who know better, need to study the original government reports to refute the strange notion that American government accounting history began with the National Municipal League and Progressivism.

Researchers might even create a historical version of *Local Government Accounting Trends and Techniques*,[7] showing with reasonable accuracy the range and frequency of early American government accounting practices. From this work, it ought to be possible to create a taxonomy of government accounting methods, and even a phylogeny, as called for by Waymire and Basu.[8] Surely this is not beyond the inclination or capabilities of accounting historians, all of whom are accustomed to meticulously account for trees in order to describe forests.

Pending such future research, this study supports the conclusion that statehood matters, both fiscally and in terms of public sector accounting quality. When a government acquires major new fiscal powers, as a territory does when it becomes a state, it can be expected to increase the price it charges for its services significantly and to improve noticeably the quality of the financial reports it provides to the citizenry.

This Leviathan dynamic of statehood offers an explanation for some of today's controversial sovereignty questions—for instance in Puerto Rico and Quebec, where popular majorities have repeatedly rejected an increase in sovereignty.

It also raises an important question about the federalist system: Why do the people sometimes choose to increase their government's level of sovereignty? Given the Leviathan dynamic set in motion by such a step, why statehood?

NOTES

1. The federal income tax was widely discussed in the years around the enactment of the 16th amendment. See, for example, Zander (an Arizona tax commissioner), "Tax Progress in Arizona," 13.

2. NV Controller, *Report*, 5.

3. Governmental Accounting Standards Board, "Concepts Statement No. 1," 1987, 20–21.

4. Brewer, *Sinews of Power*; Ezzamel, "Accounting Working for the State."
5. Kinney, "Accounting Scholarship," 278, emphasis in the original.
6. Sunder, "State of Accounting Practice and Education."
7. Cornwall, *Local Governmental Accounting*.
8. Waymire and Basu, "Economic Crisis."

Appendix

$\mathbf{M}$y calculations of the F-ratio differ from those used in most studies because no detailed annual statistics on the personal income or gross product of the states or territories exist for the 1800s or very early 1900s. The only data collected annually on the size of the economy at the time was the value of real and (some) personal property. Therefore, the denominator in the F ratio is property values.

An alternative to this state-based denominator can be used from the late nineteenth century on. Annual figures for the gross national product are available from the U.S. Census beginning in 1889. Thus, the F ratio can be modified to compare Arizona and New Mexico spending and revenues to the size of the national economy instead of the local economy, from 1889 to 1930. This controls for national trends, while the Nevada data control for regional trends. This alternative also helps check any inaccuracies springing from the use of property values as a measure of the size of the economy.

Data for the numerator variables were easier to locate. Two measures of the numerator were often available—territorial/state government expenditures and receipts.[1] Whenever possible, therefore, an F for spending and an F for revenues was calculated, so as to test the robustness of any results. No attempt was made to adjust F for modern definitions of government revenues and expenditures. Instead, the cash basis of accounting used by the governments in this study was followed. However, in cases where it could be determined that the accounts include borrowed cash as part of the revenues or loan and bond repayments as part of expenditures, those amounts were subtracted from the numerator sums.

An additional adjustment to the original data is that I deleted federal transfers to the territorial governments from the calculations of receipts. When a

187

territory became a state, it had to assume many of the spending obligations formerly paid by the United States. A territory's ability to externalize part of its tax burden to citizens of the states has frequently been cited by territorial residents as a reason for opposing statehood. Such federal money, when identifiable, was subtracted from territorial revenues.

The reason for these adjustments is that if federal transfers to the territories are included in territorial revenues, the fiscal bite taken out of the territorial economy would be overstated, tending to obscure any statehood-associated rise in F. Identifying federal transfers also made it possible to determine whether the new states simply raised local revenues just enough to offset the loss in federal transfers after statehood. I calculated F with and without such amounts to determine what changes occur in the proportion of federal funds to total receipts.

Thus, the variables used to measure the fiscal size of the territorial and state governments are the following "F" ratios:

F-Exp = total territorial or state expenditures / assessed property values

F-Rev = total territorial or state revenues (excluding certain transfers from the federal government) / assessed property values

For Arizona and New Mexico, a modification of these ratios also was calculated:

F-GNP = total territorial or state expenditures or revenues (excluding certain transfers from the federal government) / gross national product

DATA SOURCES

An important limit on the validity of any conclusions in this study is the accuracy and completeness of the data. Sources are restricted to identified, extant, usable, archival data. Hundreds of territorial, state, and local officials, many on the frontier, gathered and recorded the information a century ago with greatly varying degrees of care and expertise. These sources of error are likely random and therefore were partly controlled for by the use of many years' observations in three different states. Indeed, that is an important advantage of this study— the use of original state-level data provides a far larger number of observations than does the census, for instance, in most of the period.

A more serious potential problem is the possibility that the data contain systematic errors. Some officials included borrowed monies in revenues and repayments of principal in expenses, for instance. Furthermore, county receipts, a significant fraction of the state and local total, were sometimes included in state sums. Additionally, tax assessors often systematically mis-valued property.[2] These are the types of errors that must be caught by close reading of the accounts. In some cases, it was possible to reconcile one set of figures with another—the treasurer's to the auditor's, for instance, or the territory's to those of the U.S. Census—to help identify and correct this sort of problem. The need for such verification and reconciliation was compounded by the lack of consistency in reporting styles and content over time and across governments. This chore was very lengthy, and a disadvantage of the research design.

MEASURES OF REVENUES AND EXPENDITURES

The data collection effort for this study produced a number of fiscal ratios. Years covered for the various F ratios varied according to availability of data. All of the state data series calculated for this study are missing observations for some years. For years in which property values were unavailable, so that an F ratio could not be calculated, the numcrator value generally was not calculated, either. Following is a list of the versions of revenues and expenditures I calculated.

Measures of Revenues

Six versions of annual receipts were recorded, as described below. These measures are highly correlated with each other in the cases of New Mexico and Arizona; in Nevada, some are highly correlated.

1. *Revenue A.* Own-source state or territorial receipts, that is, excluding federal transfers.[3] When identifiablc, interfund transfers and receipts from the sale of bonds were excluded as well.
2. *Revenue B.* Own-source receipts as calculated for Revenue A plus those federal transfers recorded by the territorial or state government as well as those recorded only in *Receipts and Expenditures*.[4]
3. *Revenue Aa or Bb.* Own-source revenues as calculated for Revenue A, plus some but not all of the federal subsidies.
4. *Revenue C.* Annual receipts as collected by Sylla, Legler, and Wallis.[5] New Mexico data are provided for 1913–1916; Arizona for 1911–1916; Nevada for 1867–1917. Because of the short time periods covered for the subject states, the Sylla et al. data on revenues and expenditures were not used for the analysis of F in the present study. However, the Sylla et al. data did prove useful in checking the reasonableness of the data calculated for this study. In all three states, if interfund transfers and bond activity were not separately reported by the state officials, the Sylla team did not re-calculate revenues to exclude them.
5. *Revenue D.* Annual revenue receipts less federal transfers as calculated from U.S. Census records.[6] The Census collected these revenue data from the states and territories in 1903, in 1912/13, and annually beginning in 1915, with the exception of 1920 and 1921. Because the Census

made only two observations from the New Mexico and Arizona territorial periods, these data were not used for the main analysis in the present study. However, they are useful in making alternative versions of F for limited comparison with the main analysis described above.

6. *Revenue E.* Annual revenue receipts including federal transfers, as recorded by the U.S. Census.[7] This series is the same as Revenue D above, except that federal subventions and grants are not subtracted from the revenue receipts figure given by the Census.

Measures of Expenditures

Four versions of annual expenditures were recorded, as described below.

1. *Expenditures A.* Warrants issued. Expenditures A was calculated for New Mexico, 1891–1930, and Arizona, 1883–1930. Where identifiable, interfund transfers, loan repayments, investment bond purchases, and redemptions of bonds and certificates of indebtedness were deducted from the total.

2. *Expenditures B.* Warrants paid.

3. *Expenditures C.* Annual expenditures as calculated by Sylla, Legler, and Wallis.[8] New Mexico data are provided for 1913–1916; Arizona for 1911–1916; Nevada for 1867–1917. Because of the short time periods covered for the subject states, the Sylla et al. data on revenues and expenditures were not used for the analysis of F in the present study.

4. *Expenditures D.* "Governmental cost payments," as recorded by the U.S. Census.[9] According to the definitions of governmental and nongovernmental cost payments provided by the Census,[10] governmental cost payments conform most closely to the expenditure totals of interest in this study. Non-governmental payments include, for instance, interfund transfers, debt redemption, and investment purchases.[11]

The Census collected these expenditures data from the states and territories in 1903, in 1912/13, and annually beginning in 1915, with the exceptions of 1920 and 1921. Because the Census made only two observations from the New Mexico and Arizona territorial periods, these data were not used for the main analysis in the present study. However, they are useful in making alternative versions of F for limited comparison with the main analysis described above.

REGRESSION ANALYSES

Regression analysis supports the graphical results. A regression of F-RevA on SOVEREIGNTY finds that the status of the government explains over 90 percent of the fiscal variation in New Mexico and 58 percent in Arizona. Regressing F-RevA on a linear trend found that F-RevA rose modestly over time in New Mexico and declined slightly in Arizona, changes that were overwhelmed by the effect of SOVEREIGNTY. Neither SOVEREIGNTY nor the time trend had significant effects on F-RevA in the control state, Nevada.

The residuals from the Nevada equation, introduced to control for regional economic trends, had no explanatory power. SOVEREIGNTY explains over 90 percent of the variation in F-GNP for New Mexico and Arizona, but none for Nevada. In all of the New Mexico and Arizona equations, SOVEREIGNTY is highly statistically significant.

Note that the equation for Nevada using SOVEREIGNTY includes a first-order moving average variable, MA(1). The data series used for this study probably contain some degree of autocorrelation, as often occurs in time series.[12] The appropriate corrections have been made to the models. Adding an autoregressive term, AR(1), to the New Mexico and Arizona equations and a moving average term to the Nevada equation corrected for the autocorrelation problem; the Durbin-Watson statistics fall within the relevant ranges in each case.[13] However, the equations that include SOVEREIGNTY offer a much better fit—a higher R^2 and better statistical significance—for the observed behavior of F-RevA in New Mexico and Arizona than do the extremely simple models. The model including SOVEREIGNTY does not do a better job for Nevada.

Finally, F-RevA in New Mexico and Arizona was regressed on all the explanatory variables together, to see if, jointly, they produced equations that fit the data better. They did not. SOVEREIGNTY remained a significant term, as it is in every regression run for this study. But neither YEAR nor the Nevada residual variable had a statistically significant effect on the behavior of F-RevA in either state. The joint model for New Mexico explains about 94 percent of the F-RevA variance; the Arizona joint model explains 68 percent.

TIME PERIOD

One of the uncertainties explored in this study was the timing of the presumed increase in the government's relative cost. By hypothesis, any increase would be caused by the statehood-associated increase in the government's degree of sovereignty. However, I thought the increase might occur years before or after the date of formal statehood. The timing might be determined by when a popular majority approved of becoming a state, in which case the jump in the fiscal bite could precede statehood by years. Alternatively, it might take some years after the formal change in status for the government to exercise its new powers fully and behave as Leviathan.

Table A.1.   Determinants of Relative Fiscal Size in New Mexico, Arizona, and Nevada

Independent Variables	Dependent Variables		
	NM F-RevA	AZ F-RevA	NV F-RevA
SOVERFICNIY	.002918	.002249	−.000800
	(.0000)	(.0022)	(.3666)
YEAR	7.52E-05	−8.71E-05	.000152
	(.1518)	(.1788)	(.2635)
NV RESIDUAL	.001350	−.000749	
	(.2111)	(.5856)	
C	−.140153	.169932	−.284008
	(.1608)	(.1701)	(.2726)
AR(1)		−.232394	.568023
		(.4636)	(.0686)
R^2	.941604	.679283	.258869
N	17	16	17

Sources: See tables A.2, A.3, and A.4.

Note: P-values in parentheses. SOVEREIGNTY = 0 for 1903–1912; = 1 for 1913-1919. F-RevA = own-source revenues as a share of total property values. F-RevA observations interpolated for 1910 in New Mexico; for 1905, 1906, 1909, 1910 in Arizona; for 1903, 1904, 1906 in Nevada. NV-RESIDUAL = residual series taken from model regressing log of NV F-RevA on first-order moving average.

The study results answer the question of timing, at least for New Mexico and Arizona. The Leviathan jump in fiscal size occurred immediately after formal statehood—not before and not years afterwards.

The relevant time span was identified by graphing the behavior of F over the longest period for which data were calculated. The longer time series for F-RevA, the main variable analyzed in this study, is graphed for all three states in figure A.1.

Figure A.1 shows some of the dramatic growth in government of the 1920s, partly due to the "Good Roads" movement.[14] The effect of road-building actually began in the very early 1920s. That rise is evident in figure A.1 but is far more dramatic in the revenue series that include federal subsidies, Revenue B and E. This is because the national government poured enormous amounts of money into road building in the states in the second and third decades of the twentieth century. But the 1913–1914 bump in revenues for New Mexico and Arizona, which occurred before the Good Roads phenomenon in those states, was a clear change from the pattern of territorial days. This was the hypothesized effect of a change in sovereignty.

Thus, the period chosen for analysis eliminated the Good Roads story after 1919, and went back before statehood for a roughly commensurate number of years. Note that New Mexico and Arizona never returned to the small fiscal size of territorial days. Also note that figure A.1 illustrates once more that Nevada's fiscal pattern was quite different from that of the subject states.

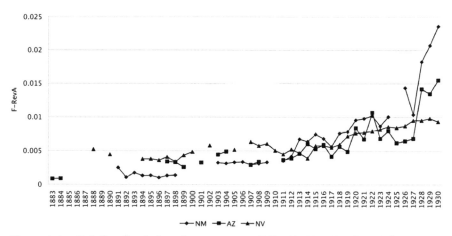

Figure A.1. Relative fiscal size of government (F-RevA), New Mexico, Arizona, Nevada, 1883–1930.

ALTERNATIVE MEASURES OF THE DEPENDENT VARIABLE: F-GNP

Annual data on the U.S. gross national product are available for the study period, 1903–1919. Variations in GNP might well explain part of the fiscal behavior of sub-national governments, including New Mexico and Arizona. However, the correlation between GNP and YEAR for this period is 0.88, so it is futile to use both of them as independent variables. Instead, a second measure of F was created, F-GNP. This is the ratio of own-source monies collected by the territory or state to the national GNP.

The correlation between the two F-GNP series for New Mexico and Arizona is 93 percent. These regression analyses are quite similar to the regressions for F-RevA. An autocorrelation problem exists that was corrected by a combination of autoregression and moving average terms. SOVEREIGNTY is a statistically significant explanatory variable in every equation for New Mexico and Arizona, but not for Nevada. The amount of New Mexico's F-GNP variance explained by SOVEREIGNTY alone is similar to the amount of F-RevA variance explained by SOVEREIGNTY alone—that is, the degree of sovereignty explains almost all the fiscal variance. For Arizona, however, SOVEREIGNTY alone explains a lot more of the F-GNP than it does of the F-RevA variance (92 percent vs. 58 percent). YEAR, which has a modest but statistically significant effect on F-RevA in the subject states, has no significant effect on F-GNP. The Nevada residual term affects New Mexico F-GNP significantly, though it does not improve the R^2 for the model. Recall that the Nevada residual has no significant effect on the F-RevA variable for either of the subject states.

DATA SERIES

Table A.2. Data Series for New Mexico's Fiscal Ratios, 1890–1930

Year	NM RevA	NM RevB	NM ExpA	NM ExpB	NM PrValA	NM F-RevA	NM F-GNP
1890					$216,138,430		
1891	$383,410	$416,410	$265,910	$393,061	153,456,325	0.00250	0.000028
1892	222,432	242,399	246,319	300,800	208,010,990	0.00107	0.000016
1893	359,977	377,977	206,061		207,874,225	0.00173	0.000026
1894	255,814	301,951	203,501		195,452,510	0.00131	0.000020
1895	274,057	329,157		310,150	205,704,015	0.00133	0.000020
1896	188,479	239,576		266,799	184,455,510	0.00102	0.000014
1897	259,908	338,849	206,580	303,998	197,390,595	0.00132	0.000018
1898	264,505	327,906	250,874	385,636	194,040,205	0.00136	0.000017
1899							
1900							
1901							
1902					193,169,965		
1903	635,842	717,560		535,831	197,984,760	0.00321	0.000028
1904	663,812	696,237		585,871	213,325,000	0.00311	0.000029
1905	656,744	721,604			200,543,020	0.00327	0.000026
1906	720,514	770,861			216,228,730	0.00333	0.000025
1907	709,353	798,729	663,619		242,545,485	0.00292	0.000023
1908	809,304	870,485	838,671		262,631,475	0.00308	0.000029
1909	977,394	1,107,925	955,712		297,321,555	0.00329	0.000029
1910							
1911	831,285	955,387	887,266		236,995,523	0.00351	0.000023
1912	900,303	1,029,265	1,174,101		217,372,362	0.00414	0.000023
1913	1,695,133	1,834,072	1,808,840		252,259,554	0.00672	0.000043
1914	1,724,552	1,813,778			271,902,119	0.00634	0.000045
1915	2,272,604	2,359,268	2,213,545		305,710,502	0.00743	0.000057
1916	2,241,271	2,329,937	2,070,644		330,387,523	0.00678	0.000046
1917	2,461,254	2,590,113	2,319,831	2,275,915	439,826,517	0.00560	0.000041
1918	3,617,267	3,738,420	3,384,412	3,380,859	476,083,345	0.00760	0.000047
1919	3,875,146	4,076,573	4,069,729	3,973,498	495,412,841	0.00782	0.000046
1920	5,136,263	5,687,029	4,957,454	5,046,060	537,395,536	0.00956	0.000056
1921	4,739,255	6,665,810	6,283,236	6,268,960	484,653,483	0.00978	0.000068
1922	5,025,139	7,034,078	6,097,650	6,126,624	492,385,833	0.01021	0.000068
1923	4,051,297	5,681,242	5,632,445	5,816,522	468,910,613	0.00864	0.000048
1924	4,603,681	6,688,337	7,137,834	7,031,153	458,751,118	0.01004	0.000054
1925					412,318,969	0.00000	
1926	5,948,187	7,341,832	6,292,793	6,266,378	414,929,703	0.01434	0.000061
1927	5,440,048	7,077,730	7,818,732	7,887,787	525,622,342	0.01035	0.000057
1928	9,612,781	11,149,534	10,826,078	10,553,737	527,447,612	0.01823	0.000099
1929	10,759,885	13,024,463	11,829,421		520,351,132	0.02068	0.000104
1930	13,536,989	14,638,522	14,642,935		574,452,020	0.02357	0.000150

Sources: Series calculations are based on data in the following sources (state sources are cited under "New Mexico" in bibliography): New Mexico Special Revenue Commission, Report, 1920; the annual or biennial reports of the state comptroller, the state tax commission, and the territorial and state auditors, traveling auditors, and treasurers; annual editions of Receipts and Expenditures, U.S. Congress, House; annual editions of Financial Statistics of States, U.S. Bureau of the Census; U.S. Bureau of the Census, Wealth, Debt, and Taxation, 1907, 1913; GNP from U.S. Bureau of the Census, Historical Statistics, part 1, series F 1.

Note: RevA = own-source revenues. RevB = own-source revenues plus federal expenditures. ExpA = warrants issued. ExpB = warrants paid. PrValA = total assessed property values adjusted to estimated true value. F-RevA = RevA / PrValA. F-GNP = RevA / U.S. GNP.

Table A.3. Data Series for Arizona's Fiscal Ratios, 1883–1930

Year	AZ RevA	AZ RevB	AZ ExpA	AZ ExpB	AZ PrValC	AZ F-RevA	AZ F-GNP
1883	$75,569		$138,942		$90,252,442	0.00084	
1884	75,569		121,589		86,365,046	0.00087	
1885							
1886							
1887			174,267		74,781,446		
1888			152,709		74,037,186		
1889							
1890							
1891			221,695		80,772,761		
1892			193,576		79,780,464		
1893					81,389,093		
1894					77,319,928		
1895				$286,333			
1896				305,303			
1897	297,560	$369,788	191,645	293,635	87,694,883	0.00339	0.000020
1898	297,560	348,207	152,687	364,968	89,924,400	0.00331	0.000019
1899	240,209	289,951	130,702	437,826	92,884,344	0.00259	0.000014
1900			270,665	397,504	96,521,331		
1901	359,468	385,318	222,765	344,937	111,010,947	0.00324	0.000017
1902			305,756	480,162	111,666,222		
1903	543,784	629,636	340,910	526,738	123,108,687	0.00442	0.000024
1904	627,270	679,108	362,386	630,629	128,798,375	0.00487	0.000027
1905					165,486,780		
1906					179,848,464		
1907	644,446	746,214	598,367	601,569	221,063,303	0.00292	0.000021
1908	775,520	870,460	739,455	737,668	230,392,976	0.00337	0.000028
1909					236,240,179		
1910					246,074,932		
1911	1,014,030	1,146,771	1,105,705		280,093,453	0.00362	0.000028
1912	1,086,964	1,224,226	1,324,922	1,300,858	280,676,382	0.00387	0.000028
1913	1,719,280	1,850,727	1,599,382	1,681,740	375,862,414	0.00457	0.000043
1914	2,453,736	2,584,104	2,404,190	2,543,356	408,540,283	0.00601	0.000064
1915	2,232,641	2,363,705	2,815,269	2,690,038	422,102,389	0.00529	0.000056
1916	2,879,952	3,056,516	2,618,821	3,068,565	488,226,371	0.00590	0.000060
1917	2,900,643	3,207,048	3,200,857	3,166,927	699,245,000	0.00415	0.000048
1918	4,700,428	4,886,647	4,249,287	4,249,287	835,916,000	0.00562	0.000062
1919	4,170,999	4,368,024	5,611,141	4,852,815	856,791,000	0.00487	0.000050
1920	7,413,324	7,865,520		6,517,684	884,455,682	0.00838	0.000081
1921	5,579,980	6,611,458		7,875,011	830,536,582	0.00672	0.000080
1922	7,824,203	9,389,229		7,964,822	733,995,000	0.01066	0.000106
1923	4,998,247	6,448,292	6,344,479		733,994,556	0.00681	0.000059
1924	5,551,790	6,719,270	5,983,117		699,142,997	0.00794	0.000066
1925	4,015,731	4,976,346	5,720,181		652,444,309	0.00615	0.000043
1926	4,210,390	4,917,774	4,802,350		653,163,397	0.00645	0.000043
1927	4,585,730	5,406,065	4,970,211		673,127,177	0.00681	0.000048
1928	9,652,206	9,918,936	9,172,136		681,736,018	0.01416	0.000100
1929	9,426,471	10,761,839	11,640,466		700,890,801	0.01345	0.000091
1930	11,054,860	13,611,598	12,199,008		714,945,809	0.01546	0.000122

Sources: Series calculations are based on data in the following sources (state sources are cited under "Arizona" in bibliography): the annual or biennial reports of the territorial board of equalization, the state tax commission, and the territorial and state auditors and treasurers; annual editions of *Receipts and Expenditures*, U.S. Congress, House; annual editions of *Financial Statistics of States*, U.S. Bureau of the Census; U.S. Bureau of the Census, *Wealth, Debt, and Taxation*, 1907, 1913; GNP from U.S. Bureau of the Census, *Historical Statistics*, part 1, series F 1.

Note: RevA = own-source revenues. RevB = own-source revenues plus federal expenditures. ExpA = warrants issued. ExpB = warrants paid. PrValC = total assessed property values adjusted to estimated true value. F-RevA = RevA / PrValC. F-GNP = RevA / U.S. GNP. For details of variables, see "Revenues, Expenditures, and Property Values," chap. 5.

Table A.4. Data Series for Nevada's Fiscal Ratios, 1880–1930

Year	NV RevA	NV RevB	NV ExpB	NV PrValAb	NV F-RevA	NV F-GNP
1880		$303,118	$295,859	$73,493,386		
1881		381,471	448,993	73,460,468		
1882		413,156	330,560	70,163,893		
1883		385,769	382,844	71,038,840		
1884		378,329	256,630	67,946,934		
1885		391,789	342,881	67,097,559		
1886		397,850	254,726	74,122,568		
1887		405,446	383,822	77,100,580		
1888	$408,812	441,200	269,096	78,504,660	0.00521	
1889				77,370,297		
1890	316,516	321,614	339,995	71,153,523	0.00445	0.000024
1891		355,162	402,141	85,927,304		
1892		387,070	321,662	89,068,904		
1893		376,723	372,164	74,951,974		
1894	357,950	361,794	330,507	94,696,177	0.00378	0.000028
1895	358,199	361,991	398,775	94,390,629	0.00379	0.000026
1896	334,077	337,942		92,776,871	0.00360	0.000025
1897	378,561	382,361	402,376	92,641,840	0.00409	0.000026
1898	311,213	315,103	338,462	93,078,879	0.00334	0.000020
1899	408,170	414,682	328,428	94,392,085	0.00432	0.000023
1900	468,348	481,469	404,263	96,829,328	0.00484	0.000025
1901		472,577	422,073	80,571,009		
1902	485,915	492,347	374,756	84,291,472	0.00576	0.000022
1903			353,757	93,904,116		
1904				104,554,593		
1905	619,300	633,399	544,096	120,580,586	0.00514	0.000025
1906						
1907	955,599	968,256	665,319	151,534,329	0.00631	0.000031
1908	958,510	967,613	800,464	167,278,870	0.00573	0.000035
1909	1,025,321	1,034,540	1,059,491	169,841,492	0.00604	0.000031
1910	919,804	943,557		183,440,848	0.00501	0.000026
1911	891,403	905,882	1,003,995	199,483,299	0.00447	0.000025
1912	1,006,888	1,020,432	990,086	193,441,301	0.00521	0.000026
1913	1,022,564	1,037,016	986,661	220,005,194	0.00465	0.000026
1914	871,038	871,038	1,044,820	225,220,719	0.00387	0.000023
1915	1,311,329	1,329,037	1,195,442	228,536,437	0.00574	0.000033
1916	1,395,798	1,415,574	1,120,393	242,875,651	0.00575	0.000029
1917	1,398,962	1,427,305	1,338,556	254,812,922	0.00549	0.000023
1918	1,655,929	1,686,317	1,320,442	278,950,945	0.00594	0.000022
1919	2,008,272	2,040,413	2,032,503	280,432,250	0.00716	0.000024
1920	2,480,216	2,996,514	3,447,337	325,876,022	0.00761	0.000027
1921	2,408,244	2,896,305	3,037,741	311,955,216	0.00772	0.000035
1922	2,407,913	3,209,285	3,210,169	304,086,308	0.00792	0.000032
1923	2,685,673	4,164,786	4,137,289	329,180,021	0.00816	0.000032
1924	2,858,578	5,051,915	4,863,945	333,383,696	0.00857	0.000034
1925	2,775,400	4,562,308	4,690,329	329,744,802	0.00842	0.000030
1926	2,914,518	3,944,679	4,015,710	335,755,419	0.00868	0.000030
1927	3,186,644	4,234,604	3,799,829	335,398,346	0.00950	0.000034
1928	3,198,042	4,285,722	4,043,089	336,886,363	0.00949	0.000033
1929	3,465,544	5,337,809	4,615,371	353,531,148	0.00980	0.000034
1930	3,187,083	4,301,056	4,322,506	342,514,238	0.00930	0.000035

Sources: Series calculations are based on data in the following sources (state sources are cited under "Nevada" in bibliography): the annual or biennial reports of the state controller and the state tax commission; annual editions of *Receipts and Expenditures*, U.S. Congress, House; annual editions of *Financial Statistics of States*, U.S. Bureau of the Census; U.S. Bureau of the Census, Wealth, Debt, and Taxation, 1907, 1913; GNP from U.S. Bureau of the Census, *Historical Statistics*, part 1, series F 1.

Note: RevA = own-source revenues. RevB = own-source revenues plus federal expenditures. ExpB = warrants paid. PrValAb = total assessed property values adjusted to estimated true value. F-RevA = RevA / PrValAb. F-GNP = RevA / U.S. GNP. For details of variables, see "Revenues, Expenditures, and Property Values," chap. 5.

NOTES

1. Generally speaking, the two measures differ by debt issued to finance long-lived projects, such as roads and canals. For instance, expenditures on such projects will be made with borrowed funds, while the receipts from issuing the related debt will not be included in the revenue variable.

2. Although the Bureau of the Census did not believe, in the early twentieth century, that this source of error materially affected "the total for the nation or for the state." (U.S. Bureau of the Census, *Wealth, Debt, and Taxation*, *Special Reports*, 6.) See also discussion of the census method for estimating the true value of real property in the same source, 8–11.

3. Revenue A calculations are based on information in the following sources (listed in the bibliography under the state names): For New Mexico, the annual or biennial reports of the territorial and state auditors, traveling auditors, and treasurers, and the state comptroller; for Arizona, the annual or biennial reports of the territorial and state auditors and treasurers; for Nevada, the annual reports of the state controller. Also consulted for the Nevada calculations were the annual editions of *Receipts and Expenditures* published by the U.S. Congress, House.

4. Revenue B calculations for all states were based in part on U.S. Congress, House, *Receipts and Expenditures*. Specific sources for each state are the same territorial and state reports listed in the footnote for Revenue A above.

5. Sylla, Legler, and Wallis, *Sources and Uses of Funds in State and Local Governments*. The Inter-university Consortium for Political and Social Research has stored these data in a downloadable database.

6. Revenue D, calculated by subtracting "subventions and grants" from "revenue receipts," is based on the following: Revenue receipts for 1903 and 1912/13, in U.S. Bureau of the Census, *Wealth, Debt, and Taxation 1913*, vol. 2, pt. 6, table 13; revenue receipts for 1915–1919, 1922–1930, in U.S. Bureau of the Census, *Financial Statistics of States, 1915–1919, 1922–1931*, table 2; subventions and grants for 1903 and 1912/13, in U.S. Bureau of the Census, *Wealth, Debt, and Taxation 1913*, vol. 2, pt. 6, tables 6 and 7; subventions and grants for 1915–1919 and 1922–1930, in U.S. Bureau of the Census, *Financial Statistics of States, 1915–1919, 1922–1931*, table 3 and, depending on the year, table 7 or 8.

7. Revenue receipts for 1903 and 1912/13, in U.S. Bureau of the Census, *Wealth, Debt, and Taxation 1913*, vol. 2, pt. 6, table 13; revenue receipts for 1915–1919, 1922–1930, in U.S. Bureau of the Census, *Financial Statistics of States, 1915–1919, 1922–1931*, table 2.

8. Sylla, Legler, and Wallis, *Sources and Uses of Funds in State and Local Governments*. The Inter-university Consortium for Political and Social Research has stored these data in a downloadable database.

9. Expenditures D figures are "governmental cost payments" as recorded by the U.S. Bureau of the Census in the following sources: for 1903 and 1912/13, in *Wealth, Debt, and Taxation 1913*, vol. 2, pt. 6, table 13; for 1915–1919, 1922–1930, in *Financial Statistics of States, 1915–1919, 1922–1931*, table 2.

10. U.S. Bureau of the Census, *Wealth, Debt, and Taxation 1913*, vol. 2, pt. 6, p. 19.

11. U.S. Bureau of the Census, *Wealth, Debt, and Taxation 1913*, vol. 2, pt. 6, table 15.

12. When F-RevA is regressed on year and the constant term c alone, the Durbin-Watson statistic approaches 1 in all three states (1.05 in New Mexico, 1.08 in Arizona, and 1.04 in Nevada). According to Gujarati, such values in these equations indicate that autocorrelation may exist (*Basic Econometrics*, 422–423, 818–822).

13. Gujarati, *Basic Econometrics*, 422–423, 818–822.

14. Higgens-Evenson, *Price of Progress*, chap. 4.

Bibliography

Aaron, H. "Some Observations on Property Tax Valuation and the Significance of Full Value Assessment." In *The Property Tax and Its Administration*, edited by A. D. Lynn, Jr. 153–166. Madison, WI: University of Wisconsin Press, 1969.

Adams, Romanzo. "Essentials to Orderly Progress in Tax Reform." *Bulletin of the National Tax Association* 6, no. 2 (November 1920): 42–43.

Alexander, Thomas G. "The Federal Land Survey System and the Mountain West, 1870–1896." In *The American Territorial System*, edited by John P. Bloom, 145–160. Athens, OH: Ohio University Press, 1973.

Allen, W. H. "The Budget as an Instrument of Financial Control." *Government Accountant* 2, no. 5 (1908): 192–200.

American Institute of Certified Public Accountants. *Local Governmental Accounting Trends & Techniques*. New York: American Institute of Certified Public Accountants, 1988–1991.

Anderson, Gary M., William F. Shughart II, and Robert D. Tollison. "Adam Smith in the Customhouse." *Journal of Political Economy* 93, no. 4 (1985): 740–759.

"Arizona Budgetary Reform." *The Bulletin of the National Tax Association* 7, no. 9 (June, 1922): 275–276.

Arizona. Auditor. . . . *Report of the State Auditor . . . for the Fiscal Year . . .* [title varies].

———. State Tax Commission. *Biennial Report of the State Tax Commission of Arizona, to the Governor of the State of Arizona* [various dates].

———. Treasurer. *Report of the State Treasurer for the Year Beginning . . . and Ending . . .* [title varies].

Arizona (Territory). Auditor. *Report of the Territorial Auditor . . . for the Fiscal Year . . .* [title varies].

———. Territorial Board of Equalization. *Proceedings of the Territorial Board of Equalization of Arizona* [irregular; title varies; sometimes contained in Auditor's report].

———. Treasurer. *Report of the Treasurer of the Territory of Arizona for the Period Beginning . . . and Ending . . .* [title varies].

Bain, Roger M. "Two Early American Treatises on Municipal Accounting." *The Canadian Chartered Accountant* 84, no. 2 (February, 1964): 130–134.

Baker, M. N. "Uniform Municipal Accounting." *Proceedings of the Milwaukee Conference for Good City Government and Sixth Annual Meeting of the National Municipal League held September 19, 20, 21, 1900 at Milwaukee, Wis.* Ed. Clinton Rogers Woodruff. Philadelphia: National Municipal League, 1900: 239–242.

Bakken, Gordon M. "Rocky Mountain Constitution Making, 1850–1912." In vol. 35, *Contributions in Legal Studies*, edited by Paul L. Murphy. New York: Greenwood Press, 1987.

Ball, Larry D. *Desert Lawmen: The High Sheriffs of New Mexico and Arizona, 1846–1912.* Albuquerque: University of New Mexico, 1992.

Benson, George C. S. *The American Property Tax: Its History, Administration, and Economic Impact.* Claremont, CA: Institute for Studies in Federalism, Lincoln School of Public Finance, 1965.

Blackmon, F. W. "The Basis of Assessment in Taxation." In *State and Local Taxation: First National Conference under the Auspices of the National Tax Association, Columbus, Ohio, November 12–15, 1907*, New York: MacMillan, 1908: 434–435.

Blandin, E. J. "Municipal Government of Cleveland." *Proceedings of the Second National Conference for Good City Government held at Minneapolis, December 8 and 10, 1894 and of the First Annual Meeting of the National Municipal League and of the Third National Conference for Good City Government held at Cleveland, May 29, 30 and 31, 1895.* Philadelphia: National Municipal League, 1895, 112–118.

Brackenborough, Susie. "Pound Foolish Penny Wise System: The Role of Accounting in the Improvement of the River Tyne, 1800–1850." *Accounting Historians Journal* 30, no. 1 (June 2003): 45–72.

Braeman, J. "Albert J. Beveridge and Statehood for the Southwest, 1902–1912." *Arizona and the West* 10, no. 4 (1968): 313–342.

Brennan, Geoffrey, and James M. Buchanan. *The Power to Tax: Analytical Foundations of a Fiscal Constitution. The Collected Works of James M. Buchanan*, vol. 9. Indianapolis: Liberty Fund, 2000. First published in 1980.

Brewer, John. *The Sinews of Power: War, Money and the English State, 1688–1783.* New York: Alfred A. Knopf, 1989.

Briffault, Richard. "Federalism." In *Oxford Companion to American Law*, edited by Kermit L. Hall, 299–303. Oxford: Oxford University Press, 2002.

Brownlee, W. Elliot. *Federal Taxation in America: A Short History*, 2nd ed. Cambridge, UK: Cambridge University Press, 2004.

Bulletin of the National Tax Association 4, no. 8 (May, 1919). Untitled article, 200.

Chan, James L. "Decisions and Informantion [*sic*] Needs of Voters, Taxpayers and Service Recipients." In *Objectives of Accounting and Financial Reporting for Governmental Units: A Research Study*, vol. 2, edited by Allan R. Drebin, James L. Chan, and Lorna C. Ferguson, 4.1–4.23. Chicago: National Council on Governmental Accounting, 1981.

Chase, Harvey S. "A Brief History of the Movement towards Uniform Municipal Reports and Accounts in the United States." *The Accountant* 31, new ser. No. 1558 (October 15, 1904): 394–399.

Cleveland, Frederick A. "Chicago's Accounting Reform." Paper presented at the Ninth Annual Conference of the National Municipal League, Detroit, Michigan, 1903. Reprinted in F. A. Cleveland, *Chapters on Municipal Administration and Accounting*. New York: Longmans, Green, 1909, 219–243.

———. "The Need for Coordinating Municipal, State and National Activities." In "Efficiency in City Government," special issue, *Annals of the American Academy of Political and Social Science* 41 (May, 1912): 23–39.

———. "Revenues and Expenses as Distinguished from Receipts and Disbursements in Municipal Accounting." *Official Record of the Proceedings of the Congress of Accountants held at the World's Fair, Saint Louis*. New York: George Wilkinson, 1904: 60–70.

Clow, Frederick R. "Suggestions for the Study of Municipal Finance." *Quarterly Journal of Economics* 10, no. 4 (July, 1896): 455–466.

Colquhoun, Philip. "The State." In *The Routledge Companion to Accounting History*, edited by John Richard Edwards & Stephen P. Walker, chapter 26. Oxford, U.K.: Routledge, 2009.

Coombs, Hugh Malcolm, and John Richard Edwards. "Record Keeping in Municipal Corporations: A Triumph for Double Entry Bookkeeping." *Accounting, Business and Financial History* 4, no. 1 (1994): 163–180.

Coopers & Lybrand. *Statistical Supplement to Financial Disclosure Practices of the American Cities*. Coopers & Lybrand, 1976.

Cornwall, S. (ed.) *Local Governmental Accounting Trends & Techniques*. New York: American Institute of Certified Public Accountants, 1988.

Crosby, A. F. "Financial Control over Municipal Receipts and Expenditures." *Proceedings of the Columbus Conference for Good City Government and Fifth Annual Meeting of the National Municipal League held November 16, 17, 18, 1899*. Ed. Clinton Rogers Woodruff. Philadelphia: National Municipal League, 1899: 148–154.

Cullis, John G., and Philip R. Jones. *Microeconomics and the Public Economy: A Defence of Leviathan.* Oxford, U.K.: Basil Blackwell, 1987.

Cushing, B. E. "A Kuhnian Interpretation of the Historical Evolution of Accounting." *The Accounting Historians Journal* 16, no. 2 (1989): 1–41.

Cuzán, Alfred G., and Charles M. Bundrick. "Fiscal Policy and Presidential Elections, 1880–1992." *Polity* 29, no. 1 (Fall 1996): 14–156.

Cuzán, Alfred G., and Richard J. Heggen. "Expenditures and Votes: In Search of Downward–Sloping Curves in the United States and Great Britain." *Public Choice* 45 (1985): 19–34.

Dargan, Marion. "New Mexico's Fight for Statehood, 1895–1912." *New Mexico Historical Review* 14 (1939): 1–33.

Daunton, Martin. *Trusting Leviathan: The Politics of Taxation in Britain, 1799–1914.* Cambridge: Cambridge University, 2001.

Doron, Michael E. "The American Institute of Accountants and the Professionalization of Auditing: The Campaign to End Temporary Audit Staff and Promote the

Natural Business Year, 1923–1960." Presented at annual meeting of the American Accounting Association, August 11, 2011, Denver, CO.

Dworak, Robert J. *Taxpayers, Taxes, and Government Spending: Perspectives on the Taxpayer Revolt*. New York: Praeger, 1980.

Dye, Victoria E. *All Aboard for Santa Fe Railway: Railway Promotion of the Southwest 1890s to 1930s*. Albuquerque: University of New Mexico Press, 2005.

Eblen, Jack E. *The First and Second United States Empires*. Pittsburgh: University of Pittsburgh Press, 1968.

Edwards, J. R., ed. *The History of Accounting: Critical Perspectives on Business and Management*. 4 vols. London: Routledge, 2000.

Elazar, Daniel J. "Federalism: Theory." In *Encyclopedia of the American Constitution*, edited by Leonard W. Levy, Kenneth L. Karst, and Dennis J. Mahoney, 704–708. New York: Macmillan, 1986.

Ernst & Whinney. *How Cities Can Improve Their Financial Reporting, Based on a Study of 100 Annual Reports*. Ernst & Whinney, 1979.

Ethridge, M. E. *The Case for Gridlock: Democracy, Organized Power, and the Legal Foundations of American Government*. Boulder, CO: Lexington Books, 2010.

Ezzamel, Mahmoud. "Accounting Working for the State: Tax Assessment and Collection during the New Kingdom, Ancient Egypt." *Accounting and Business Research* 32, no. 1 (2002): 17–39.

Fazio, Steven A. "Marcus Aurelius Smith: Arizona Delegate and Senator." *Arizona and the West* 12, no. 1 (Spring 1985): 73–98.

Fehrenbach, T. R. *Lone Star: A History of Texas and the Texans*. New York: Macmillan, 1968.

Figlewicz, Raymond E., Donald T. Anderson, and C. David Strupeck. "The Evolution and Current State of Financial Accounting Concepts and Standards in the Nonbusiness Sector." *Accounting Historians Journal* 12, no. 1 (Spring, 1985): 73–98.

Fisher, Glenn W. *The Worst Tax? A History of the Property Tax in America*. Lawrence, KS: University Press of Kansas, 1996.

Fleischman, Richard K., and R. Penny Marquette. "Municipal Accounting Reform c. 1900: Ohio's Progressive Accountants." *Accounting Historians Journal* 14, no. 1 (Spring, 1987): 83–94.

———. "Chapters in Ohio Progressivism: The Cincinnati and Dayton Bureaus of Municipal Research and Accounting Reform." *Ohio History* 97 (Summer–Autumn, 1988): 133–144.

Fletcher, F. N. "Budget and State Taxes in Nevada." *Bulletin of the National Tax Association* 7, no. 4 (January 1922): 113–115.

Florida Territorial Legislative Council. "Report of a Minority of a Select Committee of the House of Representatives." *Legislative Council Journal*. 10th sess., February 4, 1840, 358–359.

Folmar, Richard H. *Piecemeal Amendment of the Constitution of New Mexico, 1911 to 2006*, 17th rev. Santa Fe: New Mexico Legislative Council Service, 2007.

Forrester, David A. R. *Aspects of French Accounting*. Working Paper No. 64, Academy of Accounting Historians, 1985.

Fowler, James H., II. "Constitutions and Conditions Contrasted: Arizona and New Mexico, 1910. *Journal of the West* 13, no. 4 (October, 1971): 51–58.

Giroux, Gary, and Andrew J. McLelland. "Governance Structures and Accounting at Large Municipalities." *Journal of Accounting and Public Policy* 22, no. 3 (2003): 203–230.

Governmental Accounting Standards Board. *Codification of Governmental Accounting and Financial Reporting Standards.* Stamford, CT: Governmental Accounting Standards Board, 2008.

———. "Concepts Statement No. 1 of the Governmental Accounting Standards Board: Objectives of Financial Reporting." *Governmental Accounting Standards Series*, no. 037. Financial Accounting Foundation, May, 1987.

———. "GASB and the User Community." Available at http://www.gasb.org/jsp/ GASB/Page/GASBSectionPage&cid=1176156741809 (accessed July 10, 2011).

———. *Statement 34: Basic Financial Statements—and Management's Discussion and Analysis—for State and Local Governments.* Norwalk, CT: Governmental Accounting Standards Board, 1999.

———. *Why Governmental Accounting and Financial Reporting Is—and Should Be—Different.* Norwalk, CT: Governmental Accounting Standards Board, 2006. Available at http://www.gasb.org/jsp/GASB/Page/GASBSectionPage&cid= 1176156741271.

Guice, John D. W. "The Cement of Society: Law in the Mississippi Territory." *Gulf Coast Historical Review* 1 (Spring 1986): 76–99.

———. "The Role of the Territorial Supreme Courts: The Historian's View." In *The American Territorial System,* edited by John P. Bloom, 105–113. Athens, OH: Ohio University Press, 1973.

Gujarati, Damodar N. *Basic Econometrics.* 3rd ed. New York: McGraw–Hill, 1995.

Hackett, R. P. "Recent Developments in Governmental and Institutional Accounting." *Accounting Review* 8, no. 2 (June, 1933): 122–129.

Hagerman, H. J. "Foreword." *The New Mexico Tax Review* 1, no. 1 (February 1916): 1.

Harrison, Robert. "Congressional Insurgents of 1905." *Wisconsin Magazine of History* 76, no. 1 (Autumn 1992): 3–20.

Hartwell, Edward M. "The Financial Reports of Municipalities, with Special Reference to the Requirement of Uniformity." *Proceedings of the Columbus Conference for Good City Government and Fifth Annual Meeting of the National Municipal League held November 16, 17, 18, 1899.* Ed. Clinton Rogers Woodruff. Philadelphia: National Municipal League, 1899: 124–135.

———. "Report of Committee on Uniform Accounting and Statistics." In *Proceedings of the New York Conference for Good City Government and the Eleventh Annual Meeting of the National Municipal League held April 25, 26, 27 and 28, 1905, at New York.* National Municipal League, 1905: 206–234.

Haskins, Charles Waldo. "The Municipal Accounts of Chicago." In *Proceedings of the Rochester Conference for Good City Government and Seventh Annual Meeting of the National Municipal League held May 8, 9, 10, 1901 at Rochester, New York.* Philadelphia: National Municipal League, 1901: 302–314.

Hay, Leon E. "State and Local Governments (U.S., 1901–1991)." In *The History of Accounting: An International Encyclopedia*, ed. Michael Chatfield and Richard Vangermeersch. New York: Garland Publishing, 1996: 553–555.

Hayostek, Cindy. "Douglas Delegates to the 1910 Constitutional Convention and Arizona's Progressive Heritage." *Journal of Arizona History* 47, no. 4 (2006): 347–366.

Heller, William B., Philip Keefer, and Mathew D. McCubbins. "Political Structure and Economic Liberalization: Conditions and Cases from the Developing World." In *The Origins of Liberty: Political and Economic Liberalization in the Modern World*, edited by Paul W. Drake and Mathew D. McCubbins, 146–178. Princeton, NJ: Princeton University, 1998.

Henderson, H. B. "Uniform Accounting and State Examination of Public Accounts," in Woodruff, C.R. (ed.), *Proceedings of the Milwaukee Conference for Good City Government and Sixth Annual Meeting of the National Municipal League*. Ed. Clinton Rogers Woodruff. Philadelphia: NML, 247–256.

Higgens–Evenson, R. Rudy. *The Price of Progress: Public Services, Taxation, and the American Corporate State, 1877–1929*. Baltimore: Johns Hopkins University Press, 2003.

Holder, William W. *A Study of Selected Concepts for Government Financial Accounting and Reporting. NCGA Research Report*. Chicago: National Council on Governmental Accounting, 1980.

Holls, F. W. "State Boards of Municipal Control." *Proceedings of the Third [Fourth] National Conference for Good City Government and of the Second Annual Meeting of the National Municipal League held at Baltimore May 6, 7 and 8, 1896*. Philadelphia: National Municipal League, 1896: 226–235.

Holmes, William, Linda H. Kistler, and Lewis S. Corsini. *Three Centuries of Accounting in Massachusetts*. Development of Contemporary Accounting Thought. New York: Arno, 1978.

Hornung, Chuck. *Fullerton's Rangers: A History of the New Mexico Territorial Mounted Police*. Jefferson, NC: McFarland & Company, Inc., 2005.

"How States Are Admitted to the Union." *Congressional Digest* 33, no. 6–7 (June–July 1954): 164.

Ingram, Robert W., and Walter A. Robbins. *Financial Reporting Practices of Local Governments*. Stamford, CT: Governmental Accounting Standards Board of the Financial Accounting Foundation, 1987.

———. "Partial Validation of the GASB User Needs Survey: A Methodological Note." *Research in Governmental and Nonprofit Accounting: A Research Annual*, 1992.

Inman, Robert P. "Federal Assistance and Local Services in the United States: The Evolution of a New Federalist Fiscal Order." In *Fiscal Federalism: Quantitative Studies*, edited by Harvey S. Rosen. Chicago: University of Chicago, 1988.

Inman, Robert P., K. K. Raman, and Early R. Wilson. "The Information in Governmental Annual Reports: A Contemporaneous Price Reaction Approach." *Accounting Review* 64, no. 2 (April, 1989): 250–268.

James, A. E. "A Review of the Tax Levies of 1915." *New Mexico Tax Review* 1, no. 1 (February 1916): 1–10.

Jenkins, Myra Ellen, ed. *Guide to the Microfilm Edition of the Territorial Archives of New Mexico, 1846–1912.* In *The Historical Services Division of the State of New Mexico Records Center and Archives.* Territorial Archives of New Mexico, 1974.

Jones, David B., Robert B. Scott, Lisa Kimbro, and Robert W. Ingram. *The Needs of Users of Governmental Financial Reports.* Stamford, CT: Governmental Accounting Standards Board of the Financial Accounting Foundation, 1985.

Jones, Kay F. "Ana Frohmiller; Watchdog of the Arizona Treasury." *Journal of Arizona History* 25, no. 4 (1984): 349–368.

Jones, Rowan. *The History of the Financial Control Function of Local Government Accounting in the United Kingdom.* New Works in Accounting History. New York: Garland, 1992.

Key, M. David. "Progressivism and Imperialism in the American Southwest, 1880–1912." PhD diss., University of New Mexico, 2005.

Kibler, E. "The Work of the Ohio Municipal Code Commission." *Proceedings of the Columbus Conference for Good City Government and Fifth Annual Meeting of the National Municipal League held November 16, 17, 18, 1899.* Ed. Clinton Rogers Woodruff. Philadelphia: National Municipal League, 1899: 188–198.

Knauss, James Owen. "Extracts from the Times and the Floridian: Reports of Convention." Appendix 3 in *Territorial Florida Journalism.* Deland, FL: Florida Historical Society, 1926.

Kravchuk, Robert S., and William R. Voorhees. "The New Governmental Financial Reporting Model under GASB Statement No. 34: An Emphasis on Accountability." *Public Budgeting & Finance* 21, no. 3 (Fall, 2001): 1–30.

Krenkel, John H. "The Disputed Arizona Gubernatorial Election of 1916." *Journal of the West* 13, no. 4 (1974): 59–68.

Kwiatkowski, Vernon Everett. "Infrastructure Assets: An Assessment of User Needs and Recommendations for Financial Reporting." PhD diss., University of Kentucky, 1986.

Lamar, Howard R. *The Far Southwest, 1846–1912: A Territorial History,* rev ed. Albuquerque: University of New Mexico Press, 2000.

Larson, Carole. *Forgotten Frontier: The Story of Southeastern New Mexico.* Albuquerque: University of New Mexico, 1993.

Larson, Robert W. "Statehood for New Mexico, 1888–1912." *New Mexico Historical Review* 37, no. 3 (July, 1962): 161–200.

———. "Taft, Roosevelt and New Mexico Statehood." *Mid–America: An Historical Review* 60, no. 3 (July, 1985): 249–269.

———. "Territorial Politics and Cultural Impact." *New Mexico Historical Review* 60, no. 3 (July, 1985): 249–269.

Leip, David. *United States Presidential Election Results 1789–2008.* Accessed July 22, 2011, at www.uselectionatlas.org/RESULTS.

Leopard, Donald. "Joint Statehood: 1906." *New Mexico Historical Review* 34, no. 4 (October, 1959): 241–247.

Lewis, Nancy Owens, and Kay Leigh Hagan. *A Peculiar Alchemy: A Centennial History of SAR 1907–2007.* Santa Fe: School for Advanced Research, 2007.

Lynch, Mona Pauline. *Sunbelt Justice: Arizona and the Transformation of American Punishment.* Stanford, CA: Stanford Law Books, 2010.

Lyon, W. H. "Arizona Territory and the Harrison Act of 1886." *Arizona and the West* 26, no. 3 (1984): 209–224.

MacCracken, John H. "Taxation of City Real Estate and Improvements on Real Estate as Illustrated in New York City." *State and Local Taxation: First National Conference under the Auspices of the National Tax Association, Columbus, Ohio, November 12–15, 1907.* New York: MacMillan, 1908: 375–397.

Marquette, R. Penny, and Richard K. Fleischman. "Government/Business Synergy: Early American Innovations in Budgeting and Cost Accounting." *Accounting Historians Journal* 19, no. 2 (December, 1992): 123–145.

Martis, Kenneth C. *The Historical Atlas of Political Parties in the United States Congress, 1789–1989.* New York: Macmillan, 1989.

Marwick, Mitchell & Co. "Municipal Accounting." *Government Accountant* 2, no. 5 (1908): 216–219.

Matika, L. A. "The Contributions of Frederick Albert Cleveland to the Development of a System of Municipal Accounting in the Progressive Era." PhD diss., Kent State University, 1988.

McDonald, W. C. "The Tax Problem in New Mexico." *New Mexico Tax Review* 1, no. 1 (February 1916): 24–25.

McKinsey, James O. *Budgetary Control.* New York: Ronald Press, 1922.

———. "Municipal Accounting." *Journal of Accountancy* 35, no. 2 (February, 1923): 81–94.

McPherson, J. H. T. "The General Property Tax as a Source of State Revenue." In *State and Local Taxation: First National Conference under the Auspices of the National Tax Association, Columbus, Ohio, November 12–15, 1907.* New York: MacMillan, 1908: 475–484.

Mehrotra, Ajay K. "Forging Fiscal Reform: Constitutional Change, Public Policy, and the Creation of Administrative Capacity in Wisconsin, 1880–1920." *Journal of Policy History* 20 (2008): 94–112.

———. "Producing Tax Knowledge: The National Tax Association and the Administrative Apparatus of the Fiscal State." Paper presented at the annual meeting of the American Political Science Association, Boston, MA, 2002.

Melzer, Richard. "New Mexico in Caricature: Images of the Territory on the Eve of Statehood." *New Mexico Historical Review* 62, no. 4 (October 1987): 335–360.

Miller, Peter. "Governing by Numbers: Why Calculative Practices Matter." *Social Research* 68, no. 2 (2001): 379–396.

———. "On the Interrelations between Accounting and the State." *Accounting, Organizations and Society* 15, no. 4 (1990): 315–338.

Milliken, I. J. "Municipal Condition of San Francisco." *Proceedings of the Second National Conference for Good City Government held at Minneapolis, December 8 and 10, 1894, and of the First Annual Meeting of the National Municipal League and of the Third National Conference for Good City Government held at Cleveland May 29, 30 and 31, 1895.* Philadelphia: National Municipal League, 1895: 449–453.

Montoya, María E. "The Dual World of Governor Miguel A. Otero: Myth and Reality in Turn–of–the–Century New Mexico." *New Mexico Historical Review* 67, no. 1 (January, 1992): 13–31.

Moore, John H. "Local and State Governments of Antebellum Mississippi." *Journal of Mississippi History* 44, no. 2 (1982): 104–134.

Morecroft, Susan E., Edward N. Coffman, and Daniel L. Jensen. "T. Coleman Andrews: Crusader for Accountability in Government." *Accounting, Business & Financial History* 10, no. 2 (July, 2000): 245–258.

Moussalli, Stephanie D. "Florida's Frontier Constitution: The Statehood Banking, & Slavery Controversies." *Florida Historical Quarterly* 74, no. 4 (1996): 423–439.

"Municipal Accounting." *Engineering Record* 47, no. 18 (May 2, 1903): 466–467.

Nash, Gerald D. "New Mexico in the Otero Era: Some Historical Perspectives." *New Mexico Historical Review* 67, no. 1 (January 1992): 1–12.

National Municipal League. "Municipal Corporations Act." *Proceedings of the Columbus Conference for Good City Government and Fifth Annual Meeting of the National Municipal League held November 16, 17, 18, 1899.* Ed. Clinton Rogers Woodruff. Philadelphia: National Municipal League, 1899: 216–223.

Nelson, Michael A. "An Empirical Analysis of State and Local Tax Structure in the Context of the Leviathan Model of Government." *Public Choice* 49, no. 3 (1986): 283–294.

"Nevada." *The Bulletin of the National Tax Association* 11, no. 8 (May, 1921): 234.

Nevada. Auditor. *Annual Report of the State Auditor to the Governor of Nevada for the Year Ending . . .* [title varies].

———. Controller. *Annual Report of the State Controller* [title varies].

———. Tax Commission. *Biennial Report of the Nevada Tax Commission* [title varies].

"New Mexico." *The Bulletin of the National Tax Association* (February, 1917): 137.

"New Mexico." *The Bulletin of the National Tax Association* 6, no. 8 (May, 1921): 235–236.

New Mexico. Auditor. *Biennial Report of . . ., Auditor of the State of New Mexico, for the . . . 'th and . . . 'th Fiscal Years Ending . . .* [title varies].

———. Comptroller. *Biennial Report for the . . . 'th and . . . 'th Fiscal Years and of County Activities* [title varies].

———. Special Revenue Commission. *Report of the New Mexico Special Revenue Commission to the Governor and the Legislature of the State of New Mexico, Made in Accordance with Chapter 9, Fourth State Legislature Extra Session, 1920.* Santa Fe: Santa Fe New Mexican Publishing, 1920.

———. State Tax Commission. *Biennial Report of the State Tax Commission, . . . 'th and . . . 'th Fiscal Years* [title varies].

———. Traveling Auditor. *Report of the Traveling Auditor of the State of New Mexico for the Period Beginning on . . . and Ending on . . .* [title and dates vary].

———. Treasurer. *Biennial Report of the State Treasurer, . . . 'th and . . . 'th Fiscal Years, . . .* [title varies].

New Mexico (Territory). Auditor. *Report of the Territorial Auditor, . . . from . . . to . . .* [title varies].

———. Governor, Secretary, and Chief Justice. "Certificate of the Governor, Secretary, and Chief Justice of the Territory of New Mexico, as to Vote on Constitution of Proposed State of New Mexico. . . . " In U.S. Congress, House, Committee on the Territories, *The Constitution of the State of New Mexico.* . . . 61st Cong., 3d sess., doc. 1369, Feb. 10, 1911.

———. Traveling Auditor. *Report of the Traveling Auditor and Bank Examiner on Territorial Finances for the Fiscal Year Ended.* . . . [title and dates vary].

———. Treasurer. *Report of the Territorial Treasurer, from . . . to . . .* [title and dates vary].

Normand, Carol, and Charles W. Wootton. "The Recognition and Valuation of Current Assets on the Balance Sheet in the United States, 1865–1940." *Accounting Historians Journal* 28, no. 2 (December, 2001): 63–108.

Oates, Wallace E. *Property Taxation and Local Government Finance.* Cambridge, MA: Lincoln Institute of Land Policy, 2001.

Oldroyd, David, and Alisdair Dobie. "Bookkeeping." In *The Routledge Companion to Accounting History,* edited by John Richard Edwards and Stephen P. Walker, 95–119. Oxford, U.K.: Routledge, 2009.

Onuf, Peter S. "New State Equality: The Ambiguous History of a Constitutional Principle." *Publius: The Journal of Federalism* 18 (1988): 53–69.

Onuf, Peter S. *Statehood and Union: A History of the Northwest Ordinance.* Bloomington, IN: Indiana University Press, Midland Book ed., 1992. First published 1987 by Indiana University Press.

Otero, Miguel Antonio. *My Nine Years as Governor of the Territory of New Mexico, 1897–1906.* Edited by Marion Dargan. Albuquerque: University of New Mexico, 1940.

Ott, Attiat F., and Shadbegian, Ronald J. "Centralized versus Decentralized Provision and the Size of Government." In *Public Sector Budgets: A Comparative Study,* edited by Attiat F. Ott, 227–243. Brookfield, VT: Edward Elgar, 1993.

Owens, Kenneth N. "Pattern and Structure in Western Territorial Politics." In *The American Territorial System,* edited by John P. Bloom, 161–179. Athens, OH: Ohio University Press, 1973.

Palsson, Mary Dale. "The Arizona Constitutional Convention of 1910: The Election of Delegates in Pima County." *Arizona and the West* 16, no. 2 (1974): 111–124.

Paton, William Andrew, and Russell Alger Stevenson. *Principles of Accounting.* New York: Macmillan, 1918.

Peltzman, Sam. "Voters as Fiscal Conservatives." *Quarterly Journal of Economics* 107, no. 2 (1992): 327–361.

Peterson, Stephen. "Why It Worked: Critical Success Factors of a Financial Reform Project in Africa." *Faculty Research Working Paper Series,* RWP 11–019, John F. Kennedy School of Government, Harvard University, March, 2011.

Peterson, Thomas H. Jr. "Danger Sound Klaxon: The Automobile Comes to Territorial Arizona." *Journal of Arizona History* 15, no. 3 (Fall 1974): 249–268.

Picur, Ronald D., and Rowan A. Miranda. "Fiscal Information Illusion: How the Cost of Government Is Distorted." *Research in Governmental and Nonprofit Accounting* 8 (1994): 163–199.

Pomeroy, Earl S. *The Territories and the United States, 1861–1890: Studies in Colonial Administration.* Seattle: University of Washington Press, 1969, ©1947.

Potts, James H. "A Brief History of Property and Depreciation Accounting in Municipal Accounting." *Accounting Historians Journal* 9, no. 1 (Spring, 1982): 25–37.

———. "The Evolution of Budgetary Accounting Theory and Practice in Municipal Accounting from 1870." *Accounting Historians Journal* 4, no. 1 (Spring, 1977): 89–100.

———. "The Evolution of Municipal Accounting in the United States: 1900–1935." *Business History Review* 52, no. 4 (Winter, 1978): 518–536.

———. "Some Highlights in the Evolution of the Fund Concept in Municipal Accounting." *The Government Accountants Journal* 26, no. 2 (Summer, 1977): 58–62.

Powers, Le Grand. "Governmental Accounting for Efficiency and Economy of Administration." Annual Address of the President of the Association of American Government Accountants, May 27, 1909. Reprinted in *The Government Accountant* 3, no. 1 1909: 22–29.

———. "Nature and Aims of State Central Control of Municipal Accounts and Financial Reports." In *Proceedings of the New York Conference for Good City Government and the Eleventh Annual Meeting of the National Municipal League held April 25, 26, 27 and 28, 1905 at New York.* National Municipal League, 1905: 244–247.

———. "Public Indebtedness." *New Mexico Tax Review* (February 1916: 27–29).

———. "Standardizing Governmental Accounts." *The Government Accountant* 1 (no. 5, 1907): 254–262.

———. "Uniform Accounting in Its Relation to Comparative Municipal Statistics." In *Proceedings of the Chicago Conference for Good City Government and the Tenth Annual Meeting of the National Municipal League held April 27, 28 and 29, 1904 at Chicago, Illinois.* Philadelphia: National Municipal League, 1904: 230–241.

———. Untitled. *State and Local Taxation: First National Conference under the Auspices of the National Tax Association, Columbus, Ohio, November 12–15, 1907,* New York: MacMillan, 1908: 48.

Prendergast, William A. "Efficiency Through Accounting." In "Efficiency in City Government," special issue, *Annals of the American Academy of Political and Social Science* 41 (May, 1912): 43–56.

Previts, Gary John, and Richard E. Brown. "The Development of Government Accounting: A Content Analysis of the Journal of Accountancy, 1905 to 1989." *Accounting Historians Journal* 20, no. 2 (December, 1993): 119–138.

Previts, Gary John, and Barbara Dubis Merino. *A History of Accountancy in the United States: The Cultural Significance of Accounting.* Columbus, OH: Ohio State University Press, 1998.

Prince, L. Bradford. *New Mexico's Struggle for Statehood: Sixty Years of Effort to Obtain Self Government.* Santa Fe: New Mexican Printing, 1910.

Pry, Mark E. "Statehood Politics and Territorial Development: The Arizona Constitution of 1891." *Journal of Arizona History* 35, no. 4 (1994): 397–426.

Radaelli, C. M. "Taxation Research as Political Science Research." In *Taxation: An Interdisciplinary Approach to Research*, M. Lamb et al., eds., 85–103. Oxford: Oxford University, 2005.

Reid, Robert Raymond, Governor of Florida. "Statement of the Votes for and against the Constitution." In *Florida Becomes a State,* edited by Dorothy Dodd, 376–378. Tallahassee, FL: Florida Centennial Commission, Florida State Library, 1945.

Remis, James S. "Governmental Accounting Standards—A Historical Perspective." Chap. 1 in Drebin, Allan R., James L. Chan, and Lorna C. Ferguson, *Objectives of Accounting and Financial Reporting for Governmental Units: A Research Study,* vol. 2, Chicago: National Council on Governmental Accounting, 1981.

Riskin, Marci L. *The Train Stops Here: New Mexico's Railway Legacy.* Albuquerque: University of New Mexico Press, 2005.

Roosevelt, Franklin Delano. "Message from the President of the United States." *Journal of Accountancy* 64, no. 5 (November, 1937): 331–332.

Rowe, L. S. "Public Accounting under the Proposed Municipal Program." *Proceedings of the Columbus Conference for Good City Government and Fifth Annual Meeting of the National Municipal League held November 16, 17, 18, 1899.* Ed. Clinton Rogers Woodruff. Philadelphia: National Municipal League, 1899: 104–123.

Rubin, Irene S. "Who Invented Budgeting in the United States?" *Public Administration Review* 53, no. 5 (Sept.–Oct. 1993): 438–444.

Sálaz Márquez, Rubén. *The Santa Fe Ring: Land Grant History in American New Mexico.* Albuquerque: Cosmic House, 2008.

Sanders, George D. "Tiebout Migrants and the Median Voter as Users of Accounting Information." *Research in Governmental and Nonprofit Accounting* 8 (1994): 137–155.

Santana, M. C. *Puerto Rican Newspaper Coverage of the Puerto Rican Independence Party: A Content Analysis of Three Elections.* New York: Garland Publishing, 2000.

Sargiacomo, Massimo, and Delfina Gomes. "Accounting and Accountability in Local Government: Contributions from Accounting History Research." *Accounting History* 16, no. 3 (2011): 253–290.

Scheiber, Harry N. "Federalism: History." In *Encyclopedia of the American Constitution,* edited by Leonard W. Levy, Kenneth L. Karst, and Dennis J. Mahoney, 697–704. New York: Macmillan, 1986.

Schweikart, Larry. "Early Banking in New Mexico from the Civil War to the Roaring Twenties." *New Mexico Historical Review* 61, no. 1 (January, 1988): 1–24.

Seligmann, G. L, Jr. "The El Paso and Northeastern Railroad's Economic Impact on Central New Mexico." *New Mexico Historical Review* 61, no. 3 (July, 1986): 217–231.

Sells, Elijah Watts. "Corporate Management Compared with Government Control." *Government Accountant* 2, no. 2 (1908): 58–63.

Sheridan, Thomas E. *Arizona: A History.* Tucson: University of Arizona Press, 1995.

Shughart, William F. II and Laura Razzolini, eds. *The Elgar Companion to Public Choice.* Cheltenham, U.K: Edward Elgar, 2001.

Smith, Adam. *An Inquiry into the Nature and Causes of the Wealth of Nations.* London: Printed for W. Strahan and T. Cadell, 1776.

Sparling, S. E. "The Importance of Uniformity for Purposes of Comparison." *Proceedings of the Columbus Conference for Good City Government and Fifth An-*

nual Meeting of the National Municipal League held November 16, 17, 18, 1899. Ed. Clinton Rogers Woodruff. Philadelphia: National Municipal League, 1899: 136–147.

"State Supervision of Municipal Accounts, Under Existing Legislative Enactments Prior to 1913." *National Municipal Review* 2, no. 3 (July, 1913): 522–525.

"A Statistical Survey of Government Costs in New Mexico." *New Mexico Tax Review* 1, no. 1 (February, 1916): 16.

Strong, T. N. "Municipal Condition of Portland." *Proceedings of the Second National Conference for Good City Government held at Minneapolis, December 8 and 10, 1894, and of the First Annual Meeting of the National Municipal League and of the Third National Conference for Good City Government held at Cleveland May 29, 30 and 31, 1895.* Philadelphia: National Municipal League, 1895: 432–438.

Sunder, Shyam. "The State of Accounting Practice and Education." 2006. Accessed 6/01/07, http://www.som.yale.edu/faculty/Sunder/research.html#Accounting_and_Control_Pr.

Sylla, Richard E. "Long–Term Trends in State and Local Finance: Sources and Uses of Funds in North Carolina, 1800–1977." In *Long–Term Factors in American Economic Growth.* National Bureau of Economic Research, Studies in Income and Wealth, vol. 51. Chicago: University of Chicago Press, 1986.

Sylla, Richard E., John B. Legler, and John Wallis. *Sources and Uses of Funds in State and Local Governments, 1790–1915: [United States]* [Computer file]. New York, NY: New York University, Athens, GA: University of Georgia, and College Park, MD: University of Maryland [producers], 1991. Ann Arbor, MI: Inter–university Consortium for Political and Social Research [distributor], 1993.

———. *State and Local Government [United States]: Sources and Uses of Funds, City and County Data, Nineteenth Century* [Computer file]. New York, NY: Richard E. Sylla, New York University, Athens, GA: John B. Legler, University of Georgia, College Park, MD: John Wallis, University of Maryland [producers], 1994. Ann Arbor, MI: Inter–university Consortium for Political and Social Research [distributor], 1995.

Tanner, John B. "Governmental Profit and Loss." *Journal of Accountancy* 17, no. 4 (April, 1914): 264–270.

Taussig, B. J. "Results Obtainable Through Reorganization of Accounting Methods." In "Efficiency in City Government," special issue, *Annals of the American Academy of Political and Social Science* 41 (May, 1912): 57–63.

Terr. Pap.: AZ. See U.S. Department of the Interior.

Terr. Pap.: NM. See U.S. Department of the Interior.

Tiltman, Edward D. "New Mexico Constitutional Convention: Recollections." *New Mexico Historical Review* 3 (July, 1952): 177–186.

Toomey, William Michael. "Prelude to Statehood: The Southwest Territory, 1790–1796." PhD diss., University of Tennessee, Knoxville, 1991.

Treleven, J. E. "The Milwaukee Bureau of Economy and Efficiency." In "Efficiency in City Government," special issue, *Annals of the American Academy of Political and Social Science* 41 (May, 1912): 270–278.

Trimble, Marshall. *Arizona: a Panoramic History of a Frontier State*. Garden City, NY: Doubleday, 1977.

Tweedale, A. "The Accounting System of the District of Columbia." Address before the Association of American Government Accountants, October 20, 1908. Reprinted in *The Government Accountant* 2, no. 6 (October, 1908), 225–239.

United States. "Treaty of Guadalupe Hidalgo." February 2, 1848. *United States Statutes at Large* 9: 922–932.

U.S. Bureau of the Census, *Financial Statistics of the States, vols. 1915–1919, 1922–1931.* Washington, DC: GPO, 1916–1920, 1924–1933.

———. *Historical Statistics of the United States, Colonial Times to 1970,* bicentennial ed. Washington, DC: GPO, 1975.

———. *Historical Statistics of the United States, Colonial Times to 1970.* White Plains, NY: Kraus International Publications, 1989. Reprint of Bicentennial ed.

———. *Historical Statistics on Governmental Finances and Employment.* Census of Governments: 1962. Washington, DC: GPO, 1962.

———. *Wealth, Debt, and Taxation, 1913.* 2 vols. Washington, DC: GPO, 1945.

———. *Wealth, Debt, and Taxation. Special Reports of the Census Office.* Washington, DC: GPO, 1907.

———. *Wealth, Debt, and Taxation, 1913.* 2 volumes. Washington, DC: GPO, 1915.

U.S. Congress. *Annals of the Congress of the United States, 1789–1824.* 42 vols. Washington, DC, 1834–1856.

———. *Congressional Record.* 57th Cong., 1st sess., 1902. Vol. 35, pt. 5. Washington, DC.

———. *Admission of Arizona into the Union, Exhibit A, Constitution for the State of Arizona, as Adopted by the Constitutional Convention Friday October 2, 1891,* 52nd Cong., 1st sess., March 19, 1892. H. Rep. 1045.

———. House, *Admission of Oklahoma, Arizona, and New Mexico.* HR 12543, 57th Cong., 1st sess. *Congressional Record* 35, pt. 5 (May 7, 1902): H 5136.

———. *Receipts and Disbursements.* 62nd Cong., 2nd sess., 1911, H. Doc. 128, *Serial Set* 6186, 36.

———. *Receipts and Expenditures: A Combined Statement of the Receipts and Expenditures of the Government for the Fiscal Year Ended June 30. . . .* Washington, D.C.: GPO, annual. [Title varies; often called "Combined Statement of the Receipts and Disbursements, Balances, etc., of the United States" in later years.]

U.S. Congress. Senate. Committee on Territories. *Prohibiting Passage of Local or Special Laws in Territories of the United States.* 49th Cong., 1st sess., June 15, 1886. S. Rep. 1327.

U.S. Department of the Interior. *Interior Department Territorial Papers: Arizona 1868–1913.* 8 microfilm reels. Washington, D.C.: National Archives, 1962. [Abbreviated in text as *Terr. Pap.: AZ.*]

———. *Interior Department Territorial Papers: New Mexico, 1851–1914.* 15 microfilm reels. Washington, D.C.: National Archives, 1962. [Abbreviated in text as *Terr. Pap.: NM.*]

———. *Report of the Governor of Arizona.* In *Reports of the Department of the Interior for the Fiscal Year Ended June 30 1909: Administrative Reports,* Vol. II. Washington, D.C.: Government Printing Office, 1910, 531–558.

U.S. Department of the Treasury. *An Account of the Receipts and Expenditures of the United States for the Year . . . Stated in Pursuance of the Standing Order of the House of Representatives of the United States, Passed the Thirtieth Day of December, One Thousand Seven Hundred and Ninety–One.*

U.S. General Accounting Office. *Experiences of Past Territories Can Assist Puerto Rico Status Deliberations: Report to the Congress.* GGD–80–26. Washington, D.C.: March 7, 1980.

Van Cleve, Ruth G. *The Office of Territorial Affairs.* New York: Praeger, 1974.

VanderMeer, Philip. *Desert Visions and the Making of Phoenix, 1860–2009.* Albuquerque: University of New Mexico, 2010.

Walton, John M. "The Application to a Municipality of Modern Methods of Accounting and Reporting." In "Efficiency in City Government," special issue, *Annals of the American Academy of Political and Social Science* 41 (May, 1912): 64–68.

Watts, Stan. *A Legal History of Maricopa County.* Charleston, SC: Arcadia Publishing, 2007.

Waymire, Gregory, and Sudipta Basu. "Economic Crisis and Accounting Evolution." *Accounting and Business Research* 41, no. 3 (August 2011): 207–232.

Weigle, Marta. *Alluring New Mexico: Engineered Enchantment, 1821–2001.* Santa Fe: Museum of New Mexico Press, 2010.

Welsh, Cynthia Secor. "A 'Star Will Be Added': Miguel Antonio Otero and the Struggle for Statehood." *New Mexico Historical Review* 67, no. 1 (January 1992): 33–51.

Wilcox, D. F. "An Examination of the Proposed Municipal Program." *Proceedings of the Columbus Conference for Good City Government and Fifth Annual Meeting of the National Municipal League held November 16, 17, 18, 1899.* Ed. Clinton Rogers Woodruff. Philadelphia: National Municipal League, 1899: 51–62.

Williams, Daniel W. "Measuring Government in the Early Twentieth Century." *Public Administration Review* 63, no. 6 (Nov/Dec, 2003): 643–659.

Willoughby, William Franklin. *Territories and Dependencies of the United States: Their Government and Administration.* American States Series. New York: Century Co., 1905.

Wilson, Earl R. *Financial Reporting by State and Local Governments: A Survey of Preferences among Alternative Formats.* Norwalk, CT: Governmental Accounting Standards Board, 1990.

Wilson, R. Michael. *Crime & Punishment in Early Arizona.* Las Vegas: Stagecoach Books, 2004.

Winkler, F. C. "Municipal Government of Milwaukee." *Proceedings of the Second National Conference for Good City Government held at Minneapolis, December 8 and 10, 1894, and of the First Annual Meeting of the National Municipal League and of the Third National Conference for Good City Government held at Cleveland May 29, 30 and 31, 1895.* Philadelphia: National Municipal League, 1895: 119–124.

Woodruff, C. R. "Uniform Municipal Accounting and Reporting." *The Government Accountant* 1, no. 10 (February, 1908), 468–480.

Wynne, Andy. "Public Sector Accounting—Democratic Accountability or Market Rules?" *Public Money and Management* 26, no. 1 (January, 2004): 5–7.

Zander, C. M. "Assessment of Mining Property." *Bulletin of the National Tax Association* (October, 1916): 21.

———. "1918 Valuations by the Arizona Commission." *Bulletin of the National Tax Association* 4, no. 3 (December, 1918): 80–81.

———. "Tax Progress in Arizona." *Bulletin of the National Tax Association* 5, no. 1 (October, 1919): 12–15.

Zimmerman, Jerold L. "The Municipal Accounting Maze: An Analysis of Political Incentives." *Journal of Accounting Research* 165 (1977): 107–144.

Index

About the Author

Stephanie Dunham Moussalli is assistant professor of accounting at Rhodes College in Memphis, Tennessee. She has undergraduate degrees in anthropology, French education, and accounting; master's degrees in public administration and history; and a doctorate in accounting. She has worked as an accountant for GE and taught history, political science, English as a second language, French, and composition as an adjunct instructor at the college level. She and her husband live in both Memphis and Oxford, Mississippi.

CPSIA information can be obtained at www.ICGtesting.com
Printed in the USA
BVOW071409050312

284389BV00002B/2/P